Richard Jefferies
After London; or Wild England

Edinburgh Critical Editions of Nineteenth-Century Texts

Published titles
Richard Jefferies, After London; or Wild England
Mark Frost

Forthcoming titles
William Barnes, Dialect Poems in The Dorset County Chronicle
Thomas Burton and Emma Mason

Geraldine Jewsbury, Critical Essays and Reviews (1849–1870)
Anne-Marie Beller

Hartley Coleridge, The Complete Poems
Nicola Healey

George Gissing, The Private Papers of Henry Ryecroft
Thomas Ue

Visit the Edinburgh Critical Editions of Nineteenth-Century Texts
website at: edinburghuniversitypress.com/series/ecenct

Richard Jefferies
After London; or Wild England

Edited and with an introduction by Mark Frost
Including additional writings by Richard Jefferies

EDINBURGH
University Press

Edinburgh University Press is one of the leading university presses in the UK. We publish academic books and journals in our selected subject areas across the humanities and social sciences, combining cutting-edge scholarship with high editorial and production values to produce academic works of lasting importance. For more information visit our website: www.edinburghuniversitypress.com

Edinburgh University Press Ltd
The Tun – Holyrood Road
12(2f) Jackson's Entry
Edinburgh EH8 8PJ

Typeset in 11/12.5 Baskerville and Times New Roman by
Servis Filmsetting Ltd, Stockport, Cheshire,
and printed and bound in Great Britain by
CPI Group (UK) Ltd, Croydon CR0 4YY

A CIP record for this book is available from the British Library

ISBN 978 1 4744 0239 2 (hardback)
ISBN 978 1 4744 0240 8 (webready PDF)
ISBN 978 1 4744 0241 5 (epub)

Contents

Introduction

Readers not wishing to read details of the novel in advance should treat this introduction as an afterword.

Richard Jefferies's *After London; or Wild England* (1885) is a novel that simply refuses to go away, and one which is gaining an ever more prominent place in studies of Victorian culture. Published during the anxious closing decades of the nineteenth century, this disturbing novel, set in a barbaric future England, can often dazzle, sometimes infuriate, and always intrigue. It begins uncannily, casually announcing the destruction of the world's greatest metropolis:

> The old men say their fathers told them that soon after the fields were left to themselves a change began to be visible. It became green everywhere in the first spring, after London ended, so that all the country looked alike.

'One of Jefferies' masterpieces in description', according to Edward Thomas, the opening chapters explain with 'an unsuspected strength of remorseless logic and restraint' the processes involved in the destruction of London and its civilisation (1978: 233).[1] The society that suffers this cataclysmic downfall is recognisably Jefferies's, a society that 'with certain machines worked by fire [...] traversed the land swift as the swallow glides through the sky'; and capable of transmitting 'intelligence to the utmost parts of the earth along wires'. Amidst unprecedented sea level disturbance, the Thames silts up and floodwaters enter 'the cloacæ of the ancient city', so that the seemingly immortal capital, symbol of British imperial reach, was found to be 'after all only of brick, and when the ivy grew over and trees and shrubs sprang up, and, lastly, the waters underneath burst in, this huge metropolis was soon overthrown'. Using nature to destroy a city that had long fascinated and repelled him, Jefferies unsettles by invoking catastrophe; by intelligently declining to offer a clear explanation of 'the event' that led to London's demise; but also, and more profoundly, by refusing to provide an idyll in the *tabula rasa* created by the novel's opening. In his 1909 biography of Jefferies, Thomas was

---

[1] Full details of works cited can be found in the Further Reading section that follows this introduction.

certainly surprised by this: 'having described the relapse to barbarism and the loss of everything characteristic of nineteenth-century civilization, one so dogmatic and prophetic as Jefferies might have been expected to make use of this opportunity, and to show us a Utopia' (1978: 233). That he does not do so is only one way in which this uncanny novel can wrong-foot readers, but it should be unsurprising that Jefferies refuses utopia, for *After London* is a novel of disgusted alienation, an extreme imaginative wish fulfilment, and a powerful register of decidedly mixed feelings about Victorian humanity, 'a novel which, for all its concern with barbarism and wildness, is born of the crisis of modernity' (Hooker 1996: 38).

The novel refuses to go away in the sense that it stays in the mind long after a first encounter with that uncanny opening. John Fowles found *After London* 'the strangest book that Richard Jefferies ever wrote, if not the strangest book from any considerable writer of his period' (1980: vii). This abidingly productive strangeness sharply divides opinion concerning its genesis, literary worth, and generic status, and the novel has refused to disappear in the sense that it has stubbornly maintained a position in discussions of late-nineteenth-century fiction. In recent decades it has attracted increased scrutiny by scholars whose diversity of perspective reflects the novel's preoccupations with many Victorian and post-Victorian anxieties about the countryside and the city, science, industrialisation, social organisation, demographics, imperial identity, and resources.

The novel's strangeness is also related to uncertainties about its literary status, for as Angela Richardson concludes when discussing Jefferies's late novels 'they are certainly not novels in the nineteenth-century style' (1992: xiv). Odd-looking as an example of prevailing practices in nineteenth-century realism, *After London* nonetheless relates to many literary genres. Regularly cited as a dystopia, an apocalyptic novel, and a science fiction text, it has also been called a biographical novel, a Darwinian tale, a romance quest, and a novel of national identity. It has an antagonistic kinship with Victorian medievalism but also anticipates features of twentieth-century fiction. The need for a new scholarly edition of a novel that refuses to go away has become more pressing given recent rising interest in the relationship between literature and environment, and the instigation of a roughly defined school of literary theory known as ecocriticism, for the novel's futuristic evocation of 'Wild England' offers rich opportunities to think about cultural attitudes to nature. To those interested in what has been termed the Anthropocene – a proposed geological period, beginning in the nineteenth century, in which the catastrophic effects of human activity are physically evident in the geological record – *After London*'s sensitivity to human impacts on environment can certainly make it seem a pioneering 'green' text. Promiscuously entwined in many discourses, *After London* overspills its various generic and thematic categorisations, and is happily unlike any other book. Its participation in diverse traditions opens up multiple ways of approaching its strangeness and making a case for its significance within and beyond its culture.

This introduction will situate *After London* in a range of literary, scientific, and cultural contexts, examining criticisms of the novel and of Jefferies's literary identity, and the place the novel occupies in Jefferies's corpus. While acknowledging the novel's links to Jefferies's life, I would suggest that reading *After London* simply as a reflection of biography flattens its rich instability and elusive strangeness.[2] It will be more helpful to consider the generic categories in which the novel has been situated, and to celebrate the diversity of scholarly opinion on the novel by exploring the different ways in which its strangeness has been approached. For this reader, its most compelling life lies in that ancient field of human creativity, the pastoral tradition, but the novel cannot be reduced to any particular reading as so much of its compelling energy lies in its instability, multiplicity, and open-endedness.

Jefferies's corpus and the reception of *After London*

It is worth beginning by considering why there is so little consensus about the novel and about Jefferies's place in Victorian literature. While most of his works remain in print, Jefferies has never attained a prominent position in English literary history, a fact in part explained by the vexed question of what kind of an author he was. An aspirant fiction writer who commenced his career with three novels and published six more in the remainder of his brief, brilliant life, Jefferies first achieved prominence through three 1872 letters to *The Times* on agriculture in his native Wiltshire, letters which were a presentiment of his ability to produce topical, informed rural commentary for newspapers and periodicals. Early, unremunerative work with Wiltshire newspapers leant his literary style many of the traits of the journalist to whom brevity and deadlines loomed large. Indeed, the Jefferies 'nature essay', probably his quintessential literary form, arose out of

---

[2] Critics have been quick to identify the roots of Jefferies's work in his life. For biographical readings, see Besant 1888: 151–6, Thomas 1978: 55, 95, 128, 235–9, Keith 1965: 15–39, Fowles 1980: xiii, Hooker 1996: 41–5.

a financial need to produce word-limited pieces for national periodicals. Collected together as themed volumes, *The Gamekeeper at Home* (1878), *The Amateur Poacher*, and *Wild Life in a Southern County* (both 1879) announced a distinctive voice capable of evoking rural environments vividly and precisely. Thomas cites Gilbert White's *The Natural History of Selborne* (1789) as a predecessor but argues that its primarily biological focus means it carries 'a considerable dead weight of what is or was only matter of fact' (1978: 98), while Jefferies's nature writings exhibit superior imaginative power and a greater interest in human culture. Jefferies's principal income was accrued from periodical articles and their subsequent publication as collections, the best of which – *Nature Near London* (1883), *The Life of the Fields* (1884), and *The Open Air* (1885) – demonstrate a powerfully maturing style and an increasingly radical social position. During this period, he also published an extraordinary 'spiritual autobiography', *The Story of My Heart* (1883), and five novels, including two for children, *Wood Magic* (1881) and *Bevis: The Story of a Boy* (1882), inspirations for *The Wind in the Willows* (1908), *Winnie-the-Pooh* (1926), and *Swallows and Amazons* (1930), just as *After London* has been described as 'a spiritual grandparent to Narnia and Middle Earth' (Brannigan 2015: 35). Despite his prodigious output, and the favourable reception of many of his works, 'the name of Richard Jefferies is often to be found on the periphery of the English literary scene in that indistinct no-man's land that skirts the boundaries of creative literature, natural history, and rural sociology' (Keith 1965: 15).

This relative neglect, W. J. Keith suggests, 'can partly be explained as a difficulty of classification' (1965: 15), with readers often valuing or knowing only his nature writings, social commentaries, children's books, or late novels. While some venerate his autobiography, others discern a barrier to Jefferies's wider acceptance, Q. D. Leavis suggesting that 'there has always been a garden-suburb cult of *The Story of My Heart* which has assisted in discrediting him' (1989: 256), and C. Henry Warren averring that 'it has been [Jefferies's] misfortune to attract the uncritical attention of what one may call the wind-on-the-heath brethren' (1948: 25–6). Wary of this kind of territorialism, Keith claims that Jefferies's range 'should serve as a distinction rather than as an encumbrance' (1965: 15). Valuing only segments of Jefferies's corpus leads to a limited, distorted view of his ideas, and risks neglecting the possibility that his insouciant transgressions of literary boundaries are amongst the most important features of his work. To serve his 'ability to present the countryside on paper in all its variety and complexity', a variety involving 'consideration of the human inhabitants as well as of the flora and fauna', Jefferies utilises diverse literary forms (Keith 1965: 21). Combining rural journalism, nature writing, and fiction, works like *Round About a Great Estate* and *Hodge and His Masters* (both 1880) are energised by their absolute resistance to classification, and anticipate twentieth-century experiments with literary form.

The generic ambiguities of Jefferies's works are relevant to *After London*, a novel that at first glance seems an oddity within his corpus; that stands in unclear relation to other late-Victorian texts; and that struggles to satisfy the expectations of the realist novel. To Walter Besant, author of *The Eulogy of Richard Jefferies* (1888) and prolific producer of polished, popular, but often unremarkable novels, Jefferies appeared to lack basic novel-craft in failing to follow the familiar patterns of realism. Indeed, Besant entirely dismissed Jefferies's pretensions:

> He never was a novelist; he never could be one. To begin with, he knew nothing of society, nothing of men and women, except the people of a small country town [...] He wholly lacked the dramatic faculty. He could draw splendid landscapes, but he could not connect them together by the thread of human interest [...] He did not understand, so to speak, stage management. When he had got a lot of puppets in his hands, he could not make them act. And he was too self-contained to be a novelist; he could never get rid of his own personality. (1888: 151)

There is a great deal more in this vein from Besant, whose decided preference was for Jefferies's nature writings. This partiality led him to regard even the generally well-received novels of the 1880s as dysfunctional:

> The individual pictures which he presents are delightful and wonderful; they are like his short essays and articles – they may be read with enormous pleasure – but the story, what is the story? Where is it? There is none. There is only the promise of a story not worked out, left, not half untold, but hardly begun, as in 'After London' and in 'Amaryllis at the Fair'. [...] As the writer never took any interest in his characters – one understands that as clearly as if it was proclaimed upon the house-tops – so none of his readers can be expected to feel any interest. (1888: 151–2)

That Besant was emphatically wrong in so damning an analysis is widely felt, although echoes are sometimes heard, as in Andrew Rossabi's claim that Jefferies's characters 'never begin to move from within, independently of their creator' (1986: 11), but Besant's early scorn has led to a sometimes defensive tone in subsequent critical responses. Thomas, who deemed Besant's *Eulogy* 'unsympathetic and incomplete', conceded that 'as a rule Jefferies' treatment of his characters is quite external', but discerned development over time: 'though Felix himself is not more than the others a complete creature of flesh and mind, he develops into an interesting spirit rather than a man' (1978: ix, 90, 238). For Keith, Jefferies produced 'powerful but unequal novels' which in the later stages of his career 'rival those of Thomas Hardy in truth and integrity if not in control and fictional technique' (1965: 15–16, 21). Fowles believed that 'nothing, beyond an excess of sympathy, can make [Jefferies] a great novelist', but claimed that 'he did a good deal better in *After London* than most critics of the novel, ancient and modern, have been prepared to grant' (1980: xiii). Others are uninhibited by Besant's pronouncements. Darko Suvin describes *After London* as 'an important and seminal text' and 'a near masterpiece of Victorian SF' (1983: 376, 377). Leavis celebrated 'a many-sided and comprehensive genius [...] whose interests, ideas, and temperament associate him with other peculiar English geniuses', including William Cobbett, Charles Dickens, Edward Thomas, and D. H. Lawrence; and whose style and 'strikingly contemporary aspect as a social satirist' place him 'in the central and most important tradition of English prose style' (1989: 256). Counting his range as a strength, she re-evaluated his fiction, arguing that 'Jefferies wrote four novels of permanent worth', and picking out 'the superb opening' of *After London* as the pinnacle of his 'mature style' (1989: 261–2). The polarisation of opinion elicited by Jefferies's novels – with Besant and Leavis as markers of the range – signifies a productively difficult creative vigour.

Consensus remains elusive when one turns to specific criticisms of *After London*. Fowles noted that early reviewers overwhelmingly felt that 'the first section of the book [...] and the later journey into the dead heart of London were "fresh" and "striking" pieces of writing; but that the portrayal of [the protagonist] Felix Aquila in the second half of the book was a failure', and that many 'also complained about the ambiguous ending' (1980: ix). The novel has also been criticised as episodic, seemingly incomplete, and weakly characterised. In a letter of 2 April 1884, Jefferies told C. J. Longman that the novel's events 'are purposely dealt with in minute detail so that they may appear actual realities, and the incidents stand out as if they had just happened' (Besant 1888: 210). On reading the published version of the novel, however, readers may feel that Part II, 'Wild England', does not maintain the minute attention of Part I. Indeed, the depictions of the Aquila household, Felix's romance with Aurora Thyma, and the period spent in the battlefields near Aisi feel abbreviated. Felix alone is a fully defined character, and amongst the secondary characters only his father, brother Oliver, and Aurora Thyma emerge as brief individualised portraits. After we glimpse Felix's youngest brother at breakfast, and learn of his miserable position in the Court Treasury, he disappears from the narrative. Courtiers who in other hands would generate significant subplots remain 'off stage' at court, referred to in conversation but rarely depicted in the flesh. A well-researched theory has been put forward to explain such features. Examining the Longman correspondence and other biographical material, three Jefferies critics conclude that he completed a three-volume *After London* by 1882 which Cassell requested be cut down to one volume for publication (Besant 1888: 210, Thomas 1978: 233, Fowles 1980: x–xi.). Such extensive revision may help account for the various criticisms of the narrative line and characterisation.

It would ultimately be unwise to pin too much on the novel's revision, however, for some of the apparent deficiencies of *After London* are evident elsewhere and might better be regarded as markers of an unusual approach than as cause for reproach. Like *After London*, *Greene Ferne Farm* (1880) and *Amaryllis at the Fair* (1887) struggle to maintain interest in their romance plots, and the latter work, like *After London*, ends inconclusively. In each novel lingering descriptions of landscape demonstrate Jefferies's desire to produce a textual surface interwoven with moments of incidental stillness and repose that are at odds with the demands for onward narrative energy associated with realist novels. Setting thus occupies narrative space that in realist texts would usually be devoted to detailed characterisation and sustained plot development. The relationship between this vitally present but challenging environment and the protagonist-adventurer is the novel's central focus, with each achieving similarly inflated levels of prominence in ways that unsettle realist expectations. If secondary characterisation is sparse, this only intensifies the focus on the main character's interiority and restlessness, a focus that makes Felix the body around which other characters orbit, and one of Jefferies's finest achievements. That there is something odd about the narrative structure and characterisation of *After London* may reveal not just difficult editing choices but also, as I will argue later, a quiet desire for literary experimentation.

As Keith suggests, 'when in search of what is valuable in Jefferies, we should turn to his writings rather than his life' (1965: 15). If, instead of reading *After London* as a biographical novel, we place it in the context of his corpus, we gain a means to reconsider its seeming singularity. While Jefferies did not publish another work like it in theme, the novel's concerns are rooted in many of his other published and unpublished texts. These roots will become evident as we start to examine the various generic categories in which the novel has been placed, and the varied ways in which it has been interpreted. Reading the novel through science fiction, dystopia, Darwinism, romance, national identity, naturalism, and pastoral is intended as a spur to further analytical endeavours, rather than representing the limits of its interpretive potential. The readings below are variously linked to one another, and could be further combined with other readings that the inexhaustible possibilities of this uncanny novel invite.

Sci-fi

After London certainly appears less singular when one learns that Jefferies had already imaginatively destroyed the capital nearly a decade earlier. A fragment of an unfinished short story, 'The Great Snow', published here as Appendix I, was written in 1876. In this horrific tale severe winter freezes and starves its population to extinction amidst nationwide calamity. The pinnacle of this disaster is reached amidst scenes of bestial violence and depravity in which the narrator's feelings about modernity are made clear:

> Many went raving mad, and ran about naked until they dropped and died. Fanatics preached unheeded to the crowds. 'Where now' they cried, 'Where now is your mighty city that defied nature and despised the conquered elements – where now is your pride when so simple and contemptible an agent as a few flakes of snow can utterly destroy it?'

While the action of 'The Great Snow' is more immediate, and the tone more febrile, than in *After London*, the texts are closely allied in the degree to which London's destruction is lingered upon, and in their participation in emerging science fiction ideas. *After London* looks even less singular – and more like the result of an obsession – when we note that in an only recently published short story, 'Snowed Under', the capital is again brought to the very brink of wintry catastrophe (Wolfreys and Baker 1996: 19–29). This undated story, told in diary form from the perspective of an eligible society girl, is considerably more sophisticated than 'The Great Snow' and reads like a development of it. Its first-person narration and relative restraint in relating a similar train of events are in some ways far more disturbing. 'Snowed Under' reprieves London, but the helplessness of its infrastructure and its civilised inhabitants in the face of unprecedented natural emergencies is more grimly underlined. Its sci-fi elements are astutely blended with its romance plot to unsettling effect.

There are obvious reasons, then, to think of *After London* as sci-fi, although the genre itself is difficult to define as it is not restricted to a particular medium and cannot be identified by formal features. Proposed definitions speak instead of 'that branch of literature which deals with the reaction of human beings to changes in science and technology' (Asimov 1975: 92), and of narratives 'built around human beings, with a human problem, and a human solution, which would not have happened at all without its scientific content' (Atheling 1967: 14), while the genre could be described as using scientific frameworks and futuristic or distant settings to reflect the preoccupations of the moment of writing.

On such terms, *After London* certainly looks like sci-fi, and has a prominent place in accounts of the genre, which usually note that after the pioneering example of Mary Shelley's *The Last Man* (1826), British science fiction writing becomes clearly established during the century's last decades, much influenced by the overseas examples of Edgar Allan Poe and Jules Verne. *After London's* apocalyptic urges were preceded by William Hay's *The Doom of the Great City: Being the Narrative of a Survivor Written* A.D. *1942* (1880), foreseeing the capital's destruction by killer fog. Also influenced by the 'alternative history' format of George Chesney's *The Battle of Dorking* (1871), envisaging an imminent Germanic invasion, Victorian sci-fi is varied and fluid, often overlapping with popular romance, sensation fiction, supernatural tales, and the political novel. Tracing the emergence of its early subgenres, Suvin claims that by the 1880s 'alternative histories' become dominant, 'overshadowing the other two forms of Future War and Extraordinary Voyage' (1983: 362). In this genre anatomisation, *After London's* early participation underlines its importance. It certainly proceeds much further into the future than most alternative histories, has a keener scientific interest, and has a stronger claim to being a founder of what might be termed catastrophe sci-fi, for which Nicholas Daly's description of nineteenth-century volcano narratives would also serve: 'the events of such narratives turn on the annihilation of people and property; their structures are characterized by the interruption of narrative continuity; and their philosophy generally suggests the limitations of human powers' (2011: 255). The novel's creation of a near-extinction-level event, and its conjuring of a harsh landscape that dominates a violent remnant population, has certainly been reiterated ad nauseum in science fiction writing, television, and cinema in a way that reveals a powerful cultural currency.

After London was quickly followed by similar novels and stories, signs perhaps of an under-recorded early influence, and, as Suvin notes, 'Cobbett's "Great Wen" of London is the prime target' of annihilation in fiction from Chesney through to H. G. Wells's *The War of the Worlds* (1898) (1983: 374). In Henry Watson's *The Decline and Fall of the British Empire; or, The Witch's Cavern* (1890), London is again snowbound, victim of climate change in a rural backwater, while in Jingo Jones's *The Sack of London by the Highland Host: A Romance of the Period* (1900), the Scots, a distant threat in *After London*, become the prime agent of destruction. With stronger sci-fi credentials, Robert Barr's 'The Doom of London' (1895) and Grant Allen's 'The Thames Valley Catastrophe' (1897) envisage, in the former, the return of killer fog, while in the latter the countryside strikes back against urban predominance by unleashing flood basalts that entirely erase London. Replaying the destructive urges of 'The Great Snow' and *After London*, these stories also reflect their preoccupation with the breakdown of human civility in the face of epochal environmental challenges, a breakdown represented by commuters fighting on piles of dead bodies at Cannon St Station in 'The Doom of London', and by the increasing selfishness of Allen's polite bicycling protagonist. Amidst anxieties about late-Victorian imperial dominance, and emerging doubts about the long-term sustainability of industrial civilisation, such stories contemplate the resurgence amidst crisis of the most bestial elements of human nature, hidden just under its surface in a way that clearly foreshadows the post-Holocaust anxieties in John Christopher's *The Death of Grass* (1951), William Golding's *The Lord of the Flies* (1954), and, as Brannigan suggests (2015: 3–4), J. G. Ballard's *The Drowned World* (1962).

It should of course be no surprise to find that the most potent symbol of British power should be the preferred recipient of cataclysm in Victorian sci-fi, or that the locus of hyper-destruction has passed on to other cities, but it is a telling measure of the ambivalence with which many late Victorians observed themselves. While the novel's sci-fi credentials are clear, much is going on within its pages that does not look much like science fiction. A richer understanding of *After London* can only be achieved by thinking through its further literary allegiances.

Dystopia and neo-medievalism

In order to think about the novel in relation to dystopianism it is worth beginning with its unusually prominent representation of environment. While its convincing descriptions of the greening of post-London England draw upon Jefferies's detailed observations of environmental forces and organic behaviour, we should also notice that 'Wild England' is dangerous, threatening, and malign. An environment dominated by enormous forests and a vast lake across central southern England is the haunt of evolutionary descendants of domestic and farm animals, and of human and semi-human groups implacably hostile to travellers. Contesting the notion that *After London* revels in 'the destruction of civilization and the opportunity it provides for a return to an idyllic, barbaric existence', Caroline Sumpter perceptively suggests that 'although it sometimes indulges in the fantasies of the Boy's Own adventure, the barbaric future in *After London* is […] far from idyllic' (Parrinder 1995: 64, Sumpter 2011: 316). Part II, where the inequity of the barbarous courtly society is dissected, only confirms the novel's dystopian impulses. As John Brannigan notes, 'there is nothing remotely utopian about the archipelagic England which takes the place of its drowned antecedent', and something ironic in the fact that after the startling changes described in the early chapters 'life after London – floral, faunal, and human – is not so different from life before London' (2015: 35). Drawn to destroy present society, Jefferies struggled to conceive of a positive alternative in a novel whose consolations are only ever provisional or partial.

This pessimism initially seems odd, because Jefferies's work is often far more optimistic in celebrating the redemptive possibilities of nature or in pointing out positive changes in rural England. For Fowles it is certainly puzzling that 'the supposedly "sensitive" nature writer, author in 1883 of a passionate explosion, *The Story of My Heart*, against machine thinking and machine society', contemplates 'the miseries of a future world bereft of higher knowledge and technology' (1980: vii). This is not to suggest that Jefferies idealises rural life, or that he was unaware of limits to nature's redemptive power, nor is it to neglect the fact that like many other post-Darwinian writers he was troubled by a vision of an indifferent materialist environment. It is, however, to suggest that pessimism elsewhere in Jefferies is never as pronounced or sustained as in *After London*. Having destroyed the apotheosis of industrial modernity, the green world that follows is grudgingly yielding resources to a population scarcely able to maintain marginal cultivated zones. Post-event society is autocratic and corrupt; technologically incompetent and economically reliant on slavery; threatened from within by courtly intrigues and from without by invading forces; and riven by social and geographical fractures. Jefferies is distinctively modern in not simply imagining the utter destruction of urban modernity, but in experiencing guilty pleasures when doing so. Although apocalyptic visions have ancient roots Jefferies was amongst the first (but by no means the last) to conjure a less annihilatory but perhaps more masochistic vision in which an incomplete apocalypse leads to a fragmented, dysfunctional human population. He is in this an augury of a widespread dystopian impulse, rooted in anxieties about population growth, development, and urbanisation, a phenomenon manifest in feelings of alienation from society, other people, the built environment, and nature.

Modern as it is, Jefferies's dystopian turn is also strongly shaped by his disenchantment with neo-medievalism, a powerfully optimistic strand of nineteenth-century aesthetic and social discourse. Most obviously represented by Walter Scott's novels, the poetry of Keats and Tennyson, the architectural theories of A. W. Pugin and John Ruskin, Pre-Raphaelite art, and Thomas Carlyle's politics, neo-medievalism also inspired antiquarians, archaeologists, sculptors, the Arts and Crafts Movement, and building conservationists. Neo-medievalists variously promoted a positive vision of the Middle Ages as a golden age of art, design, beauty, and social cohesion, a consolatory construction presented in deliberate contradistinction to Victorian liberal modernity. Occasionally Jefferies seems to reflect this outlook: in *The Gamekeeper at Home* (1878) he says of the titular figure, 'freedom and constant contact with nature have made him every inch a man; and here in this nineteenth century of civilised effeminacy may be seen some relic of what men were in the old feudal days when they dwelt practically in the woods'; while an April 1878 diary entry complains 'the World has grown so innocent it has become a miserable place to live in. This last half-century has been dreadfully namby-pamby' (Jefferies 1978: 12, Looker 1948: 35). Jefferies reaches not for an image of feudal civility and beauty, however, but for a model of practical outdoor masculinity associated with violence. Such moments of nostalgia are also comparatively rare. A more general antipathy is evident in a splenetic diary outburst in which he lambasts 'the *Mediaevalism* of the XIX Century' and its '*Mediaevaleissance*', and suggests that feudal and Victorian societies were equally useless: 'Ridiculous! We have not advanced one single atom. We can do nothing for ourselves' (Looker 1948: 54).

It is surprising, therefore, to hear the oft-related story of the influence of *After London* on Ruskinian disciple and arch-neo-medieval-ist William Morris. Edward Carpenter recalled Morris 'arriving from the train with Jefferies's book *After London* in his hands' in 1885, and claimed that 'the book delighted him with its prophecy of an utterly ruined and deserted London, gone down in swamps and malaria, with brambles and weeds spreading through slum streets and fashionable squares' (1916: 217). Around this time Morris enthused to Georgiana Burne-Jones that 'absurd hopes curled round my heart as I read it' and, a fortnight later, that 'I have no more faith than a grain of mustard seed in the future history of "civilization", which I *know* now is doomed to destruction'. Fresh from *After London*, he reflected 'how often it consoles me to think of barbarism once more flooding the world, and real feelings and passions, however rudimentary, taking the place of our wretched hypocrisies' (Mackail 1899: 144). Carpenter noted that Morris 'hated modern civilisation, and London as its representative, with a fierce hatred – its shams, its hypocrisies, its stuffy indoor life, its cheapjack style, its mean and mongrel ideals' (1916: 217). But when he came to write his own future novel, *News from Nowhere* (1891), Morris chose not to flood the streets and fashionable squares of London but to green them. While Morris was 'never weary of praising' *After London* (Mackail 1899: 144), the narrator of *News from Nowhere* time-travels to a clean, low-density city harmoniously connected by the salmon-filled Thames to the rural economy. In effortless communalism, freed from the miseries of paid labour, resourceful Londoners pursue the rediscovered pleasures of craft work.

'Nowhere' is a typically neo-medieval claim for the values and achievements of the Middle Ages, but in *After London* 'Jefferies did not imagine an ideal society rising to flourish in the wake of the old, just a rather familiar anarchic and violent past returning to haunt an English people who could now only dimly recall having been at the centre of a global empire' (Brannigan 2015: 2). Its isolated, fractious communities have reverted to a past that looks medieval, but London's demise does not release a creative Renaissance. Rather we witness a technologically impoverished society incapable of fairly basic manufacture, a society in which velvet, satin, tobacco, and wine are 'almost unobtainable', while china and printed books have become rare relics of an unfathomable past. Jefferies also refuses to idealise feudal order, presenting instead a hierarchical society that apes chivalric values but promotes a thinly disguised system of slavery in order to bolster a venal court. Jefferies was simply less inclined than Morris to idealise feudal life, as we sense from a passage in *Hodge and His Masters* in which he describes a hedger working with a billhook. Jefferies's praise of the craft involved in their creation is overshadowed by invocations of medieval brutality:

> A dreadful weapon that simple tool must have been in the old days before the advent of the arquebus. For with the exception of the spike, which is not needed for hedge work, it is almost an exact copy of the brown bill of ancient warfare [...] Wielded by a sinewy arm, what gaping gashes it must have slit through helm and mail and severed bone! Watch the man there – he slices off the tough thorn as though it were straw. (Jefferies 1992b: 168)

The passage unsettles by superimposing agricultural and military uses of the billhook, and the peaceful rustic with the sinewy-armed medieval soldier. There is in this a shadowed sense of potential reversion, of billhook to vicious weapon, of hedger to frenzied killer, and – in *After London*, a book obsessed with reversion – of poor humanity to the devolved bushmen whose club or 'spud' – a conceptual relative of the hedger's billhook – is a multifunctional killing tool.

Comparisons between Jefferies and Morris help to define relations between utopian and dystopian writings. While 'Jefferies yielded nothing to Morris in terms of apocalyptic longings', his dystopian turn should be seen as 'honesty' rather than pathological pessimism (Fowles 1980: xvii). The comparison is framed yet more helpfully by John Plotz:

> In response to what moved him in Jefferies, Morris conjured a quasimedieval realm from which capitalism has been banished and in which human desires are thereby totally reshaped. But both parts of *After London* follow a very different logic. Everything will change, without anything important changing. Species and mores do alter, but the laws that determine both speciation and the behavior of people in society remain unaltered. (2015: 40)

It is this 'stasis in flux', to use Plotz's apt phrase, that supplies the novel's distinctive dystopianism, rejecting the Enlightenment argument that by positively altering the social environment human nature becomes perfectible. Sumpter, reading the novel through the influence on Jefferies of political theorist Niccolo Machiavelli, argues that the resulting pragmatism of his position 'endorsed neither a liberal nor a Marxist vision of progress: in fact, he encouraged his readers to question whether progress was possible at all' (2011: 316). A rejection both of the progressive idea of linear progress and of the neo-medieval belief in progress-through-return, this new world is as venal as the old, and human nature as recognisable to Machiavelli as it is to the narrator of *After London*:

Men for ever trample upon men, each pushing to the front; nor is there safety in remaining in retirement, since such are accused of biding their time and of occult designs. Though the population of these cities all counted together is not equal to the population that once dwelt in a single second rate city of the ancients, yet how much greater are the bitterness and the struggle!

A Jefferies diary entry for March 1883 proclaimed 'that we must begin again like the Caveman. No knowledge at present of use since it does not help. We must destroy the idea of our knowing anything. We must fully acknowledge that we know nothing and begin again' (Looker 1948: 128); but *After London* asks whether beginning again is futile. It is here that we begin to tease out differences between Jefferies's approach and that of many twentieth-century dystopias. As Keith notes, Jefferies's vision does 'not partake of the calculated evil of the inverted Utopias of Huxley and Orwell', or, we might add, of their inspiration, Yevgeny Zamyatin's *We* (1924) (1965: 118). These novels focus on the disastrous power of centralised ideologies and insist on small, enduring powers of individual resistance. In *After London*, by contrast, 'we see a new struggling civilization making the same tragic mistakes and blunders as the old [in] a vision (and this is crucial) not of evil but of ignorance' (Keith 1965: 118). If 'beginning again only brings us back [to] the same tyranny and misery', then 'Jefferies's novel embodies a brutal vision of human and animal struggle' in which dystopia is 'the product of a wolfish human nature, compelled to repeat the mistakes of the past' (Sumpter 2011: 315–16).

In summer 1884, encapsulating decidedly dystopian feelings, a richly dark diary entry worried obsessively away at the latest London news:

> Little village. Mediaeval London. The Thames. Putrid black water, decomposed human body under the paddle wheel. Deeds of darkness, the body. Nine Elms, sewn up in sack. Children miserable, tortured just the same. The tyranny of the nobles now paralleled by the County Court. Machinery for extortion. The sewers system and the W.C. water. The ground prepared for the Cholera plague and fever, zymotic, killing as many as the plague. The 21 parishes of the Lower Thames Sewage Scheme without any drainage at all. The whole place prepared for disease and pestilence. Cruelty of hospital system to patient and for surrounding inhabitants.
> This W. C. Century. (Looker 1948: 180–1)

Haunted by epidemic disease, and preoccupied with waste and pollution, this remorseless Dickensian vision fulminates against assaults on that traditional symbol of purity and healing, water. Jefferies's horror at its debasement by human folly approaches Ruskin's furious denunciation of the despoiling of the Wandel springs in *The Crown of Wild Olive* (1873). Such concerns are refracted in that most watery of novels, *After London*, and one of its few partial consolations is the creation of a vast lake of almost entirely pure water. It is partial consolation because while the narrator regrets 'that it has so often proved only the easiest mode of bringing the miseries of war', he notes that 'men are never weary of sailing to and fro upon it [...] and in the evening we walk by the beach, and from the rising grounds look over the waters, as if to gaze upon their loveliness were reward to us for the labour of the day'.

Jefferies's dystopian preoccupation with London is widely evident. As Henry Salt observes, 'some of the very best of Jefferies' short essays are devoted to London scenes', and this preoccupation intensified after 1877 when he moved with his family to semi-rural Surbiton to be closer to the capital's publishing worlds (1894: 59). In *Nature Near London*, an obvious manifestation of this preoccupation, Jefferies is often surprised by the abundance of wildlife around London but never reconciled to its uncanny size, presence, and powers of attraction. As he notes in one essay, 'the inevitable end of every footpath round about London is London. All paths go thither', because 'the proximity of the immense City [...] induces a mental, a nerve-restlessness' that means 'you cannot dream for long, you must up and away, and, turn in which direction you please, ultimately it will lead you to London' (Jefferies 2012: 20). Ambivalence about London is also revealed in the piece published here as Appendix II, an undated fragment from the British Library. This offers a pained discursion on Jefferies's feeling that while 'everyone else has fully made up his mind and knows exactly what he is going to do', he remains a 'little', 'despicable', and 'paltry' outsider in the crowds, 'the only man in London who is not quite decided'. His eventual decision – to squeeze into a doorway to avoid the driven crowds – neatly underlines his isolation. 'The Modern Thames', one of six London essays in *The Open Air*, is a darkly comic account of his relationship with the waterway and is, for readers of *After London*, perhaps the most suggestive of his other writings. Jefferies had 'looked forward to living by the river with delight, anticipating the long rows I should have past the green eyots', the opportunities to 'gather many a flower and notice many a plant', to 'converse with the ancient men of the ferries and listen to their river lore', to observe 'a ruin or a timbered house', and to end with 'the delicious ease of floating home carried by the stream, repassing all that had pleased before' (2004: 117, 118). Instead he discovers a river both unruly and foolishly regulated, clogged with pleasure craft, courting couples, dangerous barges, and ignorant sportsmen. Intent on forensic investigation of present ills, the essay expresses elegiac longing for an older environment as he describes the loss from the river of otters, 'the last and largest of the wild creatures who once roamed so freely in the forests which enclosed Londinium', that 'fort in the woods and marshes [...] which to this day, though drained and built over, enwrap the nineteenth-century in thick mists' (Jefferies 2004: 115). Representing London as a disturbing element in a still-potent natural landscape, the fate of the river's wildlife symbolises moral turpitude: 'London ought to take the greatest interest in the otters of its river. The shameless way in which every otter that dares to show itself is shot, trapped, beaten to death, and literally battered out of existence, should rouse the indignation of every lover of nature' (Jefferies 2004: 115). Because a cultivated and commercialised Thames is now overrun by a morally savage people who care not for 'a living link going back to the days of Cassivelaunus' (2004: 115), Jefferies's response in *After London* was to use the unruly waters of the Thames to cleanse London of its population and to try to return its landscape to marsh and wood.

However, this attempt is only partly successful, and the novel's dystopianism is emphasised by the manner in which London continues to threaten long after its demise. While the novel 'envisages with equanimity and indeed with relief the total obliteration of the bourgeois civilization', the enduring stupidity of Jefferies's society is given a potent symbol in 'the terrible oozy mass and miasma of the marshes covering what was London' (Suvin 1983: 373). Although flooded, the city remains malign:

> It is a vast stagnant swamp, which no man dare enter, since death would be his inevitable fate. There exhales from this oozy mass so fatal a vapour that no animal can endure it. The black water bears a greenish-brown floating scum, which for ever bubbles up from the putrid mud of the bottom [...] When the vapour is thickest, the very wildfowl leave the reeds, and fly from the poison. There are no fishes, neither can eels exist in the mud, nor even newts. It is dead.

The passage's focus on the deathly qualities of London's afterlife is matched by a keen sense of its potent volatility, so inexhaustible

are the noxious Victorian gases that regularly poison the lake. As
Brannigan observes, the city is 'as foul and repugnant under water
as it was above' (2015: 2). London can be destroyed but what it
symbolises is ineradicable. It is difficult to imagine a more dystopian
conclusion than this.

Darwinian novel

Jefferies's dystopian turn involves 'a milieu in which plants, animals,
physical landscapes, and human society are greatly altered without
fundamentally changing the underlying rules that govern action'.
Dystopia and Darwinism are intimate bedfellows in the novel, and
critics have been keen to examine its evolutionary roots and content.
While Part I is the prime locus of evolutionary activity in the novel,
with the opening chapter's evocation of the intensively competitive
response of flora and fauna to the sudden opportunities opened up
by 'the event' perhaps its most intense manifestation, evolution profoundly shapes the novel's anxious and abidingly pessimistic pres-
entation of human affairs.

Jefferies's urge to Darwinise is an essentially ecological impulse
because it is interested in the interactions of organisms with each
other and with environment. This has roots in deep historical anal-
yses of rural landscape and culture. In *Wild Life in a Southern County*
Jefferies pauses his descriptions of the Wiltshire Downs to muse on
their long history, and in doing so invokes a vision of reforestation
that clearly anticipates 'Wild England':

> In endeavouring [...] for a moment to glance back into the
> unwritten past, and to reconstruct the conditions of some four-
> teen or fifteen centuries since, it must not be forgotten that the
> downs may then have presented a different appearance. There is
> a tradition lingering still that they were in the olden times almost
> covered with wood [...] I may even go further and say that, if left
> to itself, it would in a few generations revert to that condition; for
> this reason, that when a clump of trees is planted here, experi-
> ence has shown that it is not so much the wind or the soil which
> hinders their growth as the attacks of animals wild and tame.

If agriculture ceased, Jefferies suggests, 'these wide, open downs
become again a vast forest, as doubtless they were when the beaver
and the wild boar and the wolf roamed over the country' (1937:
39–40). *After London*'s vision of reversion to natural forms emerged
during such musings, playing persistently throughout Jefferies's work,

sometimes conjuring up images of himself as a lone backwoodsman, for whom 'there could be no greater pleasure [...] than to wander with a matchlock through one of the great forests or wild tracts that still remain in England' (1978: 350).

The relapsed world of *After London* is founded on many such environmental investigations. During an excursion for *Nature Near London*, he notices at the base of a river bridge that 'the current had scooped away the sand of the bottom by the central pier, exposing the brickwork to some depth'. Carefully observing a seemingly mundane interaction of the built and natural environment, Jefferies discerns silting processes and 'the same undermining process that goes on by the piers of bridges over great rivers' (2012: 46). From this it is merely an inspired imaginative jump to this passage from the fifth chapter of *After London*:

> By the changes of the sea level and the sand that was brought up there must have grown great banks, which obstructed the stream. I have formerly mentioned the vast quantities of timber, the wreckage of towns and bridges which was carried down by the various rivers, and by none more so than by the Thames. These added to the accumulation, which increased the faster because the foundations of the ancient bridges held it like piles driven in for the purpose [...] The waters of the river, unable to find a channel, began to overflow up into the deserted streets, and especially to fill the underground passages and drains, of which the number and extent was beyond all the power of words to describe. These, by the force of the water, were burst up, and the houses fell in.

Jefferies's ecological impulses result in *After London* in attempts to make imaginative projections of fluctuating animal population dynamics under new environmental circumstances. Human depopulation and widespread starvation amongst domestic pets permit rodent plagues to devastate agriculture, but then, in line with Malthusian and Darwinian logic, 'the extraordinary multiplication of these creatures was the means of providing food for the cats that had been abandoned in the towns, and came forth into the country in droves'. Adapting to their new environment, 'they became, in a very short time, quite wild, and their descendants now roam the forests' as a new rapidly evolved feline species. This ecological projection is essentially an extension of a passage in an earlier work describing a gamekeeper's wife adept at making rugs from the skins of cats killed by her husband: 'The majority were wild – that is, had taken up their residence in the woods, reverting to their natural state, and causing great havoc among the game. Feasting like this and in the joys of freedom, many had grown to a truly enormous size' (Jefferies 1978: 21). Evolutionary intimations accompany the reference to prodigious growth when 'reverting to their natural state', but Jefferies goes further in musing on 'the extraordinary number of cats which stray abroad and get their living by poaching':

> In the preserves say from ten to twenty miles round London the cats thus killed must be counted by thousands [...] In one little copse not more than two acres in extent, and about twelve miles from Hyde Park Corner, fifteen cats were shot in six weeks [...] When two or three wild or homeless animals take up their abode in a wood, they speedily attract half a dozen hitherto tame ones; and, if they were not destroyed, it would be impossible to keep either game or rabbits. (1978: 21–2)

In the same volume, Jefferies refers to domestic owls, kept in cereal districts to control populations of mice which 'if undisturbed [...] multiply in such numbers as would scarcely be credited' (1978: 30). These jittery reflections reveal that after Darwin Jefferies is as unsettled as delighted by the natural world, and that 'Wild England' involves imaginative extensions of such investigations. That the rapid evolution of *After London* unconvincingly neglects the extended timescales of Darwinism is less interesting than what this reveals about Jefferies's attitudes to nature and humanity.

These attitudes can be approached via *The Story of My Heart*, a work that attempts to communicate Jefferies's ardent desire for transcendent communion with the natural world, while conceding doubts about the consolations of nature. In an intense passage accepting that 'a great part, perhaps the whole, of nature and of the universe is distinctly anti-human' or 'outre-human', Jefferies cannot escape a conception of nature as ineffably other when presented with the exotic discoveries of modern science:

> How extraordinary, strange, and incomprehensible are the creatures captured out of the depths of the sea! The distorted fishes; the ghastly cuttles; the hideous eel-like shapes; the crawling shell-encrusted things; the centipede-like beings; monstrous forms, to see which gives a shock to the brain. They shock the mind because they exhibit an absence of design. There is no idea in them. (2008: 64)

In this familiar post-Darwinian nausea at an environment rendered uncanny and meaningless, such creatures 'call up a vague sense of chaos, chaos which the mind revolts from [...] It is like looking into chaos' (Jefferies 2008: 65). Despite his passionate longing for natural communion, Jefferies cannot escape a vision of indifferent materialism:

> There is nothing human in nature. The earth, though loved so dearly, would let me perish on the ground, and neither bring forth food nor water. Burning in the sky the great sun, of whose company I have been so fond, would merely burn on and make no motion to assist me. (2008: 61)

As Robert Macfarlane observes, Jefferies 'knew that nature might cure but that it might also be brutally mute, shocking in its disinterest' (2012: xxi). For many late Victorians evolutionary theory weakened or destroyed Rousseauvian and Romantic impulses to see nature as meaningful, connected, and kind, a site of inspiration and self-improvement for individuals, a direct connection to divinity, and a model for harmonious community. Through Darwin-influenced eyes nature can dissolve into meaningless matter, and appears competitive, indifferent, and distinctly other. As such, its status as a site of healing, comfort, and cultural insight is at the very least complicated. An important avenue to utopianism is cut off if one follows Darwin to a vision of nature as remorseless and disconnected from human life. 'Wild England' is inhospitable to its remnant human populace, a Darwinian environment in both its evolutionary upheavals and its anti-human qualities as a wilderness at once superabundant and unyielding. For that great Darwinian scholar Gillian Beer, 'Jefferies' work condenses fears which in the 1870s and 1880s intensified in the wake of Darwinian controversy: fears that decadence may be an energy as strong as development, and extinction a fate more probable than progress' (2000: 135).

Visions of ecological reversion lent urgent impetus to apocalyptic urges that form out of Jefferies's disenchantment with modernity. His Darwinism, like that of so many of his contemporaries, is social as well as environmental, centring on a wider *fin-de-siècle* anxiety, given perhaps its keenest edge in Max Nordau's *Degeneration* (1892) but evident across the whole range of European cultural production during this period, that human nature and civilisation are degenerative when put to the test. These anxieties are evident in a March 1884 diary entry describing a neglectful mother observed during a walk: 'Incomprehensible stupidity. The uselessness of attempting anything for the good of others when such asses [...] The people are so stupid. "I've given up the Human Race myself"' (Looker 1948:

166). Stronger Darwinian overtones are evident in April 1878 as he recorded an encounter with unsavoury drunks: 'see how easily and rapidly men would revert to the conditions of savage life. Give these a knobkerrie and assegai or bow and they are the same' (Looker 1948: 35). From such observations sprang the degenerative human elements of *After London*.

That Jefferies's Darwinist turn was at once scientific and social is clear in the manner in which evolution is made to affect human as well as animal populations. Environmental change fails to provide fertile conditions for human development, and humanity has fragmented into separate but equally dubious groups. Felix's mainstream society retains certain traditional markers of advancement, but is immoral and in permanent crisis. Felix, representing the best of that society, demonstrates talent as a designer, explorer, military strategist, and leader, so that much of the novel's slender optimism about the future is paradoxically projected on to the potential of an individual who is atypical of his culture and disregarded by it.

In an antagonistic relationship with the main human population are the gipsies and Bushmen, who initially seem clearly inferior, but ultimately destabilise the novel's racial scales. The Bushmen, descendants of beggars and the feckless ('a degraded class of persons who refused to avail themselves of the benefits of civilization'), are the imaginative kinsfolk of 'the scum of manufacturing towns' described by Jefferies in *The Gamekeeper at Home*, urban degenerates who ravage countryside game preserves in brutal armed gangs that 'display no skill, relying on their numbers, arms, and known desperation of character to protect them from arrest' (1978: 121). Persistently bestialised in a way that suggests a subordinate position in the novel's racial hierarchy, the Bushmen are 'like the black wood-dogs' in their 'fits of savage frenzy [that] destroy thrice as much as they can devour'. However, their advanced hunting skills and ability to move undetected provocatively implies that they are best-placed to thrive in the new conditions: in the Darwinian sense of adaptation, they now occupy the pinnacle of human development, their savagery a perfect evolutionary response to a savage, indifferent forest environment. Just as Jefferies prefers dystopia to utopia, so his engagement with evolutionary theory refuses its progressive connotations in favour of a competitive, anti-human vision of environment, and a degenerative vision of humanity in which hierarchical racial and social thinking is radically unsettled.

Romance

The ways that we have thought about the novel so far involve claims about content, but when one interprets the novel as a romance – as some critics believe we should – form and theme must both be considered. In the April 1884 letter to Longman, Jefferies described *After London* as 'in no sense a novel, more like a romance, but a romance of a *real* character' (Thomas 1978: 232). Keith devotes a chapter of his 1965 study to *Wood Magic, Bevis*, and *After London* as romances, arguing that Felix 'is really an extension of the Bevis of the earlier books', and that 'it would almost be possible to read these romances as a trilogy tracing the development of a single character – as a young child, as a growing youth, and as a man' (1965: 100). In these novels Keith discerns the helpful impact of 'dream-world' imaginative play on contemporary 'real world' concerns, with the demands of the latter ultimately predominating, and making *After London* 'a romance of the agricultural depression' in which 'country society has been deserted by the townsmen and left to its fate' (1965: 99, 117).

There remain reasons to consider *After London* as romance if one wishes to go beyond Keith's loose definition of the term. Chivalric romance, rooted in early medieval French literature, became a dominant high-culture poetic form, emerging from the related epic and the 'Chanson de Geste' after *The Song of Roland* (778). Retaining the epic's central quest framework, the romance evinces a greater preoccupation with courtly love and religious virtue. In a typical romance a valiant knightly protagonist, alone or with fellows, pursues a quest, defeating human and supernatural foes while maintaining chivalric values. Folklore, courtly garden locations, hunting scenes, and wilderness travel are all common elements of a genre that for English readers is best represented by *Sir Gawain and the Green Knight* (fourteenth century), Malory's *Le Morte d'Arthur* (1485), and Spenser's *The Faerie Queene* (1590–6).

Considered in these terms, *After London* can seem to be a self-conscious manifestation of the genre. While Suvin believes 'the focus on the boy-man hero, his courtly love, and his kingship' makes Part II a 'pure quest-romance' (1983: 375), one may feel sceptical when closely measuring Felix's credentials as a romance hero. While aristocratic, he is hardly an example of powerful masculinity when compared to his brother Oliver, to whom 'all the blood and bone and thew and sinew of the house seemed to have fallen', along with 'all the utter recklessness and warrior's instinct'. The younger brother is a fine knight, while the archer Felix labours under the weapon's lower-class associations. His temperament, moreover, makes him an unlikely hero:

> Felix made friends of none, and was equally despised by nominal friends and actual enemies. Oliver was open and jovial; Felix reserved and contemptuous, or sarcastic in manner. His slender frame, too tall for his width, was against him; he could neither lift the weights nor undergo the muscular strain readily borne by Oliver. It was easy to see that Felix, although nominally the eldest, had not yet reached his full development.

But it is this 'full development' that interests the novel, while Oliver, the obvious chivalric figure, disappears once Felix embarks on his quest.

The novel also does a mixed job of fulfilling other romance criteria. Although he has a clearly defined beloved in Aurora, Felix's pretensions as a courtly lover are questionable. His family's poverty makes him a poor match, and in his scenes with Aurora – which do take place in the appropriate garden setting – he is inarticulate, inconsiderate, and self-absorbed, suffering an unmasculine emotional outburst in which there is more flavour of the domestic novel than the romance. *After London* follows the quest's focus on wilderness journeys but has limited supernatural content: Felix reads a manuscript describing forest folklore spirits, but meets no supernatural foes, resists supernatural explanations, and is indifferent to Aurora's religious feeling. His combats are neither heroic nor preternatural: he is attacked by a Bushman, defeats gipsies in battle, is beaten out of camp by common soldiers, and nearly dies as a result of gas exposure. Of such deeds chivalric tales are rarely told. Difficult to reach, deadly, and generating its own folklore, London is a promising quest location, but while it tests Felix physically and mentally, its seemingly supernatural effects are always traced to material causes. The novel's ending fails to provide the clear resolution usually present in romance, while the society it describes is at heart unchivalric.

Crucially, Jefferies's seemingly self-conscious turn to a genre synonymous with the Middle Ages only emphasises his refusal to idealise the past. This is also evident in *Bevis*, as the two boys cheerfully decide on a period in which to set their war games:

> 'Let's have bow and arrow time,' said Mark; 'it's much nicer – and you sell the prisoners for slaves and get heaps of money, and do just as you like, and plough up the cities that don't please you.' (Jefferies 1976: 76)

Just as the boys want 'bow and arrow time' complete with plunder and offhand brutality, so *After London* conjures a bow and arrow hero living in a society rooted in slavery rather than chivalry. Jefferies, for whom human stupidity is geographically and temporally universal, finds the Middle Ages neither more barbarous nor more virtuous than any other period. His partial use of romance indicates a desire for fairytale hope, but its inconclusive ending, flawed society, and modern hero disclose scepticism about such fantasies.

Geography, nation, and power

Scholars have become increasingly involved in thinking about the ways in which landscape representation is not neutrally involved in disinterested accounts of environment, but participates in constructions of landscape that reveal the prevailing attitudes and ideological conditions of particular societies. Both Michael Bunce and Roger Ebbatson argue that nineteenth-century idealisations of the country and 'dialectical representations of the city as a pathologised environment' flourished as a reaction to urban capitalism and 'the consequent rise of the middle class to power' (Bunce 1994, Ebbatson 2005: 10). Ebbatson also espies in literary representations of landscape 'a complex process of signification of national identity based in binary tropes' in which 'a sense of stable cartographic models is perpetually undermined by cultural uncertainties and disorienting fragmentations' (2005: 1). In a parallel manner Brannigan's *Archipelagic Modernism* suggests that the 'nation texts' on which he focuses (covering the years 1890–1970) are 'as much concerned with biopolitical, evolutionary, and eugenics debates about social organisation as they were preoccupied with the geopolitical landscape of the British and Irish archipelago' (2015: 4). The ability of environment to act as a 'carrier' of a 'complex set of visual or verbal connotations', Ebbatson suggests, means that while landscape is often used in attempts to build a coherent ideology of nationhood, this unstable process is an ironically inevitable result of a crisis of coherence and belonging under capitalism: 'modernity and the industrial revolution cut humanity off from persistence and continuity, creating a rift between the self and the environment' that appears as points of tension or contradiction within texts (2005: 3). *After London* is interesting in this regard because, as we have seen, it replicates the 'pathologised environment' of London but refuses to replace it with an 'idealised rural image', thus resisting many of the nation-building endeavours Ebbatson describes.

A crisis in nineteenth-century literature's urge to construct national identity through landscape is reflected in *After London*. International relations are certainly important here, although they have taken a distinctly regionalist turn, with a patchwork of small, fragmented English states incapable of joint action in the face of threats from Welsh, Irish, and Scottish forces. As Brannigan points out, in a novel written during 'intense philosophical debate about "Home Rule" for Ireland [...] the return of Irish, Welsh, and Scottish political liberty is equated with the decline of "British" civilisation, and with the vulnerability of a weakened and isolated England to attack from its vengeful neighbours' (2015: 5), anxieties also evident in the glut of 'invasion novels' following *The Battle of Dorking*. If Brannigan is right, the fragmented political fabric of *After London* anticipates the yet greater cultural anxieties expressed in post-WWI modernism: 'the flood which scours a new archipelagic geography out of England is a revolutionary agent, purging the land of its industrial and commercial blight, even if it cannot usher in the new' (2015: 2). Suggesting links with T. S. Eliot's *The Waste Land* (1922), Brannigan regards *After London* as thematically and culturally 'proto-modernist', both 'an ecological fantasy' and 'a precursor to the modernist obsession with cataclysm and obliteration' (2015: 2). The hopelessly fragmented nationalities of *After London* also strongly endorse Ebbatson's claim that during this period 'the concept of Englishness is thus produced out of trauma but becomes a potent constellation of values throughout a period especially marked by a crisis of representation' (2005: 3). For Brannigan, *After London* records Jefferies's disillusionment with dominant 'narratives of progress, expansion, and enlightenment' that would be brought to severe crisis by WWI, but (as we have already seen) 'Jefferies's diluvian fantasy about the dissolution of Anglocentric power [...] contains no nostalgia for lost glories' (2015: 2).

In this context the ethnic groups of *After London* become significant. Rather than being constructed as savages who serve to solidify and define English national identity, the Gaelic invaders and the English are described in decidedly ambivalent ways. We learn that 'twice already vast armies have swept along threatening to entirely overwhelm the whole commonwealth', and that Welsh ships 'sail about the Lake committing direful acts of piracy', while the Irish seizure of Chester has heightened their threat. English myopia is underlined by the decision to hire Gaelic mercenaries 'who swarm in the palaces, in the council-chambers of the republics, and, opening the doors of the houses, help themselves to what they will'. Terrified by external threats, the narrator nonetheless concludes that 'no blame can, upon a just consideration, be attributed to either of these nations that endeavour to oppress us' because 'the ancients from whom we are descended held them in subjection many hundred years, and took from them all their liberties'. In this reminder of English oppression, the Welsh become potentially heroic in retaining their language, customs, and 'aspirations to recover their own'. There is, at any rate, an acknowledgement of multiple national perspectives, a sympathetic engagement that is of a piece with Jefferies's resistance to national stereotypes in his depiction, in *Wild Life in a Southern County*, of itinerant Irish labourers who are 'industrious, work well, drink little', 'bear generally a good character', and demonstrate 'a pleasing attachment to the employer who has once given them work and treated them with a little kindness' (1937: 321).

If notions of inherent national superiority are radically debunked by the novel, something similar occurs in racial or evolutionary terms, as we have already seen in the case of the Bushmen. Gipsies, the other principal denizens of the forest, feature regularly in Jefferies's other writings on the countryside, again described with greater sympathy than that shown by many contemporary accounts, and in ways that rarely rehearse their exotic constructions. In *After London*, admittedly, they are shadowy, exotic figures who 'attack every traveller, and every caravan or train of waggons which they feel strong enough to master'. We learn that 'vengeance is their religion and their social law, which guides all their actions among themselves', but where Bushmen have devolved, gipsies are recognisably human, but distinct from mainstream society, and with a clear belief in their own sense of superiority:

> The Romany looks on the Bushman as a dog, and slaughters him as such. In turn, the despised human dog slinks in the darkness of the night into the Romany's tent, and stabs his daughter or his wife, for such is the meanness and cowardice of the Bushman that he would always rather kill a woman than a man.

Nomadic gipsy society is socially complex, divided into functioning groups according to allegiances to a particular 'king, queen, or duke', and regulated by the 'strange ceremonies and incantations' of sorcerers and sorceresses. The mystical prominence of women in gipsy society certainly recapitulates orientalist tropes, but also reveals claims to a distinctive culture. Against a backdrop of late-Victorian obsession with race, breeding, and eugenics, it is ironic that the gipsy claim to superiority over the English is racial:

> They boast that their ancestry goes back so much farther than the oldest we can claim, that the ancients themselves were but

modern to them. Even in that age of highest civilization, which immediately preceded the present, they say (and there is no doubt of it) that they preserved the blood of their race pure and untainted, that they never dwelt under permanent roofs, nor bowed their knees to the prevalent religion. They remained apart, and still continue after civilization has disappeared, exactly the same as they were before it commenced.

Yet another example of 'stasis in flux', the continuity of gipsy culture may offer a more functional model than that of Felix's courtly society: their lifestyle, like that of the Bushmen, is better adapted to thrive in post-apocalyptic conditions than either Jefferies's 'namby-pamby' Victorians or Felix's countrymen, and their culture is at least as socially cohesive. The novel's preoccupations with race and nation are ultimately in tune with the pessimism we have traced elsewhere, but underline the range of contemporary contexts with which the novel engages, and the scepticism with which Jefferies approaches Englishness, nationhood, and race.

Experimental novel

Earlier I was at pains to engage with criticisms of the novel's characterisation and structure, and to suggest that these appear to be flaws if we judge the novel as part of the realist tradition. That they might be better considered as illustrative of a partially-realised desire for literary experimentation is supported by Plotz's observation that the novel's disenchantment with notions of historical progress is enacted at a formal level: the novel's 'stasis in flux' applies equally to the social situation and 'to individual characters, who remain essentially the same over time rather than adapting to the immediate ramifications of plot as the realist novel demands' (2015: 40).

Plotz's scepticism about *After London*'s realist credentials leads him to an original reading of the novel as an example of literary naturalism. Naturalism, generally thought to have been conceived by Émile Zola out of dissatisfaction with the focus and approach of the prevailing 'bourgeois novel', seeks to broaden fictional focus by turning to aspects of modern life that were felt to have been ignored or sentimentalised. Poverty, prostitution, alcoholism, and crime become staples in naturalist novels from Zola's vast Rougon-Macquart cycle onwards, as well as being evident in poetry, theatre, and the visual arts during the *fin de siècle*. Naturalism involves more than shifts of subject, however, for it aims for scientifically detached scrutiny of the effects of environment on individuals. Naturalism is a fluid label – it can equally seem a culmination of realism and a rejection of it – but for Plotz studies of the movement are hamstrung, firstly by regarding it as a 'narrow literary byway traversed by only a few novels', and secondly by suggestions that most British writers 'somehow missed the naturalist turn' (2015: 32, 33). Redefining naturalism as involving 'a new set of connected ideas, modes, and techniques responding to Darwinian thought', Plotz espies a broader movement 'that pervasively shaped fiction between 1859 and World War I' (2015: 32). While pointing out its kinship with both realism and modernism, Plotz argues that naturalism sharply contrasts 'with the realist and modernist prioritization of felt individual experience as the evidentiary matrix on which their accounts of the world are based' (2015: 33). In practice, the naturalist alternative involves a dual goal: firstly, 'showing the inevitable (or well-nigh inevitable) working out of physical and social laws would unveil the whole picture of an oppressive social system'; and secondly, 'replacing novelistic narrative with description (oscillating between the enormous and the minute) fostered contemplation of everyday life *sub specie aeternitatis*' (Plotz 2015: 37).

In terms of naturalism's attempts to describe the enormous (the whole social environment) and the minute (individual lives), Plotz finds that while '*After London* comes across initially as a hodgepodge, not even clearly a novel', its stylistic features and alternative history format make it a candidate for what he terms 'speculative naturalism' (2015: 35). The disparate elements of the novel combine in commitment to naturalist modes, through its Darwinian interest in the relationship between organisms and their environment, and through the narrative's 'palpable oscillation between microscopic description and macroscopic abstraction' in Parts I and II (Plotz 2015: 35, 36). Plotz's approach provides responses to criticisms of the novel's apparently shaky narrative line – now understood as the interplay of naturalism's macrocosms and microcosms – and of its distant characterisation – which becomes a necessary feature of naturalist detachment. Naturalism is also evident in Jefferies's use of what he describes as 'intermezzos' and Plotz as 'moments in which natural beauty materializes, Wordsworth-like, to disrupt narrative flow and to deliver timeless, plotless, developmentless aesthetic pleasure' (2015: 35). Use of intermezzos – so irksome and inexplicable to realists like Besant – 'holds out the prospect of a world that counters the blighted course of human events with a beauty that is not standoffish, in that it comprehends all natural life, including human life when considered apart from its despair inducing narrative dimension' (2015: 45). In realism such moments are irritating. In naturalism they are part of the whole point.

Plotz's compelling reading invites further reassessment of Jefferies's place within late-Victorian fiction, opening up fresh comparisons with Thomas Hardy (with whom he is often bracketed) and other British writers of a broadly naturalistic bent, including George Gissing and Arthur Morrison, whose bleak scrutiny of working-class poverty, and deep-seated suspicions about human nature, might be fruitfully placed alongside the forensic social analysis of 'Wild England'. A naturalist reading also invites assessment of whether the novel is involved in other modes of anti-realist experimentation. To do so we need to develop our earlier allusions to the difficulties of the novel's protagonist. The problem of Felix, I'd like to suggest, is not a matter of the author's characterisation skills or the novel's structure, but rather an indication of the emergence of a hero who is both of his author's time and an anticipation of the future.

Despite Felix's adventurous nature, intelligence, and ingenuity, he is a difficult hero with evident flaws. As the narrator concedes, his 'unbending independence and pride of spirit, together with scarce concealed contempt for others, had resulted in almost isolating him from the youth of his own age, and had caused him to be regarded with dislike by the elders'. The self-absorbed Felix – 'too quick to take offence where none was really intended' – is profoundly out of step with his peers – a diminutive scholar in a society that despises knowledge and praises strength, and an extremely ambitious individual with no friends, allies, or financial support for his remarkable plans. His weakness in reading social situations and power dynamics is often evident: at Aisi, on trial for unwisely uttering seditions about the King's military strategy, Felix avoids the death penalty by revealing his own strategic acumen, only to immediately misread the mood of the court to the extent that he is beaten out of camp.

As we have seen, Felix is also an unsatisfactory lover: during his visit to Thyma Castle, he is crippled by jealousy as better-positioned suitors pay their attentions to Aurora, and treats her badly, failing to recognise either the familial constraints under which she is placed or the secret love tokens that she leaves him. He is more doubtful about Aurora's true feelings than he should be, given that he claims to know and value her best. While the narrator leaves no doubt about Felix's love, we are never clearly shown how this feels or reassured that his passion is not primarily egotistical. While Felix develops and learns lessons during the course of his adventures (as a realist or romance hero should) he does so painfully slowly, and by the end retains key faults with which he begins – his pride, contemptuousness, and sense of isolation. Felix's lack of external validation by his peers is the principal spur for his quest, but in the closing chapters he is almost as dissatisfied to be received as a demi-God by his newly acquired followers, and it is difficult to follow Keith in concluding that he 'develops from a thwarted youth into a triumphant superman' (1965: 121). Rather, as Thomas suggests, Felix is dissatisfied with the 'embarrassing authority' gained by what he regards as ordinary talents (1978: 237). What he most dearly prizes – an estimation of his character that accords with his own self-image – remains elusive. Unfairly despised or unrealistically venerated, Felix remains alienated from almost everyone he meets:

> Felix's own position was bitter in the extreme. He felt he had talent. He loved deeply, he knew that he was in turn as deeply beloved; but he was utterly powerless [...] He could not start as a merchant without money; he could not enclose an estate and build a house or castle fit for the nuptials of a noble's daughter without money.

This is partly a typical spur of the quest format, the reason for his decision to 'go forth into the world', but it is more than this, as the extremity of language and feeling in the continuing passage demonstrates:

> Slowly the iron entered into his soul. This hopelessness, helplessness, embittered every moment. His love increasing with the passage of time rendered his position hateful in the extreme. The feeling within that he had talent which only required opportunity stung him like a scorpion.

Felix's mixture of egomania and self-loathing, and the manner in which his ambitions cannot be realised within his restrictive society, have suggested an intriguing parallel with the 'superfluous man' of Russian nineteenth-century literature, from Nikolai Gogol, Ivan Turgenev, and Ivan Goncharov to Fyodor Dostoyevsky and Anton Chekhov (Hooker 1996: 44). *After London*'s preoccupation with the effects of a restrictive society on the aspirations of a talented but alienated individual suggests a distant but intriguing kinship between Felix and the tortured idealists of these writers. Like Kirsanov, Raskolnikov, Oblomov, and the rest, Felix finds that his advanced education and progressive views are redundant, a hindrance rather than an aid because they merely provide the means to express the hopelessness of his position without providing any outlet for his energies. One could indeed go further, framing Felix as an anticipation of the predilection in some modernist works for the unlikeable and unworthy protagonist; or of the anguished central figures in existentialist fiction. Alienated, nauseated by others, and craving isolation, Felix is unable to achieve the overcoming promised by existentialist theory because he cannot fully embrace his own freedom of choice or forego his abiding preoccupation with how others perceive him. In these respects, Felix certainly looks more modern than many of his peers in late-Victorian British fiction.

With this in mind we can also reassess the novel's inconclusive close. While Besant's inevitable denunciation of the ending is typically unperceptive, Suvin's reading of 'a setting where his usual sensitive, thoughtful, impractical, discontented, and proud young misfit can work out his destiny to a happy ending impossible in capitalist civilization' is equally unrealistic (Besant 1888: 211, Suvin 1983: 375). To the more perceptive Fowles, 'the inconclusive ending' is 'entirely consistent with the underlying purpose of the novel': 'firmly announcing the future will turn out well, or the reverse, may numb man's age-old terror of not knowing [...] but it is not in harmony with reality' (1980: xx). For Fowles, 'Jefferies took the hardest option', an option, it seems clear, that further deepens Jefferies's credentials as a quietly experimental writer in anticipating the vogue for such endings amongst modernist and postmodern writing (1980: xx).

(Anti-)Pastoral novel

At the start of this introduction I suggested that *After London* merits attention as an 'Anthropocene novel', that is to say a work preoccupied with the destructive impact of human life on environment. The novel's pioneering reflections are intriguing, but we must remember that while Jefferies destroys London out of disgust at its indifferent exploitation of environment, this exploitation is not the physical cause of the capital's catastrophic end. In other words, Jefferies may regard London's downfall as fitting punishment, but its demise is caused by natural phenomena rather than human activity. We must be careful, therefore, in regarding this as an early warning about climate change, even though Wild England's climate and geography are much altered. Nonetheless, the novel's preoccupation with London is very much of its time in its anxieties about 'man's apparently uncontrollable effect on the environment around him, through population growth and consequential growth in resource consumption' (Bramwell 1989: 25). This zeitgeist is most commonly associated with John Ruskin's 'The Storm Cloud of the Nineteenth Century', a lecture given the year before *After*

London was published, in which Ruskin, in apocalyptic mode, offered one of the first claims about human-induced climate change:

> This wind is the plague-wind of the eighth decade of years in the nineteenth century; a period which will assuredly be recognized in future meteorological history as one of phenomena hitherto unrecorded in the courses of nature, and characterized pre-eminently by the almost ceaseless action of this calamitous wind. (1908: 31)

Ruskin ascribed these meteorological disturbances to coal-burning, but also saw the storm clouds he espied from his house in Cumbria as supernatural punishment for human folly:

> It looks partly as if it were made of poisonous smoke; very possibly it may be: there are at least two hundred furnace chimneys in a square of two miles on every side of me. But mere smoke would not blow to and fro in that wild way. It looks as if it were made of dead men's souls. (1908: 33)

As Vicky Albritton and Fredrik Albritton Jonsson suggest, the disturbances described by Ruskin can be ascribed to the 1883 eruption of Krakatoa and the end of the 'little ice age', but they point out that he 'was not wrong in his intuition that industrial civilization could for the first time alter the fabric of the natural world on a planetary scale' (2016: 15, 38–41, 42; see also Wheeler 1995). Jefferies's shared fears about the disastrous long-term impacts of human nature on the environment take physical and symbolic form in the ineradicable malignancy of London's flooded storehouse of poison. To a twenty-first-century readership acutely aware of the catastrophically enduring effects of industrial, agricultural, and commercial development this vision is powerful, but should not lead us to neglect the novel's specifically nineteenth-century concerns. It is in this sense that we need to understand Keith's claim that 'although [*After London*] is in many respects a new venture for Jefferies, the alternative title will remind us that the device is a daring and successful method of viewing his more usual field from a new angle' (1965: 115–16). This usual field – attempts to describe the totality of natural and rural experience – makes *After London* a thought-experiment in the consequences of continuing as Victorian society had thus far proceeded. *After London* becomes a candidate as one of the first Anthropocene novels insofar as it is reshaped by the preoccupations of later readers, but there is an older, more potent conceptual framework, the pastoral tradition, through which we can examine *After London*.

In whatever form it assumes, pastoral (or bucolic) is a product of civilisation, culture, and modernity, where modernity is defined not in terms of debates over the emergence of a defined historical era, but as the affective experience of every generation in being situated at the leading edge of social, political, cultural, and technological change, feeling that they bear an unprecedented burden of change, and seeking an escape from this predicament in constructions of alternative rural values. Running through pastoral's rich variety of modes is a contrast between rural simplicity and purity and urban complexity and vice, often also structured as a contrast between the present and the past. It is no coincidence, Garrard points out, that 'the emergence of the bucolic idyll correlates closely with large-scale urbanisation in the Hellenic period', doing so precisely to register the social shock-waves of this upheaval and growing anxieties about the apparently growing separation of city and country (2012: 39). Ironically, this sophisticated literary tradition, revolving around dreams of a simple, harmonious relationship between humanity and nature, can only exist in conditions of urban modernity.

Its first and core mode, the pastoral idyll, constructs an existing peopled landscape in which the abundant bounty of nature is effortlessly available to an innocent humankind, and in which, in Hesiod's *Works and Days* (7th c. BCE), even the marks of a plough or axe are represented as impious assaults on divine nature. Idylls are also extraordinarily vulnerable to dissolution, their fecundity and fragility equal markers of a volatile literary space. In Theocritus's *Idylls* (3rd c. BCE) the idyll is temporally present, but the various pastoral songs are enacted at the end of a day's labour, windows of poetic beauty between struggle with landscape and economics in a recognisable early Greek society. A truly effortless idyll is thus not available to Theocritus's goatherd singers, and even the Golden Age of *Works and Days* is no longer a present idyll: lost through human greed and folly, successively less exalted ages have followed until the poet's debased, nostalgic iron present. The gates of innocent, effortless Eden are likewise guarded implacably by flaming swords. In such moments we perceive the second, perhaps dominant, mode of this tradition, the pastoral elegy, a form characterised by regretful loss, and registering persistent nostalgic urges in acts of memory and of creativity to construct and memorialise lost idylls. In a register of its unstable power and temporal gymnastics, elegy protectively encases an idyll that is at once vividly present and irretrievably absent.

The intimately connected idyll and elegy are limited and partial reflections of the landscapes and economies of their writers, but pow-

erful indicators of how societies respond to their own changing circumstances. An enduring cultural impulse to elegise generates two
further modes: a belief that the lost idyll is recoverable leads to pastoral utopianism, while a belief that the disharmony that lost the idyll
in the first place is accelerating generates apocalyptic tropes. Because
pastoral is a persistent but evolving form, with 'a capacity to move
out of its old haunts in the Arcadian pastures and to inhabit the
ordinary country landscapes of the modern world', it remains part of
a self-reflexive tradition but also associated with particular moderni-
ties (Marinelli 1971: 3). As we learn from Bunce and Ebbatson, the
nineteenth century is particularly fertile ground for pastoral because
of accelerated urbanisation, industrialisation, and social change. The
period witnessed aspirations to locate, preserve, or construct idylls,
and neo-medievalism was only one instance of pastoral utopian urges.
At the same time, real and perceived destruction of landscapes gave
added energy to pastoral elegy, and to anti-pastoral literature. Seeking
to rebut the idealising tendencies of pastoral forms, anti-pastoralism
claims that environmental harmony has always been impossible, and
that pastoral impulses are too often conservative. Strongly shaped by
George Crabbe's polemical poem *The Village* (1783), anti-pastoralism
was invigorated in the Victorian period by Malthusianism, religious
scepticism, Darwinism, and attempts to understand profound social,
demographic, and environmental change. As Raymond Williams so
brilliantly argues, idylls and elegies have often been used to naturalise
hegemonic and repressive social structures and economic arrange-
ments in the countryside. Countering idylls and elegies, the various
strands of anti-pastoral either attempt, following Crabbe, to focus on
the sufferings of agriculturalists, or attempt to otherwise explain the
impossibility of harmonious co-existence. Given all of this, it should
be unsurprising that pastoral offers wide-ranging opportunities to
think through *After London*.

While Jefferies's nature essays regularly register delight at the natural world, he refused to idealise the countryside. Thomas's assessment of *Wild Life in a Southern County* – that Jefferies observes 'without
a tinge of pastoral or other sentiment' (1978: 120) – is as true of his
subsequent work. Claiming that 'Jefferies never had time for the
romantic view, then held by soft-centred middle-class intellectuals of
all persuasions from socialism to Anglo-Catholicism, of rural innocence as a viable antidote to urban evil', Fowles's characterisation of
After London suggests that at a time of agricultural depression the central pastoral contrast between city and country is in crisis: 'the book
damns all attempts to draw up battle-lines, or social solutions, on such

simplistic and sentimental grounds. London, uncontrolled capital in both social and economic senses, is evil; but fragmented rural poverty is no better' (1980: xvii). Keith reaches similar conclusions:

> Instead of the town overwhelming the country, it is the country that has survived and destroyed the town. [...] We are presented with a collection of scattered, isolated communities which have lost the inventions and sophistications of our own age [...] Man returns to Nature not through any desire on his part, but because Nature returns to him. (1965: 116)

In the same way, in his survey of the effects of education on rural life in *Hodge and His Masters*, Jefferies denies that a simpler, rural innocence has been lost and sympathises with the desire of farm girls to move to the cities: 'you cannot blame these girls [...] for thinking of something higher, more refined, and elevating than the cheese-tub or the kitchen' (1992b: 82). These insights suggest the destabilisation of a central assumption of pastoral – the superiority of rural over urban – and we can also see Jefferies's pessimism as a refusal to recreate the idyll, to construct a pastoral utopia, or even to elegise the past – for the past is corrupt London, indistinct in this reading from the corrupt present. Pastoral's reliance on temporal and spatial contrasts is elided in *After London* in a way that is both disorienting and unremittingly sceptical.

What we have already observed of the rapid evolutionary development, and the unyielding and dangerous state, of 'Wild England' can also now be read, through pastoral, as a further destabilisation of belief in the possibility of harmony between humanity and environment. Like Darwin's *On the Origin of Species*, *After London* threatens pastoral by introducing thinly populated or unpeopled landscapes that are either uncultivated or incapable of cultivation. Pastoral, the cultivated garden, is at odds with an alternative construction, the 'empty' wilderness, that was becoming more vivid as a result of increased access to travel and travel literature, and in particular because of westward expansion into the so-called wildernesses of North America.

That the anti-pastoralism of *After London* is social, environmental, and Darwinian marks the novel as a product of particular historical anxieties, but also vitally connected to our own because, as Brannigan argues, 'Jefferies understood something of the necessity of a new politics of planetary ecology, and understood too how ecology is inseparable from questions of social organisation' (2015: 17). Brannigan uses pastorally inflected language to claim that '*After London* is an exception in Jefferies's oeuvre, which more characteristically registers the diversity, richness, and wonder of the natural world [...] and seeks to champion a more harmonious co-existence of human life with other forms of ecology' (2015: 17). However, as I have tried to argue, *After London* is not exceptional in its scepticism about the possibility of harmony, something evident in a passage Brannigan quotes from *The Story of My Heart* in which Jefferies describes natural abundance in terms that are both pastoral and Darwinian:

> This our earth this day produces sufficient for our existence. This our earth produces not only a sufficiency, but a superabundance, and pours a cornucopia of good things down upon us. Further, it produces sufficient for stores and granaries to be filled to the rooftree for years ahead. I verily believe that the earth in one year produces enough food to last for thirty. (2008: 174)

Pastoral abundance pours forth from a fertile nature to a grateful humanity, but in Darwin the hyper-abundance is always checked by remorseless environmental competition. In a post-Malthusian, post-Darwinian, and capitalist context, Jefferies discovers, the earth's 'superabundance' does not reach everyone:

> Why, then, have we not enough? Why do people die of starvation, or lead a miserable existence on the verge of it? Why have millions upon millions to toil from morning to evening just to gain a mere crust of bread? Because of the absolute lack of Organisation by which such labour should produce its effect, the absolute lack of distribution, the absolute lack even of the very idea that such things are possible. Nay, even to mention such things, to say that they are possible, is criminal with many. (2008: 174)

In many nature essays Jefferies demonstrates that 'superabundance' is dependent upon the hardships of agricultural labour, and underlines the limitations of nature's consolations for labourers destined to work themselves to death. Jefferies's depictions of rural labour are particularly important if we want to read his work through pastoral. While his conservative 1872 letters to *The Times* paint a decidedly idyllic portrait of Wiltshire labour, Jefferies's views shifted markedly, so that by 1884 his critical depiction of landowners in *The Dewy Morn* typified a hardening radicalism and an intense sympathy for rural labour. This is strongly evident in an important passage from 'Sunlight in a London Square', from *The Life of the Fields*, where, in a typically pastoral fashion, he uses a city focus to form contrasts with the countryside, but then, in typically anti-pastoral fashion, places labour at the forefront in a way that rejects idyllic thinking:

So men laboured of old time, whether with plough or sickle or pruning hook, in the days when Augustan Virgil heard the garrulous swallow, still garrulous. An endless succession of labour, under the brightness of summer, under the gloom of winter; to my thought it is a sadness even in the colour and light and glow of this hour of sun, this ceaseless labour, repeating the same furrow, reiterating the blow, the same furrow, the same stroke – shall we never know how to lighten it, how to live with the flowers, the swallows, the sweet, delicious shade, and the murmur of the stream? (1884b: 212)

In a passage deliberately invoking Virgil's *Eclogues* (1st c. BCE), Jefferies finds continuities in the life of the swallow and in the ceaseless suffering of those rural labourers more normally idealised, rusticated, or occluded in the idyll. The Darwinian overtones of those 'reiterated blows' only emphasise the degree to which Jefferies refuses the consolation of idyll and elegy alike. 'One of the New Voters' (1885) also exposed the pitilessness of rural labour and its unpalatable social consequences. Both essays witness Jefferies's rejection of the pastoral myth of effortless abundance, for in his aspiration to describe the totality of countryside existence he often 'sees no way out; no way of blunting the contrast between the golden sun and wheat and the harvest slave' (Thomas 1978: 197). As Jefferies attempted to answer the question he posed in 'Sunlight in a London Square', he did not entirely reject the possibility of a better future for country and city:

I hope that at some time, by dint of bolder thought and freer action, the world shall see a race able to enjoy it without stint, a race able to enjoy the colours of the garden of life. To look backwards with the swallow there is sadness, to-day with the fleck of cloud there is unrest; but forward, with the broad sunlight, there is hope. (1884b: 213)

Hope in the future, while typically muted, and based on no particular grounds, is at least not extinguished.

Given the strongly anti-pastoral positions of much of Jefferies's later work, one should be cautious in expecting pastoral consolations from *After London*. The grounds for such an expectation lie, of course, in the fact that Felix's new prospects begin with his encounter with a simple race of shepherds, but when one examines this encounter, pastoral possibilities seem immediately to be endangered by the presence of Felix as a disturbing agent. This is particularly evident when considering his future plans, which envisage the militarisation of the Downs environment and of a people who 'had no other arms themselves but spears and knives' with which to protect themselves from persistent low-level conflict with gipsies. In one such conflict Felix's brilliant archery – a form of fighting with which the shepherds and gipsies are 'utterly unfamiliar' – eventually prompts over 6,000 tribesfolk to swear fealty to him. Earlier in the novel Felix's plans for a fortress at a strategic location on the lake lead to nothing, but with his new authority comes the opportunity to similarly fortify the Downs:

> He mentioned his scheme to the shepherds; they did not greatly care for it, as they had always been secure without it, the rugged nature of the country not permitting horsemen to penetrate. But they were so completely under his influence that to please him they set about the work. He had to show them how to make a palisade; they had never seen one, and he made the first part of it himself.

The shepherds' well-founded scepticism is based on sound knowledge of terrain, but gives way to a dutiful compliance with the technologically advanced newcomer that implies the start of a troubling pattern of social transformation. Earlier in the novel, as we noted, Felix's misery arose from his thwarted desire to 'enclose an estate and build a house or castle fit for the nuptials of a noble's daughter'. Felix's new position thus fulfils an urge for recognition, status, and power that looks distinctly patriarchal. His plans for a fortress and port, if realised, would lead to urbanisation and drastic changes to the social composition and customs of the tribes. As Fowles observes, Felix can never 'truly fit the pastoral simplicity of his shepherd-tribe's life' (1980: xix), and this is precisely because his leadership and romantic aspirations are, as Hooker observes, 'bound up with a concept of manhood which is founded on "taking possession" – of place, of people, and of his beloved' (1996: 49). The novel's romance quest, steeped in a construction of masculinity ultimately based on conquest, exists in tension with any pastoral possibilities the plot attempts to pursue.

Such a reading, through pastoral, may lead us to revisit some of the ways in which we have already approached the novel, suggesting, for example, the possibility that its Gaelophilic admissions of the historic failures of England do not mean that Felix escapes the imperialist connotations of Victorian nation building. It appears impossible for Felix to imagine a territory not defined by military strength, and there is limited sense of cultural exchange because Felix's knowledge of herbs, meteorology, and crafts, received as signs of supernatural power, renders the shepherds passive recipients of advanced knowledge.

Developing Hooker's observation that the novel is 'imbued with the spirit of imperialism in its concept of manhood and leadership' (1996: 51), it becomes possible to think of Felix's encounter with the tribes in terms of encounters between indigenous peoples and European and American settlers, and in doing so to relinquish any fading hope of pastoral comfort in the novel. In such a reading, the inconclusive ending – in which Felix sets off through the forest to attempt to win the hand of Aurora and return to his nascent shepherd kingdom – may offer relief only in the possibility that Felix will fail in his quest and offer no further disturbance to a fragile rural community. This represents the first of two potential ways of reading the ending of the novel through pastoral, a reading in which the demands of a martial romance are antagonistic to the pastoral culture of the shepherds. The other, finally more positive, reading is one in which hope is attached, on the assumption of Felix's successful return, to the redemptive possibilities of that culture in its interactions with Felix and the more sensible, sensitive, and socially active Aurora.

Jefferies's generally anti-pastoral position disinclines him to provide much material on which such hopes can fix, but we might also note that he rather characteristically refuses to foreclose the possibility of an optimistic outcome that avoids the worst excesses imagined in our first reading of the ending. Given that he has received the voluntary allegiance of thousands of followers, Felix has no plans for military conquest, and his vision does not entirely replicate the knightly structures of his old world: he adopts a role as 'war leader', astutely leaving traditional local rulers in peacetime authority, while his archery skills suggest a different kind of warfare to the muddled, asinine chivalry seen at Aisi. Given Jefferies's refusal to provide a clear ending, much rests on whether readers can conceive the possibility of a new way of living life after London that is neither an idealised realm of effortless pastoral plenty – we witness how hard the tribes work for their sustenance – nor simply a replication of the hateful disorder of courtly society, but a pragmatic synthesis of two worlds, a nascent realm of social experimentation that might, for readers drawn towards utopian possibilities, even offer a model community capable of finally ending the country's long relapse into barbarism while learning how to thrive in Wild England.

Further Reading

Albritton, Vicky and Fredrik Albritton Jonsson (2016), *Green Victorians: The Simple Life in John Ruskin's Lake District*, Chicago: Chicago University Press.

Allen, Grant (1897), 'The Thames Valley Catastrophe', *Strand Magazine*, 14.

Asimov, Isaac (1975), 'How Easy to See the Future!', *Natural History*, 84.4, 92–6.

Atheling Jr, William (1967), *The Issue at Hand*, Chicago: Advent.

Ballard, J. G. (1962), *The Drowned World*, New York: Berkley.

Barr, Robert (1895), 'The Doom of London', in *The Face and the Mask*, New York: Frederick A. Stokes, pp. 65–78.

Beer, Gillian (2000), *Darwin's Plots: Evolutionary Narrative in Darwin, George Eliot and Nineteenth-Century Fiction*, 2nd edn, Cambridge: Cambridge University Press.

Besant, Walter (1888), *The Eulogy of Richard Jefferies*, London: Chatto & Windus.

Bramwell, Anna (1989), *Ecology in the 20th Century*, New Haven and London: Yale University Press.

Brannigan, John (2015), *Archipelagic Modernism: Literature in the Irish and British Isles, 1890–1970*, Edinburgh: Edinburgh University Press.

Bunce, Michael (1994), *The Countryside Ideal: Anglo-American Images of Landscape*, London: Routledge.

Carpenter, Edward (1916), *My Days and Dreams*, London: Allen & Unwin.

Chesney, George Tompkyns [1871] (1914), *The Battle of Dorking*, London: Grant Richards.

Christopher, John (1951), *The Death of Grass*, London: Michael Joseph.

Crabbe, George [1783] (1886), 'The Village', in *Poems*, London: Cassell.

Daly, Nicholas (2011), 'The Volcanic Disaster Narrative: From Pleasure Garden to Canvas, Page, and Stage', *Victorian Studies*, 53.2, 255–85.

Darwin, Charles (1859), *On the Origin of Species by Means of Natural Selection, or the Preservation of Favoured Races in the Struggle for Life*, London: John Murray.

Ebbatson, Roger (2005), *An Imaginary England: Nation, Landscape and Literature, 1840–1920*, Aldershot: Ashgate.

Eliot, T. S. (1922), *The Waste Land*, New York: Horace Liverwright.

Fowles, John (1980), 'Introduction', in Richard Jefferies, *After London, or Wild England*, Oxford: Oxford University Press, pp. vii–xxi.

Garrard, Greg (2012), *Ecocriticism*, 2nd edn, Abingdon: Routledge.

Golding, William (1954), *The Lord of the Flies*, London: Faber and Faber.

Grahame, Kenneth (1908), *The Wind in the Willows*, London: Methuen.

Hay, William Delisle (1880), *The Doom of the Great City: Being the Narrative of a Survivor Written* A.D. *1942*, London: Newman.

Hesiod [7th c. BCE] (2008), *Theogony* and *Works and Days*, trans. M. L. West, Oxford: Oxford World Classics.

Hooker, Jeremy (1996), *Writers in a Landscape*, Cardiff: University of Wales Press.

Jefferies, Richard (1884a), *The Dewy Morn*, London: Richard Bentley and Son.

—— (1884b), *The Life of the Fields*, London: Chatto & Windus.

—— [1879] (1937), *Wild Life in a Southern County*, London: Thomas Nelson.

—— [1882] (1976), *Bevis: The Story of a Boy*, abridged edn, ed. Brian Jackson, Harmondsworth: Puffin.

—— [1878, 1879] (1978), *The Gamekeeper at Home* and *The Amateur Poacher*, ed. Richard Fitter, Oxford: Oxford University Press.

—— [1880] (1986), *Greene Ferne Farm*, ed. Andrew Rossabi, London: Grafton Books.

—— [1880] (1987), *Round About a Great Estate*, ed. John Fowles, Bradford on Avon: Ex Libris Press.

—— [1887] (1992a), *Amaryllis at the Fair*, Stroud: Alan Sutton.

—— [1880] (1992b), *Hodge and His Masters*, ed. Angela Richardson, Stroud: Alan Sutton.

—— [1881] (1995), *Wood Magic*, Ware: Wordsworth.

—— [1885] (2004), *The Open Air*, Fairfield: 1st World Library.

—— [1883] (2008), *The Story of My Heart: My Autobiography*, London: Faber and Faber.

—— [1883] (2012), *Nature Near London*, ed. Robert Macfarlane, London: Harper Collins.

Jones, Jingo (1900), *The Sack of London by the Highland Host: A Romance of the Period*, London: Simpkin, Marshall & Co.

Keith, W. J. (1965), *Richard Jefferies: A Critical Study*, London: University of Toronto Press.

Leavis, Q. D. [1938] (1989), 'Lives and Works of Richard Jefferies', in *Q. D. Leavis: Collected Essays*, ed. G. Singh, 3 vols, Cambridge: Cambridge University Press, vol. 3, pp. 254–63.

Looker, Samuel J. (1948), *The Nature Diaries and Note-Books of Richard Jefferies*, London: Grey Walls Press.

Macfarlane, Robert (2012), 'Introduction', in Richard Jefferies, *Nature Near London*, London: Harper Collins, pp. xi–xxv.

Mackail, J. W. (1899), *The Life of William Morris*, 2 vols, London: Longman, Green & Co.

Malory, Thomas (1485), *Le Morte d'Arthur*, Westminster: William Caxton.

Marinelli, Peter V. (1971), *Pastoral*, London: Methuen.

Milne, A. A. (1926), *Winnie-the-Pooh*, London: Methuen.

Morris, William (1891), *News from Nowhere*, London: Reeves and Turner.

Nordau, Max (1895), *Degeneration*, trans. from the 2nd German edn, London: William Heinemann.

Parrinder, Patrick (1995), 'From Mary Shelley to *The War of the Worlds*: The Thames Valley Catastrophe', in David Seed (ed.), *Anticipations: Essays on Early Science Fiction and its Predecessors*, Syracuse, NY: Syracuse University Press, pp. 58–74.

Plotz, John (2015), 'Speculative Naturalism and the Problem of Scale: Richard Jefferies's *After London*, after Darwin', *Modern Language Quarterly*, 76.1, 31–56.

Ransome, Arthur (1930), *Swallows and Amazons*, London: Jonathan Cape.

Richardson, Angela (1992), 'Introduction', in Richard Jefferies, *Hodge and His Masters*, Stroud: Alan Sutton, pp. vii–xv.

Rossabi, Andrew (1986), 'Introduction', in Richard Jefferies, *Greene Ferne Farm*, London: Grafton Books, pp. 9–12.

Ruskin, John (1873), *The Crown of Wild Olive*, London: George Allen.

——[1884] (1908), 'The Storm Cloud of the Nineteenth Century', in *The Library Edition of John Ruskin's Works*, ed. E. T. Cook and Alexander Wedderburn, 39 vols, London: George Allen, vol. 34, pp. 7–41.

Salt, Henry (1894), *Richard Jefferies: A Study*, London: Swan Sonneschein.

Shelley, Mary (1826), *The Last Man*, London: Henry Colburn.

Sir Gawain and the Green Knight [14th c.] (2008), trans. Tony Harrison, Oxford: Oxford World Classics.

Spenser, Edmund (1596), *The Faerie Queene*, London.

Sumpter, Caroline (2011), 'Machiavelli Writes the Future: History and Progress in Richard Jefferies's *After London*', *Nineteenth-Century Contexts*, 33.4, 315–31.

Suvin, Darko (1983), *Victorian Science Fiction in the UK: The Discourses of Knowledge and of Power*, Boston: G. K. Hall & Co.

Theocritus [3rd c. BCE] (2008), *Idylls*, trans. Richard Hunter, Oxford: Oxford World Classics.

Thomas, Edward [1909] (1978), *Richard Jefferies*, London: Faber and Faber.

Virgil [1st c. BCE] (2009), *The Eclogues* and *The Georgics*, trans. C. Day Lewis, Oxford: Oxford World Classics.

Warren, C. Henry (1948), 'Richard Jefferies', *New English Review*, 1, 25–31.

Watson, Henry Crocker Marriott (1890), *The Decline and Fall of the British Empire; or, The Witch's Cavern*, London: Trischler.

Wheeler, Michael (1995), 'Introduction', in Wheeler (ed.), *Ruskin and Environment*, Manchester: Manchester University Press, pp. 1–9.

White, Gilbert (1789), *The Natural History of Selborne*, London: Benjamin White.

Williams, Raymond [1973] (1985), *The Country and the City*, London: Hogarth Press.

Wolfreys, Julian and William Baker (1996), *Literary Theories: A Case Study in Critical Performance*, Basingstoke: Palgrave Macmillan.

A Richard Jefferies Chronology

1840 Foundation of Royal Agricultural Society; start of period of intensive modernisation and mechanisation of farming.

1843 Swindon connected to railway system.

1846 Repeal of the Corn Laws.

1848 Richard Jefferies born, 6 November, at Coate Farmhouse, near Swindon.

1859 Charles Darwin, *On the Origin of Species*.

1863 Jefferies leaves school.

1864 Jefferies and friend run away to France, intending to reach Russia.

1866 Jefferies becomes reporter with the *North Wilts Herald*.

1867 Jefferies suffers first symptoms of tuberculosis; Second Reform Act extends suffrage to all male householders.

1870s Period of agricultural depression begins (to 1890s).

1871 George Chesney, *The Battle of Dorking*.

1872 Jefferies's three agricultural letters to *The Times* published, November; first farming union formed; Thomas Hardy begins writing career.

1873 Jefferies begins career placing essays with *Fraser's Magazine*, *The Pall Mall Gazette*, *The Standard*, *New Quarterly Journal*, *Longman's Magazine*, *Live Stock Journal*, the *Manchester Guardian*, *Graphic*, and others; *Reporting, Editing, and Authorship*.

1874 Jefferies marries Jessie Baden; *The Scarlet Shawl*.

1875 Jefferies's first child, Richard Harrold, born; *Restless Human Hearts*.

1876 'The Great Snow' (unpublished).

1877 Jefferies family moves to Tolworth, Surbiton; *World's End*.

1878 *The Gamekeeper at Home*.

1879 *Wild Life in a Southern County*; *The Amateur Poacher*.

1880 Jefferies's second child, Jessie Phyllis, born; *Hodge and His Masters*; *Round About a Great Estate*; *Greene Ferne Farm*; William Hay, *The Doom of the Great City*.

1881 Beginning of final decline of Jefferies's health; moves to West Brighton to convalesce; *Wood Magic*.

1882 *Bevis: The Story of a Boy*.

1883 Jefferies's third child, Richard Oliver, born; *Nature Near London*; *The Story of My Heart*.

1884 Moves to Eltham; *Red Deer*; *The Life of the Fields*; *The Dewy Morn*; John Ruskin, 'The Storm Cloud of the Nineteenth Century'.

1885 Jefferies permanently invalided; Richard Oliver Jefferies dies; *After London*; *The Open Air*.

1886 Moves to Sussex; receives a Royal Literary Fund grant.

1887 Dies, 14 August; buried in Broadwater and Worthing Cemetery; *Amaryllis at the Fair*.

1888 Walter Besant, *The Eulogy of Richard Jefferies*.

1889 *Field and Hedgerow*.

1891 William Morris, *News from Nowhere*.

1892 *The Toilers of the Field*.

1895 Robert Barr, 'The Doom of London'.

1897 Grant Allen, 'The Thames Valley Catastrophe'.

1901 Death of Queen Victoria.

A Note on the Text

The following text follows the first edition published by Cassell & Company in 1885. There are no variant editions. Original spellings are maintained except where obvious typographical errors in the original were identifiable. There has also been no attempt to amend Jefferies's regularly inconsistent use of hyphens, nor his often idiosyncratic punctuation. A few explanatory footnotes have been added to the text where clarification was deemed necessary.

I am indebted to the production team at Edinburgh University Press for their work in putting this edition together, and to Professor Julian Wolfreys, editor of the series, for approving the edition; and eternally grateful to Professor Michael Wheeler, whose introduction to *Ruskin and Environment* (1995) first alerted me to the existence of this intriguing novel.

After London; or Wild England
by Richard Jefferies

Part I

The Relapse into Barbarism

CHAPTER I

THE GREAT FOREST

THE old men say their fathers told them that soon after the fields were left to themselves a change began to be visible. It became green everywhere in the first spring, after London ended, so that all the country looked alike.

The meadows were green, and so was the rising wheat which had been sown, but which neither had nor would receive any further care. Such arable fields as had not been sown, but where the last stubble had been ploughed up, were overrun with couch-grass, and where the short stubble had not been ploughed, the weeds hid it. So that there was no place which was not more or less green; the footpaths were the greenest of all, for such is the nature of grass where it has once been trodden on, and by-and-by, as the summer came on, the former roads were thinly covered with the grass that had spread out from the margin.

In the autumn, as the meadows were not mown, the grass withered as it stood, falling this way and that, as the wind had blown it; the seeds dropped, and the bennets became a greyish-white, or, where the docks and sorrel were thick, a brownish-red. The wheat, after it had ripened, there being no one to reap it, also remained standing, and was eaten by clouds of sparrows, rooks, and pigeons, which flocked to it and were undisturbed, feasting at their pleasure. As the winter came on, the crops were beaten down by the storms, soaked with the rain, and trodden upon by herds of animals.

Next summer the prostrate straw of the preceding year was concealed by the young green wheat and barley that sprang up from the grain sown by dropping from the ears, and by quantities of docks, thistles, oxeye daisies, and similar plants. This matted mass grew up through the bleached straw. Charlock, too, hid the rotting roots in the fields under a blaze of yellow flower. The young spring meadow-grass could scarcely push its way up through the long dead grass and bennets of the year previous, but docks and thistles, sorrel, wild carrots, and nettles, found no such difficulty.

Footpaths were concealed by the second year, but roads could be traced, though as green as the sward, and were still the best for walking, because the tangled wheat and weeds, and, in the meadows, the long grass, caught the feet of those who tried to pass through. Year by year the original crops of wheat, barley, oats, and beans asserted their presence by shooting up, but in gradually diminished force, as nettles and coarser plants, such as the wild parsnips, spread out into the fields from the ditches and choked them.

Aquatic grasses from the furrows and water-carriers extended in the meadows, and, with the rushes, helped to destroy or take the place of the former sweet herbage. Meanwhile the brambles, which grew very fast, had pushed forward their prickly runners farther and farther from the hedges till they had now reached ten or fifteen yards. The briars had followed, and the hedges had widened to three or four times their first breadth, the fields being equally contracted. Starting from all sides at once, these brambles and briars in the course of about twenty years met in the centre of the largest fields.

Hawthorn bushes sprang up among them, and, protected by the briars and thorns from grazing animals, the suckers of elm-trees rose and flourished. Sapling ashes, oaks, sycamores, and horse-chestnuts, lifted their heads. Of old time the cattle would have eaten off the seed leaves with the grass so soon as they were out of the ground, but now most of the acorns that were dropped by birds, and the keys that were wafted by the wind, twirling as they floated, took root and grew into trees. By this time the brambles and briars had choked up and blocked the former roads, which were as impassable as the fields.

No fields, indeed, remained, for where the ground was dry, the thorns, briars, brambles, and saplings already mentioned filled the space, and these thickets and the young trees had converted most part of the country into an immense forest. Where the ground was naturally moist, and the drains had become choked with willow roots, which, when confined in tubes, grow into a mass like the brush of a fox, sedges and flags and rushes covered it. Thorn bushes were there too, but not so tall; they were hung with lichen. Besides the flags and reeds, vast quantities of the tallest cow-parsnips or 'gicks'* rose five or six feet

---

* Hogweed (*Heracleum sphondylium*), a native umbelliferous plant, not to be confused with its relative, Giant Hogweed (*Heracleum mantegazzianum*), the notoriously phototoxic plant introduced to Britain as a tall and spectacular garden novelty and now widely naturalised. 'Gicks' (sometimes 'Gix') is a dialect word, confined to Gloucestershire and Jefferies's native Wiltshire, often used to describe the dry stalks of tall umbelliferous plants. It is used regularly in Jefferies's works.

high, and the willow herb with its stout stem, almost as woody as a shrub, filled every approach.

By the thirtieth year there was not one single open place, the hills only excepted, where a man could walk, unless he followed the tracks of wild creatures or cut himself a path. The ditches, of course, had long since become full of leaves and dead branches, so that the water which should have run off down them stagnated, and presently spread out into the hollow places and by the corner of what had once been fields, forming marshes where the horsetails, flags, and sedges hid the water.

As no care was taken with the brooks, the hatches upon them gradually rotted, and the force of the winter rains carried away the weak timbers, flooding the lower grounds, which became swamps of larger size. The dams, too, were drilled by water-rats, and the streams percolating through, slowly increased the size of these tunnels till the structure burst, and the current swept on and added to the floods below. Mill-dams stood longer, but, as the ponds silted up, the current flowed round and even through the mill-houses, which, going by degrees to ruin, were in some cases undermined till they fell.

Everywhere the lower lands adjacent to the streams had become marshes, some of them extending for miles in a winding line, and occasionally spreading out to a mile in breadth. This was particularly the case where brooks and streams of some volume joined the rivers, which were also blocked and obstructed in their turn, and the two, overflowing, covered the country around; for the rivers brought down trees and branches, timbers floated from the shore, and all kinds of similar materials, which grounded in the shallows or caught against snags, and formed huge piles where there had been weirs.

Sometimes, after great rains, these piles swept away the timbers of the weir, driven by the irresistible power of the water, and then in its course the flood, carrying the balks before it like battering rams, cracked and split the bridges of solid stone which the ancients had built. These and the iron bridges likewise were overthrown, and presently quite disappeared, for the very foundations were covered with the sand and gravel silted up.

Thus, too, the sites of many villages and towns that anciently existed along the rivers, or on the lower lands adjoining, were concealed by the water and the mud it brought with it. The sedges and reeds that arose completed the work and left nothing visible, so that the mighty buildings of olden days were by these means utterly buried. And, as has been proved by those who have dug for treasures, in our time the very foundations are deep beneath the earth, and not to be got at for the water that oozes into the shafts that they have tried to sink through the sand and mud banks.

From an elevation, therefore, there was nothing visible but endless forest and marsh. On the level ground and plains the view was limited to a short distance, because of the thickets and the saplings which had now become young trees. The downs only were still partially open, yet it was not convenient to walk upon them except in the tracks of animals, because of the long grass which, being no more regularly grazed upon by sheep, as was once the case, grew thick and tangled. Furze, too, and heath covered the slopes, and in places vast quantities of fern. There had always been copses of fir and beech and nut-tree covers, and these increased and spread, while bramble, briar, and hawthorn extended around them.

By degrees the trees of the vale seemed as it were to invade and march up the hills, and, as we see in our time, in many places the downs are hidden altogether with a stunted kind of forest. But all the above happened in the time of the first generation. Besides these things a great physical change took place; but, before I speak of that, it will be best to relate what effects were produced upon animals and men.

In the first years after the fields were left to themselves, the fallen and over-ripe corn crops became the resort of innumerable mice. They swarmed to an incredible degree, not only devouring the grain upon the straw that had never been cut, but clearing out every single ear in the wheat-ricks that were standing about the country. Nothing remained in these ricks but straw, pierced with tunnels and runs, the home and breeding-place of mice, which thence poured forth into the fields. Such grain as had been left in barns and granaries, in mills, and in warehouses of the deserted towns, disappeared in the same manner.

When men tried to raise crops in small gardens and enclosures for their sustenance, these legions of mice rushed in and destroyed the produce of their labour. Nothing could keep them out, and if a score were killed, a hundred more supplied their place. These mice were preyed upon by kestrel hawks, owls, and weasels; but at first they made little or no appreciable difference. In a few years, however, the weasels, having such a superabundance of food, trebled in numbers, and in the same way the hawks, owls, and foxes increased. There was then some relief, but even now at intervals districts are invaded, and the granaries and the standing corn suffer from these depredations.

This does not happen every year, but only at intervals, for it is noticed that mice abound very much more in some seasons than others. The extraordinary multiplication of these creatures was the means of providing food for the cats that had been abandoned in the towns, and came forth into the country in droves. Feeding on the mice, they became, in a very short time, quite wild, and their descendants now roam the forests.

In our houses we still have several varieties of the domestic cat, such as the tortoiseshell, which is the most prized, but when the above-mentioned cats became wild, after a while the several varieties disappeared, and left but one wild kind. Those which are now so often seen in the forest, and which do so much mischief about houses and enclosures, are almost all greyish, some being striped, and they are also much longer in the body than the tame. A few are jet black; their skins are then preferred by hunters.

Though the forest cat retires from the sight of man as much as possible, yet it is extremely fierce in defence of its young, and instances have been known where travellers in the woods have been attacked upon unwittingly approaching their dens. Dropping from the boughs of a tree upon the shoulders, the creature flies at the face, inflicting deep scratches and bites, exceedingly painful, and sometimes dangerous, from the tendency to fester. But such cases are rare, and the reason the forest cat is so detested is because it preys upon fowls and poultry, mounting with ease the trees or places where they roost.

Almost worse than the mice were the rats, which came out of the old cities in such vast numbers that the people who survived and saw them are related to have fled in fear. This terror, however, did not last so long as the evil of the mice, for the rats, probably not finding sufficient food when together, scattered abroad, and were destroyed singly by the cats and dogs, who slew them by thousands, far more than they could afterwards eat, so that the carcases were left to decay. It is said that, overcome with hunger, these armies of rats in some cases fell upon each other, and fed on their own kindred. They are still numerous, but do not appear to do the same amount of damage as is occasionally caused by the mice, when the latter invade the cultivated lands.

The dogs, of course, like the cats, were forced by starvation into the fields, where they perished in incredible numbers. Of many species of dogs which are stated to have been plentiful among the ancients, we have now nothing but the name. The poodle is extinct, the Maltese terrier, the Pomeranian, the Italian greyhound, and, it is believed, great numbers of crosses and mongrels have utterly disappeared. There was none to feed them, and they could not find food for themselves, nor could they stand the rigour of the winter when exposed to the frost in the open air.

Some kinds, more hardy and fitted by nature for the chase, became wild, and their descendants are now found in the woods. Of these, there are three sorts which keep apart from each other, and are thought not to interbreed. The most numerous are the black. The black wood-dog is short and stoutly made, with shaggy hair, sometimes marked with white patches.

There can be no doubt that it is the descendant of the ancient sheep-dog, for it is known that the sheep-dog was of that character, and it is said that those who used to keep sheep soon found their dogs abandon the fold, and join the wild troops that fell upon the sheep. The black wood-dogs hunt in packs of ten or more (as many as forty have been counted), and are the pest of the farmer, for, unless his flocks are pro-tected at night within stockades or enclosures, they are certain to be attacked. Not satisfied with killing enough to satisfy hunger, these dogs tear and mangle for sheer delight of blood, and will destroy twenty times as many as they can eat, leaving the miserably torn carcases on the field. Nor are the sheep always safe by day if the wood-dogs happen to be hungry. The shepherd is, therefore, usually accompanied by two or three mastiffs, of whose great size and strength the others stand in awe. At night, and when in large packs, starving in the snow, not even the mastiffs can check them.

No wood-dog, of any kind, has ever been known to attack man, and the hunter in the forest hears their bark in every direction without fear. It is, nevertheless, best to retire out of their way when charging sheep in packs, for they then seem seized with a blind fury, and some who have endeavoured to fight them have been thrown down and seriously mauled. But this has been in the blindness of their rush; no instance has ever been known of their purposely attacking man.

These black wood-dogs will also chase and finally pull down cattle, if they can get within the enclosures, and even horses have fallen vic-tims to their untiring thirst for blood. Not even the wild cattle can always escape, despite their strength, and they have been known to run down stags, though not their usual quarry.

The next kind of wild wood-dog is the yellow, a smaller animal, with smooth hair inclining to a yellow colour, which lives principally upon game, chasing all from the hare to the stag. It is as swift, or nearly as swift, as the greyhound, and possesses greater endurance. In coursing the hare, it not uncommonly happens that these dogs start from the brake and take the hare, when nearly exhausted, from the hunter's hounds. They will in the same way follow a stag, which has been almost run down by the hunters, and bring him to bay, though in this case they lose their booty, dispersing through fear of man, when the hunters come up in a body.

But such is their love of the chase, that they are known to assemble from their lairs at the distant sound of the horn, and, as the hunters ride through the woods, they often see the yellow dogs flitting along side by side with them through bush and fern. These animals sometimes hunt singly, sometimes in couples, and as the season advances, and winter approaches, in packs of eight or twelve. They never attack sheep or cattle, and avoid man, except when they perceive he is engaged in the chase. There is little doubt that they are the descendants of the dogs which the ancients called lurchers, crossed, perhaps, with the greyhound, and possibly other breeds. When the various species of dogs were thrown on their own resources, those only withstood the exposure and hardships which were naturally hardy, and possessed natural aptitude for the chase.

The third species of wood-dog is the white. They are low on the legs, of a dingy white colour, and much smaller than the other two. They neither attack cattle nor game, though fond of hunting rabbits. This dog is, in fact, a scavenger, living upon the carcases of dead sheep and animals, which are found picked clean in the night. For this purpose it haunts the neighbourhood of habitations, and prowls in the evening over heaps of refuse, scampering away at the least alarm, for it is extremely timid. It is perfectly harmless, for even the poultry do not dread it, and it will not face a tame cat, if by chance the two meet. It is rarely met with far from habitations, though it will accompany an army on the march. It may be said to remain in one district. The black and yellow dogs, on the contrary, roam about the forest without apparent home. One day the hunter sees signs of their presence, and perhaps may, for a month afterwards, not so much as hear a bark.

This uncertainty in the case of the black dog is the bane of the shepherds; for, not seeing or hearing anything of the enemy for months together, in spite of former experience their vigilance relaxes, and suddenly, while they sleep, their flocks are scattered. We still have, among tame dogs, the mastiff, terrier, spaniel, deer-hound, and greyhound, all of which are as faithful to man as ever.

CHAPTER II

WILD ANIMALS

WHEN the ancients departed, great numbers of their cattle perished. It was not so much the want of food as the inability to endure exposure that caused their death; a few winters are related to have so reduced them that they died by hundreds, many mangled by dogs. The hardiest that remained became perfectly wild, and the wood cattle are now more difficult to approach than deer.

There are two kinds, the white and the black. The white (sometimes dun) are believed to be the survivors of the domestic roan-and-white, for the cattle in our enclosures at the present day are of that colour. The black are smaller, and are doubtless little changed from their state in the olden times, except that they are wild. These latter are timid, unless when accompanied by a calf, and are rarely known to turn upon their pursuers. But the white are fierce at all times; they will not, indeed, attack man, but will scarcely run from him, and it is not always safe to cross their haunts.

The bulls are savage beyond measure at certain seasons of the year. If they see men at a distance, they retire; if they come unexpectedly face to face, they attack. This characteristic enables those who travel through districts known to be haunted by white cattle to provide against an encounter, for, by occasionally blowing a horn, the herd that may be in the vicinity is dispersed. There are not often more than twenty in a herd. The hides of the dun are highly prized, both for their intrinsic value, and as proofs of skill and courage, so much so that you shall hardly buy a skin for all the money you may offer; and the horns are likewise trophies. The white or dun bull is the monarch of our forests.

Four kinds of wild pigs are found. The most numerous, or at least the most often seen, as it lies about our enclosures, is the common thorn-hog. It is the largest of the wild pigs, long-bodied and flat-sided, in colour much the hue of the mud in which it wallows. To the agriculturist it is the greatest pest, destroying or damaging all kinds of crops, and routing up the gardens. It is with difficulty kept out by palisading, for if there be a weak place in the wooden framework, the strong snout of the animal is sure to undermine and work a passage through.

As there are always so many of these pigs round about inhabited places and cultivated fields, constant care is required, for they instantly discover an opening. From their habit of haunting the thickets and bush which come up to the verge of the enclosures, they have obtained the name of thorn-hogs. Some reach an immense size, and they are very prolific, so that it is impossible to destroy them. The boars are fierce at a particular season, but never attack unless provoked to do so. But when driven to bay they are the most dangerous of the boars, on account of their vast size and weight. They are of a sluggish disposition, and will not rise from their lairs unless forced to do so.

The next kind is the white hog, which has much the same habits as the former, except that it is usually found in moist places, near lakes and rivers, and is often called the marsh-pig. The third kind is perfectly black, much smaller in size, and very active, affording by far the best sport, and also the best food when killed. As they are found on the hills where the ground is somewhat more open, horses can follow freely, and the chase becomes exciting. By some it is called the hill-hog, from the locality it frequents. The small tusks of the black boar are used for many ornamental purposes.

These three species are considered to be the descendants of the various domestic pigs of the ancients, but the fourth, or grey, is thought to be the true wild boar. It is seldom seen, but is most common in the south-western forests, where, from the quantity of fern, it is called the fern-pig. This kind is believed to represent the true wild boar, which was extinct, or merged in the domestic hog among the ancients, except in that neighbourhood where the strain remained.

With wild times, the wild habits have returned, and the grey boar is at once the most difficult of access, and the most ready to encounter either dogs or men. Although the first, or thorn-hog, does the most damage to the agriculturist because of its numbers, and its habit of haunting the neighbourhood of enclosures, the others are equally injurious if they chance to enter the cultivated fields.

The three principal kinds of wild sheep are the horned, the thyme, and the meadow. The thyme sheep are the smallest, and haunt the highest hills in the south, where, feeding on the sweet herbage of the ridges, their flesh is said to acquire a flavour of wild thyme. They move in small flocks of not more than thirty, and are the most difficult to approach, being far more wary than deer, so continuously are they hunted by the wood-dogs. The horned are larger, and move in greater numbers; as many as two hundred are sometimes seen together. They are found on the lower slopes and plains, and in the woods. The meadow sheep have long shaggy wool, which is made into various articles of clothing, but they are not numerous. They haunt river sides, and the shores of lakes and ponds. None of these are easily got at, on account of the wood-dogs; but the rams of the horned kind are reputed to sometimes turn upon the pursuing pack, and butt them to death. In the extremity of their terror whole flocks of wild sheep have been driven over precipices and into quagmires and torrents.

Besides these, there are several other species whose haunt is local. On the islands, especially, different kinds are found. The wood-dogs will occasionally, in calm weather, swim out to an island and kill every sheep upon it.

From the horses that were in use among the ancients the two wild species now found are known to have descended, a fact confirmed by their evident resemblance to the horses we still retain. The largest wild horse is almost black, or inclined to a dark colour, somewhat less in size than our present waggon horses, but of the same heavy make. It is, however, much swifter, on account of having enjoyed liberty for so long. It is called the bush-horse, being generally distributed among thickets and meadow-like lands adjoining water.

The other species is called the hill-pony, from its habitat, the hills, and is rather less in size than our riding-horse. This latter is short and thickset, so much so as not to be easily ridden by short persons without high stirrups. Neither of these wild horses are numerous, but neither are they uncommon. They keep entirely separate from each other. As many as thirty mares are sometimes seen together, but there are districts where the traveller will not observe one for weeks.

Tradition says that in the olden times there were horses of a slender build whose speed outstripped the wind, but of the breed of these famous racers not one is left. Whether they were too delicate to withstand exposure, or whether the wild dogs hunted them down is uncertain, but they are quite gone. Did but one exist, how eagerly it would be sought out, for in these days it would be worth its weight in gold, unless, indeed, as some affirm, such speed only endured for a mile or two.

It is not necessary, having written thus far of the animals, that anything should be said of the birds of the woods, which every one knows were not always wild, and which can, indeed, be compared with such poultry as are kept in our enclosures. Such are the bush hens, the wood turkeys, the galenas, the peacocks, the white duck and white goose, all of which, though now wild as the hawk, are well known to have been once tame.

There were deer, red and fallow, in numerous parks and chases of very old time, and these, having got loose, and having such immense tracts to roam over unmolested, went on increasing till now they are beyond computation, and I have myself seen a thousand head together. Within these forty years, as I learn, the roe deer, too, have come down from the extreme north, so that there are now three sorts in the woods. Before them the pine marten came from the same direction, and, though they are not yet common, it is believed they are increasing. For the first few years after the change took place there seemed a danger lest the foreign wild beasts that had been confined as curiosities in menageries should multiply and remain in the woods. But this did not happen.

Some few lions and tigers, bears, and other animals did indeed escape, together with many less furious creatures, and it is related that they roamed about the fields for a long time. They were seldom met with, having such an extent of country to wander over, and after a while entirely disappeared. If any progeny were born, the winter frosts must have destroyed it, and the same fate awaited the monstrous serpents which had been collected for exhibition. Only one animal now exists which is known to owe its origin to those which escaped from the dens of the ancients. It is the beaver, whose dams are now occasionally found upon the streams by those who traverse the woods. Some of the aquatic birds, too, which frequent the lakes, are thought to have been originally derived from those which were formerly kept as curiosities.

In the castle yard at Longtover may still be seen the bones of an elephant which was found dying in the woods near that spot.

CHAPTER III

MEN OF THE WOODS

So far as this, all that I have stated has been clear, and there can be no doubt that what has been thus handed down from mouth to mouth is for the most part correct. When I pass from trees and animals to men, however, the thing is different, for nothing is certain and everything confused. None of the accounts agree, nor can they be altogether reconciled with present facts or with reasonable supposition; yet it is not so long since but a few memories, added one to the other, can bridge the time, and, though not many, there are some written notes still to be found. I must attribute the discrepancy to the wars and hatreds which sprang up and divided the people, so that one would not listen to what the others wished to say, and the truth was lost.

Besides which, in the conflagrations which consumed the towns, most of the records were destroyed, and are no longer to be referred to. And it may be that even when they were proceeding, the causes of the changes were not understood. Therefore, what I am now about to describe is not to be regarded as the ultimate truth, but as the nearest to which I could attain after comparing the various traditions. Some say, then, that the first beginning of the change was because the sea silted up the entrances to the ancient ports, and stopped the vast commerce which was once carried on. It is certainly true that many of the ports are silted up, and are now useless as such, but whether the silting up preceded the disappearance of the population, or whether the disappearance of the population and the consequent neglect caused the silting, I cannot venture to positively assert.

For there are signs that the level of the sea has sunk in some places, and signs that it has become higher in others, so that the judicious historian will simply state the facts, and refrain from colouring them with his own theory as Silvester has done. Others again maintain that the supply of food from over the ocean suddenly stopping caused great disorders, and that the people crowded on board all the ships to escape starvation, and sailed away, and were no more heard of.

It has, too, been said that the earth, from some attractive power exercised by the passage of an enormous dark body through space, became tilted or inclined to its orbit more than before, and that this, while it lasted, altered the flow of the magnetic currents, which, in an imperceptible manner, influence the minds of men. Hitherto the stream of human life had directed itself to the westward, but when this reversal of magnetism occurred, a general desire arose to return to the east. And those whose business is theology have pointed out that the wickedness of those times surpassed understanding, and that a change and sweeping away of the human evil that had accumulated was necessary, and was effected by supernatural means. The relation of this must be left to them, since it is not the province of the philosopher to meddle with such matters.

All that seems certain is, that when the event took place, the immense crowds collected in cities were most affected, and that the richer and upper classes made use of their money to escape. Those left behind were mainly the lower and most ignorant, so far as the arts were concerned; those that dwelt in distant and outlying places; and those who lived by agriculture. These last at that date had fallen to such distress that they could not hire vessels to transport themselves. The exact number of those left behind cannot, of course, be told, but it is on record that when the fields were first left neglected (as I have already described), a man might ride a hundred miles and not meet another. They were not only few, but scattered, and had not drawn together and formed towns as at present.

Of what became of the vast multitudes that left the country, nothing has ever been heard, and no communication has been received from them. For this reason I cannot conceal my opinion that they must have sailed either to the westward or to the southward where the greatest extent of ocean is understood to exist, and not to the eastward as Silvester would have it in his work upon the 'Unknown Orb', the dark body travelling in space to which I have alluded. None of our vessels in the present day dare venture into those immense tracts of sea, nor, indeed, out of sight of land, unless they know they shall see it again so soon as they have reached and surmounted the ridge of the horizon. Had they only crossed to the mainland or continent again, we should most likely have heard of their passage across the countries there.

It is true that ships rarely come over, and only to two ports, and that the men on them say (so far as can be understood) that their country is equally deserted now, and has likewise lost its population. But still, as men talk unto men, and we pass intelligence across great breadths of land, it is almost certain that, had they travelled that way, some echo of their footsteps would yet sound back to us. Regarding this theory, therefore, as untenable, I put forward as a suggestion that the ancients really sailed to the west or to the south.

As, for the most part, those who were left behind were ignorant, rude, and unlettered, it consequently happened that many of the marvellous things which the ancients did, and the secrets of their science, are known to us by name only, and, indeed, hardly by name. It has happened to us in our turn as it happened to the ancients. For they were aware that in times before their own the art of making glass malleable had been discovered, so that it could be beaten into shape like copper. But the manner in which it was accomplished was entirely unknown to them; the fact was on record, but the cause lost. So now we know that those who to us are the ancients had a way of making diamonds and precious stones out of black and lustreless charcoal, a fact which approaches the incredible. Still, we do not doubt it, though we cannot imagine by what means it was carried out.

They also sent intelligence to the utmost parts of the earth along wires which were not tubular, but solid, and therefore could not transmit sound, and yet the person who received the message could hear and recognise the voice of the sender a thousand miles away. With certain machines worked by fire, they traversed the land swift as the swallow glides through the sky, but of these things not a relic remains to us. What metalwork or wheels or bars of iron were left, and might have given us a clue, were all broken up and melted down for use in other ways when metal became scarce.

Mounds of earth are said to still exist in the woods, which originally formed the roads for these machines, but they are now so low, and so covered with thickets, that nothing can be learnt from them; and, indeed, though I have heard of their existence, I have never seen one. Great holes were made through the very hills for the passage of the iron chariot, but they are now blocked by the falling roofs, nor dare any one explore such parts as may yet be open. Where are the wonderful structures with which the men of those days were lifted to the skies, rising above the clouds? These marvellous things are to us little more than the fables of the giants and of the old gods that walked upon the earth, which were fables even to those whom we call the ancients.

Indeed, we have fuller knowledge of those extremely ancient times than of the people who immediately preceded us, and the Romans and the Greeks are more familiar to us than the men who rode in the iron chariots and mounted to the skies. The reason why so many arts and sciences were lost was because, as I have previously said, the most of those who were left in the country were ignorant, rude, and unlettered. They had seen the iron chariots, but did not under-
and the method of their construction, and could not hand down
e knowledge they did not themselves possess. The magic wires of

intelligence passed through their villages, but they did not know how to work them.

The cunning artificers of the cities all departed, and everything fell quickly into barbarism; nor could it be wondered at, for the few and scattered people of those days had enough to do to preserve their lives. Communication between one place and another was absolutely cut off, and if one perchance did recollect something that might have been of use, he could not confer with another who knew the other part, and thus between them reconstruct the machine. In the second generation even these disjointed memories died out.

At first it is supposed that those who remained behind existed upon the grain in the warehouses, and what they could thresh by the flail from the crops left neglected in the fields. But as the provisions in the warehouses were consumed or spoiled, they hunted the animals, lately tame and as yet but half wild. As these grew less in number and difficult to overtake, they set to work again to till the ground, and cleared away small portions of the earth, encumbered already with brambles and thistles. Some grew corn, and some took charge of sheep. Thus, in time, places far apart from each other were settled, and towns were built; towns, indeed, we call them to distinguish them from the champaign, but they are not worthy of the name in comparison with the mighty cities of old time.

There are many that have not more than fifty houses in the enclosure, and perhaps no other station within a day's journey, and the largest are but villages, reckoning by antiquity. For the most part they have their own government, or had till recently, and thus there grew up many provinces and kingdoms in the compass of what was originally but one. Thus separated and divided, there came also to be many races where in the first place was one people. Now, in briefly recounting the principal divisions of men, I will commence with those who are everywhere considered the lowest. These are the Bushmen, who live wholly in the woods.

Even among the ancients, when every man, woman, and child, could exercise those arts which are now the special mark of nobility, i.e. reading and writing, there was a degraded class of persons who refused to avail themselves of the benefits of civilization. They obtained their food by begging, wandering along the highways, crouching around fires which they lit in the open, clad in rags, and exhibiting countenances from which every trace of self-respect had disappeared. These were the ancestors of the present men of the bushes.

They took naturally to the neglected fields, and forming 'camps' as they call their tribes, or rather families, wandered to and fro, easily subsisting upon roots and trapped game. So they live to this day, having become extremely dexterous in snaring every species of bird and animal, and the fishes of the streams. These latter they sometimes poison with a drug or plant (it is not known which), the knowledge of which has been preserved among them since the days of the ancients. The poison kills the fishes, and brings them to the surface, when they can be collected by hundreds, but does not injure them for eating.

Like the black wood-dogs, the Bushmen often in fits of savage frenzy destroy thrice as much as they can devour, trapping deer in wicker-work hedges, or pitfalls, and cutting the miserable animals in pieces, for mere thirst of blood. The oxen and cattle in the enclosures are occasionally in the same manner fearfully mutilated by these wretches, sometimes for amusement, and sometimes in vengeance for injuries done to them. Bushmen have no settled home, cultivate no kind of corn or vegetable, keep no animals, not even dogs, have no houses or huts, no boats or canoes, nothing that requires the least intelligence or energy to construct.

Roaming to and fro without any apparent aim or object, or any particular route, they fix their camp for a few days wherever it suits their fancy, and again move on, no man knows why or whither. It is this uncertainty of movement which makes them so dangerous. To-day there may not be the least sign of any within miles of an enclosure. In the night a 'camp' may pass, slaughtering such cattle as may have remained without the palisade, or killing the unfortunate shepherd who has not got within the walls, and in the morning they may be nowhere to be seen, having disappeared like vermin. Face to face the Bushman is never to be feared; a whole 'camp' or tribal family will scatter if a traveller stumbles into their midst. It is from behind a tree or under cover of night that he deals his murderous blow.

A 'camp' may consist of ten or twenty individuals, sometimes, per-haps, of forty, or even fifty, of various ages, and is ruled by the eldest, who is also the parent. He is absolute master of his 'camp' but has no power or recognition beyond it, so that how many leaders there may be among them it is not possible even to guess. Nor is the master known to them as king, or duke, nor has he any title, but is simply the oldest or founder of the family. The 'camp' has no law, no established custom; events happen, and even the master cannot be said to reign. When he becomes feeble, they simply leave him to die.

They are depraved, and without shame, clad in sheepskins chiefly, if clad at all, or in such clothes as they have stolen. They have no cere-monies whatever. The number of these 'camps' must be considerable, and yet the Bushman is seldom seen, nor do we very often hear of their depredations, which is accounted for by the extent of country they wander over. It is in severe winters that the chief danger occurs; they then suffer from hunger and cold, and are driven to the neighbourhood of the enclosures to steal. So dexterous are they in slipping through the bushes, and slinking among the reeds and osiers, that they will pass within a few yards without discovering their presence, and the signs of their passage can be detected only by the experienced hunter, and not always by him.

It is observed that whatever mischief the Bushman commits, he never sets fire to any ricks or buildings; the reason is because his nature is to slink from the scene of his depredations, and flame at once attracts people to the spot. Twice the occurrence of a remarkably severe winter has caused the Bushmen to flock together and act in an approach to concert in attacking the enclosures. The Bushmen of the north, who were even more savage and brutal, then came down, and were with difficulty repulsed from the walled cities. In ordinary times we see very little of them. They are the thieves, the human vermin of the woods.

Under the name of gipsies, those who are now often called Romany and Zingari were well known to the ancients. Indeed, they boast that their ancestry goes back so much farther than the oldest we can claim, that the ancients themselves were but modern to them. Even in that age of highest civilization, which immediately preceded the present, they say (and there is no doubt of it) that they preserved the blood of their race pure and untainted, that they never dwelt under permanent roofs, nor bowed their knees to the prevalent religion. They remained apart, and still continue after civilization has disappeared, exactly the same as they were before it commenced.

Since the change their numbers have greatly increased, and were they not always at war with each other, it is possible that they might go far to sweep the house people from the land. But there are so many tribes, each with its king, queen, or duke, that their power is divided, and their force melts away. The ruler of the Bushman families is always a man, but among the gipsies a woman, and even a young girl often exercises supreme authority, but must be of the sacred blood. These kings and dukes are absolute autocrats within their tribe, and can order by a nod the destruction of those who offend them. Habits of simplest obedience being enjoined on the tribe from the earliest childhood, such executions are rare, but the right to command them is not for a moment questioned.

Of the sorcerers, and particularly the sorceresses, among them, all have heard, and, indeed, the places where they dwell seem full of mystery and magic. They live in tents, and though they constantly remove from district to district, one tribe never clashes with or crosses another, because all have their especial routes, upon which no intrusion is ever made. Some agriculture is practised, and flocks and herds are kept, but the work is entirely done by the women. The men are always on horse-back, or sleeping in their tents.

Each tribe has its central camping-place, to which they return at intervals after perhaps wandering for months, a certain number of persons being left at home to defend it. These camps are often situated in inaccessible positions, and well protected by stockades. The territory which is acknowledged to belong to such a camp is extremely limited; its mere environs only are considered the actual property of the tribe, and a second can pitch its tents within a few hundred yards. These stockades, in fact, are more like store-houses than residences; each is a mere rendezvous.

The gipsies are everywhere, but their stockades are most numerous in the south, along the sides of the green hills and plains, and especially round Stonehenge, where, on the great open plains, among the huge boulders, placed ages since in circles, they perform strange ceremonies and incantations. They attack every traveller, and every caravan or train of waggons which they feel strong enough to master, but they do not murder the solitary sleeping hunter or shepherd like the Bushmen. They will, indeed, steal from him, but do not kill, except in fight. Once, now and then, they have found their way into towns, when terrible massacres have followed, for, when excited, the savage knows not how to restrain himself.

Vengeance is their idol. If any community has injured or affronted them, they never cease endeavouring to retaliate, and will wipe it out in fire and blood generations afterwards. There are towns which have thus been suddenly harried when the citizens had forgotten that any cause of enmity existed. Vengeance is their religion and their social law, which guides all their actions among themselves. It is for this reason that they are continually at war, duke with duke, and king with king. A deadly feud, too, has set Bushman and gipsy at each other's throat, far beyond the memory of man. The Romany looks on the Bushman as a dog, and slaughters him as such. In turn, the despised human dog slinks in the darkness of the night into the Romany's tent, and stabs his daughter or his wife, for such is the meanness and cowardice of the Bushman that he would always rather kill a woman than a man.

There is also a third class of men who are not true gipsies, but have something of their character, though the gipsies will not allow hat they were originally half-breeds. Their habits are much the same, cept that they are foot men and rarely use horses, and are therefore called the foot gipsies. The gipsy horse is really a pony. Once only have the Romany combined to attack the house people, driven, like the Bushmen, by an exceedingly severe winter, against which they had no provision.

But then, instead of massing their forces and throwing their irresistible numbers upon one city or territory, all they would agree to do was that, upon a certain day, each tribe should invade the land nearest to it. The result was that they were, though with trouble, repulsed. Until lately, no leader ventured to follow the gipsies to their strongholds, for they were reputed invincible behind their stockades. By infesting the woods and lying in ambush they rendered communication between city and city difficult and dangerous, except to bodies of armed men, and every waggon had to be defended by troops.

The gipsies, as they roam, make little secret of their presence (unless, of course, intent upon mischief), but light their fires by day and night fearlessly. The Bushmen never light a fire by day, lest the ascending smoke, which cannot be concealed, should betray their whereabouts. Their fires are lit at night in hollows or places well surrounded with thickets, and, that the flame may not be seen, they will build screens of fir boughs or fern. When they have obtained a good supply of hot wood coals, no more sticks are thrown on, but these are covered with turf, and thus kept in long enough for their purposes. Much of their meat they devour raw, and thus do not need a fire so frequently as others.

CHAPTER IV

THE INVADERS

THOSE who live by agriculture or in towns, and are descended from the remnant of the ancients, are divided, as I have previously said, into numerous provinces, kingdoms, and republics. In the middle part of the country the cities are almost all upon the shores of the Lake, or within a short distance of the water, and there is therefore more traffic and communication between them by means of vessels than is the case with inland towns, whose trade must be carried on by caravans and waggons. These not only move slowly, but are subject to be interrupted by the Romany and by the banditti, or persons who, for moral or political crimes, have been banished from their homes.

It is in the cities that cluster around the great central lake that all the life and civilization of our day are found; but there also begin those wars and social convulsions which cause so much suffering. When was the Peninsula at peace? and when was there not some mischief and change brewing in the republics? When was there not a danger from the northern mainland?

Until recent years there was little knowledge of, and scarcely any direct commerce or intercourse between, the central part and the districts either of the extreme west or the north, and it is only now that the north and east are becoming open to us; for at the back of the narrow circle of cultivated land, the belt about the Lake, there extend immense forests in every direction, through which, till very lately, no practicable way had been cut. Even in the more civilised central part it is not to this day easy to travel, for at the barriers, as you approach the territories of every prince, they demand your business and your papers; nor even if you establish the fact that you are innocent of designs against the State, shall you hardly enter without satisfying the greed of the officials.

A fine is thus exacted at the gate of every province and kingdom, and again at the gateways of the towns. The difference of the coinage, such as it is, causes also great loss and trouble, for the money of one kingdom (though passing current by command in that territory) is not received at its nominal value in the next on account of the alloy it contains. It is, indeed, in many kingdoms impossible to obtain sterling money. Gold there is little or none anywhere, but silver is the standard of exchange, and copper, bronze, and brass, sometimes tin, are the metals with which the greater number of the people transact their business.

Justice is corrupt, for where there is a king or a prince it depends on the caprice of a tyrant, and where there is a republic upon the shout of the crowd, so that many, if they think they may be put on trial, rather than face the risk at once escape into the woods. The League, though based ostensibly on principles the most exalted and beneficial to humanity, is known to be perverted. The members sworn to honour and the highest virtue are swayed by vile motives, political hatreds, and private passions, and even by money.

Men for ever trample upon men, each pushing to the front; nor is there safety in remaining in retirement, since such are accused of biding their time and of occult designs. Though the population of these cities all counted together is not equal to the population that once dwelt in a single secondrate city of the ancients, yet how much greater are the bitterness and the struggle!

Yet not content with the bloodshed they themselves cause, the tyrants have called in the aid of mercenary soldiers to assist them. And, to complete the disgrace, those republics which proclaim themselves the very home of patriotic virtues, have resorted to the same means. Thus we see English cities kept in awe by troops of Welshmen, Irish, and even the western Scots, who swarm in the palaces, in the council-chambers of the republics, and, opening the doors of the houses, help themselves to what they will. This, too, in the face of the notorious fact that these nations have sworn to be avenged upon us, that their vessels sail about the Lake committing direful acts of piracy, and that twice already vast armies have swept along threatening to entirely overwhelm the whole commonwealth.

What infatuation to admit bands of these same men into the very strongholds and the heart of the land! As if upon the approach of their countrymen they would remain true to the oaths they have sworn for pay, and not rather admit them with open arms. No blame can, upon a just consideration, be attributed to either of these nations that endeavour to oppress us. For, as they point out, the ancients from whom we are descended held them in subjection many hundred years, and took from them all their liberties.

Thus the Welsh, or, as they call themselves, the Cymry, say that the whole island was once theirs, and is theirs still by right of inheritance. They were the original people who possessed it ages before the arrival of those whom we call the ancients. Though they were driven into the mountains of the far distant west, they never forgot their language, ceased their customs, or gave up their aspirations to recover their own. This is now their aim, and until recently it seemed as if they were about to accomplish it. For they held all that country anciently called Cornwall, having crossed over the Severn, and marched down the southern shore. The rich land of Devon, part of Dorset (all, indeed, that is inhabited), and the most part of Somerset, acknowledged their rule. Worcester and Hereford and Gloucester were theirs; I mean, of course, those parts that are not forest.

Their outposts were pushed forward to the centre of Leicestershire, and came down towards Oxford. But thereabouts they met with the forces of which I will shortly speak. Then their vessels every summer sailing from the Severn, came into the Lake, and, landing wherever there was an opportunity, they destroyed all things and carried off the spoil. Is it necessary to say more to demonstrate the madness which possesses those princes and republics which, in order to support their own tyranny, have invited bands of these men into their very palaces and forts?

As they approached near what was once Oxford and is now Sypolis, the armies of Cymry came into collision with another of our invaders, and thus their forward course to the south was checked. The Irish, who had hitherto abetted them, turned round to defend their own usurpations. They, too, say that in conquering and despoiling my countrymen they are fulfilling a divine vengeance. Their land of Ireland had been for centuries ground down with an iron tyranny by our ancestors, who closed their lips with a muzzle, and led them about with a bridle, as their poets say. But now the hateful Saxons (for thus both they and the Welsh designate us) are broken, and delivered over to them for their spoil.

It is not possible to deny many of the statements that they make, but that should not prevent us from battling with might and main against the threatened subjection. What crime can be greater than the admission of such foreigners as the guards of our cities? Now the Irish have their principal rendezvous and capital near to the ancient city of Chester, which is upon the ocean, and at the very top and angle of Wales. This is their great settlement, their magazine and rallying-place, and thence their expeditions have proceeded. It is a convenient port, and well opposite their native land, from which reinforcements continually arrive, but the Welsh have ever looked upon their possession of it with jealousy.

At the period when the Cymry had nearly penetrated to Sypolis xford, the Irish, on their part, had overrun all the cultivated and bited country in a south and south-easterly line from Chester, through Rutland to Norfolk and Suffolk, and even as far as Luton. They would have spread to the north, but in that direction they were met by the Scots, who had all Northumbria. When the Welsh came near Sypolis, the Irish awoke to the position of affairs.

Sypolis is the largest and most important city upon the northern shore of the Lake, and it is situated at the entrance to the neck of land that stretches out to the straits. If the Welsh were once well posted there, the Irish could never hope to find their way to the rich and cultivated south, for it is just below Sypolis that the Lake contracts, and forms a strait in one place but a furlong wide. The two forces thus came into collision, and while they fought and destroyed each other, Sypolis was saved. After which, finding they were evenly matched, the Irish withdrew two days' march northwards, and the Cymry as far westwards.

But now the Irish, sailing round the outside of Wales, came likewise up through the Red Rocks, and so into the Lake, and in their turn landing, harassed the cities. Often Welsh and Irish vessels, intending to attack the same place, have discerned each other approaching, and, turning from their proposed action, have flown at each other's throats. The Scots have not harassed us in the south much, being too far distant, and those that wander hither come for pay, taking service as guards. They are, indeed, the finest of men, and the hardiest to battle with. I had forgotten to mention that it is possible the Irish might have pushed back the Welsh, had not the kingdom of York suddenly reviving, by means which shall be related, valiantly thrust out its masters, and fell upon their rear.

But still these nations are always upon the verge and margin of our world, and wait but an opportunity to rush in upon it. Our countrymen groan under their yoke, and I say again that infamy should be the portion of those rulers among us who have filled their fortified places with mercenaries derived from such sources.

The land, too, is weak, because of the multitude of bondsmen. In the provinces and kingdoms round about the Lake there is hardly a town where the slaves do not outnumber the free as ten to one. The laws are framed for the object of reducing the greater part of the people to servitude. For every offence the punishment is slavery, and the offences are daily artificially increased, that the wealth of the few in human beings may grow with them. If a man in his hunger steal a loaf, he becomes a slave; that is, it is proclaimed he must make good to the State the injury he has done it, and must work out his trespass. This is not assessed as the value of the loaf, nor supposed to be confined to the individual from whom it was taken.

The theft is said to damage the State at large, because it corrupts the morality of the commonwealth; it is as if the thief had stolen a loaf, not from one, but from every member of the State. Restitution must, therefore, be made to all, and the value of the loaf returned in labour a thousandfold. The thief is the bondsman of the State. But as the State cannot employ him, he is leased out to those who will pay into the treasury of the prince the money equivalent to the labour he is capable of performing. Thus, under cover of the highest morality, the greatest iniquity is perpetrated. For the theft of a loaf, the man is reduced to a slave; then his wife and children, unable to support themselves, become a charge to the State, that is, they beg in the public ways.

This, too, forsooth, corrupts morality, and they likewise are seized and leased out to any who like to take them. Nor can he or they ever become free again, for they must repay to their proprietor the sum he gave for them, and how can that be done, since they receive no wages? For striking another, a man may be in the same way, as they term it, forfeited to the State, and be sold to the highest bidder. A stout brass wire is then twisted around his left wrist loosely, and the ends soldered together. Then a bar of iron being put through, a half turn is given to it, which forces the wire sharply against the arm, causing it to fit tightly, often painfully, and forms a smaller ring at the outside. By this smaller ring a score of bondsmen may be seen strung together with a rope.

To speak disrespectfully of the prince or his council, or of the nobles, or of religion, to go out of the precincts without permission, to trade without license, to omit to salute the great, all these and a thousand others are crimes deserving of the brazen bracelet. Were a man to study all day what he must do, and what he must not do, to escape servitude, it would not be possible for him to stir one step without becoming forfeit! And yet they hypocritically say that these things are done for the sake of public morality, and that there are no slaves (not permitting the word to be used), and no man was ever sold.

It is, indeed, true that no man is sold in open market, he is leased instead; and, by a refined hypocrisy, the owner of slaves cannot sell them to another owner, but he can place them in the hands of the notary, presenting them with their freedom, so far as he is concerned. The notary, upon payment of a fine from the purchaser transfers them to him, and the larger part of the fine goes to the prince. Debt alone under their laws must crowd the land with slaves, for, as wages are scarcely known, a child from its birth is often declared to be in debt. For its nourishment is drawn from its mother, and the wretched mother is the wife of a retainer who is fed by his lord. To such a degree is this tyranny carried! If any owe a penny, his doom is sealed; he becomes a bondsman, and thus the estates of the nobles are full of men who work during their whole lives for the profit of others. Thus, too, the woods are filled with banditti, for those who find an opportunity, never fail to escape, notwithstanding the hunt that is invariably made for them, and the cruel punishment that awaits recapture. And numbers, foreseeing that they must become bondsmen, before they are proclaimed forfeit, steal away by night, and live as they may in the forests.

How, then, does any man remain free? Only by the favour of the nobles, and only that he may amass wealth for them. The merchants, and those who have license to trade by land or water, are all protected by some noble house, to whom they pay heavily for permission to live in their own houses. The principal tyrant is supported by the nobles, that they in their turn may tyrannise over the merchants, and they again over all the workmen of their shops and bazaars.

Over their own servants (for thus they call the slaves, that the word itself may not be used), who work upon their estates, the nobles are absolute masters, and may even hang them upon the nearest tree. And here I cannot but remark how strange it is, first, that any man can remain a slave rather than die; and secondly, how much stranger it is that any other man, himself a slave, can be found to hunt down or to hang his fellow; yet the tyrants never lack executioners. Their castles are crowded with retainers who wreak their wills upon the defenceless. These retainers do not wear the brazen bracelet; they are free. Are there, then, no beggars? Yes, they sit at every corner, and about the gates of the cities, asking for alms.

Though begging makes a man forfeit to the State, it is only when he has thews and sinews, and can work. The diseased and aged, the helpless and feeble, may break the law, and starve by the roadside, because it profits no one to make them his slaves. And all these things are done in the name of morality, and for the good of the human race, as they constantly announce in their councils and parliaments.

There are two reasons why the mercenaries have been called in; first, because the princes found the great nobles so powerful, and can keep them in check only by the aid of these foreigners; and secondly, because the number of the outlaws in the woods has become so great that the nobles themselves are afraid lest their slaves should revolt, and, with the aid of the outlaws, overcome them.

Now the mark of a noble is that he can read and write. When the ancients were scattered, the remnant that was left behind was, for the most part, the ignorant and the poor. But among them there was here and there a man who possessed some little education and force of mind. At first there was no order; but after thirty years or so, after a generation, some order grew up, and these men, then become aged, were naturally chosen as leaders. They had, indeed, no actual power then, no guards or armies; but the common folk, who had no knowledge, came to them to decide their disputes, to advise them what to do, to pronounce some form of marriage, to keep some note of property, and to unite them against a mutual danger.

These men in turn taught their children to read and write, wishing that some part of the wisdom of the ancients might be preserved. They themselves wrote down what they knew, and these manuscripts, transmitted to their children, were saved with care. Some of them remain to this day. These children, growing to manhood, took more upon them, and assumed higher authority as the past was forgotten, and the original equality of all men lost in antiquity. The small enclosed farms of their fathers became enlarged to estates, the estates became towns, and thus, by degrees, the order of the nobility was formed. As they intermarried only among themselves, they preserved a certain individuality. At this day a noble is at once known, no matter how coarsely he may be dressed, or how brutal his habits, by his delicacy of feature, his air of command, even by his softness of skin and fineness of hair.

Still the art of reading and writing is scrupulously imparted to all their legitimate offspring, and scrupulously confined to them alone. It is true that they do not use it except on rare occasions when necessity demands, being wholly given over to the chase, to war, and politics, but they retain the knowledge. Indeed, were a noble to be known not to be able to read and write, the prince would at once degrade him, and the sentence would be upheld by the entire caste. No other but the nobles are permitted to acquire these arts; if any attempt to do so, they are enslaved and punished. But none do attempt; of what avail would it be to them?

All knowledge is thus retained in the possession of the nobles; they do not use it, but the physicians, for instance, who are famous, are so, because, by favour of some baron, they have learned receipts in the ancient manuscripts which have been mentioned. One virtue, and one only, adorns this exclusive caste: they are courageous to the verge of madness. I had almost omitted to state that the merchants know how to read and write, having special license and permits to do so, without which they may not correspond. There are few books, and still fewer to read them; and these all in manuscript, for though the way to print is not lost, it is not employed since no one wants books.

CHAPTER V

THE LAKE

THERE now only remains the geography of our country to be treated of before the history is commenced. Now the most striking difference between the country as we know it and as it was known to the ancients is the existence of the great Lake in the centre of the island. From the Red Rocks (by the Severn) hither, the most direct route a galley can follow is considered to be about 200 miles in length, and it is a journey which often takes a week even for a vessel well manned, because the course, as it turns round the islands, faces so many points of the compass, and therefore the oarsmen are sure to have to labour in the teeth of the wind, no matter which way it blows.

Many parts are still unexplored, and scarce anything known of their extent, even by repute. Until Felix Aquila's time, the greater portion, indeed, had not even a name. Each community was well acquainted with the bay before its own city, and with the route to the next, but beyond that they were ignorant, and had no desire to learn. Yet the Lake cannot really be so long and broad as it seems, for the country could not contain it. The length is increased, almost trebled, by the islands and shoals, which will not permit of navigation in a straight line. For the most part, too, they follow the southern shore of the mainland, which is protected by a fringe of islets and banks from the storms which sweep over the open waters.

Thus rowing along round the gulfs and promontories, their voyage is thrice prolonged, but rendered nearly safe from the waves, which rise with incredible celerity before the gales. The slow ships of commerce, indeed, are often days in traversing the distance between one port and another, for they wait for the wind to blow abaft,* and being heavy, deeply laden, built broad and flat-bottomed for shallows, and bluff at the bows, they drift like logs of timber. In canoes the hunters, indeed, sometimes pass swiftly from one place to another, venturing farther out to sea than the ships. They could pass yet more quickly were it not for the inquisition of the authorities at every city and port, who not only levy dues and fees for the treasury of the prince, and for their own

---

* Near to the stern.

rapacious desires, but demand whence the vessel comes, to whom she belongs, and whither she is bound, so that no ship can travel rapidly unless so armed as to shake off these inquisitors.

The canoes, therefore, travel at night and in calm weather many miles away from the shore, and thus escape, or slip by daylight among the reedy shallows, sheltered by the flags and willows from view. The ships of commerce haul up to the shore towards evening, and the crews, disembarking, light their fires and cook their food. There are, however, one or two gaps, as it were, in their usual course which they cannot pass in this leisurely manner; where the shore is exposed and rocky, or too shallow, and where they must reluctantly put forth, and sail from one horn of the land to the other.

The Lake is also divided into two unequal portions by the straits of White Horse, where vessels are often weather-bound, and cannot make way against the wind, which sets a current through the narrow channel. There is no tide; the sweet waters do not ebb and flow; but while I thus discourse, I have forgotten to state how they came to fill the middle of the country. Now, the philosopher Silvester, and those who seek after marvels, say that the passage of the dark body through space caused an immense volume of fresh water to fall in the shape of rain, and also that the growth of the forests distilled rain from the clouds. Let us leave these speculations to dreamers, and recount what is known to be.

For there is no tradition among the common people, who are extremely tenacious of such things, of any great rainfall, nor is there any mention of floods in the ancient manuscripts, nor is there any larger fall of rain now than was formerly the case. But the Lake itself tells us how it was formed, or as nearly as we shall ever know, and these facts were established by the expeditions lately sent out.

At the eastern extremity the Lake narrows, and finally is lost in the vast marshes which cover the site of the ancient London. Through these, no doubt, in the days of the old world there flowed the river Thames. By the changes of the sea level and the sand that was brought up there must have grown great banks, which obstructed the stream. I have formerly mentioned the vast quantities of timber, the wreckage of towns and bridges which was carried down by the various rivers, and by none more so than by the Thames. These added to the accumulation, which increased the faster because the foundations of the ancient bridges held it like piles driven in for the purpose. And before this the river had become partially choked from the cloacæ of the ancient city which poured into it through enormous subterranean aqueducts and drains.

After a time all these shallows and banks became well matted together by the growth of weeds, of willows, and flags, while the tide, ebbing lower at each drawing back, left still more mud and sand. Now it is believed that when this had gone on for a time, the waters of the river, unable to find a channel, began to overflow up into the deserted streets, and especially to fill the underground passages and drains, of which the number and extent was beyond all the power of words to describe. These, by the force of the water, were burst up, and the houses fell in.

For this marvellous city, of which such legends are related, was after all only of brick, and when the ivy grew over and trees and shrubs sprang up, and, lastly, the waters underneath burst in, this huge metropolis was soon overthrown. At this day all those parts which were built upon low ground are marshes and swamps. Those houses that were upon high ground were, of course, like the other towns, ransacked of all they contained by the remnant that was left; the iron, too, was extracted. Trees growing up by them in time cracked the walls, and they fell in. Trees and bushes covered them; ivy and nettles concealed the crumbling masses of brick.

The same was the case with the lesser cities and towns whose sites are known in the woods. For though many of our present towns bear the ancient names, they do not stand upon the ancient sites, but are two or three, and sometimes ten miles distant. The founders carried with them the name of their original residence.

Thus the low-lying parts of the mighty city of London became swamps, and the higher grounds were clad with bushes. The very largest of the buildings fell in, and there was nothing visible but trees and hawthorns on the upper lands, and willows, flags, reeds, and rushes on the lower. These crumbling ruins still more choked the stream, and almost, if not quite, turned it back. If any water ooze past, it is not perceptible, and there is no channel through to the salt ocean. It is a vast stagnant swamp, which no man dare enter, since death would be his inevitable fate.

There exhales from this oozy mass so fatal a vapour that no animal can endure it. The black water bears a greenish-brown floating scum, which for ever bubbles up from the putrid mud of the bottom. When the wind collects the miasma, and, as it were, presses it together, it becomes visible as a low cloud which hangs over the place. The cloud does not advance beyond the limit of the marsh, seeming to stay there by some constant attraction; and well it is for us that it does not, since at such times when the vapour is thickest, the very wildfowl leave the reeds, and fly from the poison. There are no fishes, neither can eels exist in the mud, nor even newts. It is dead.

The flags and reeds are coated with slime and noisome to the touch; there is one place where even these do not grow, and where there is nothing but an oily liquid, green and rank. It is plain there are no fishes in the water, for herons do not go thither, nor the kingfishers, not one of which approaches the spot. They say the sun is sometimes hidden by the vapour when it is thickest, but I do not see how any can tell this, since they could not enter the cloud, as to breathe it when collected by the wind is immediately fatal. For all the rottenness of a thousand years and of many hundred millions of human beings is there festering under the stagnant water, which has sunk down into and penetrated the earth, and floated up to the surface the contents of the buried cloacæ.

Many scores of men have, I fear, perished in the attempt to enter this fearful place, carried on by their desire of gain. For it can scarcely be disputed that untold treasure lies hidden therein, but guarded by terrors greater than fiery serpents. These have usually made their endeavours to enter in severe and continued frost, or in the height of a drought. Frost diminishes the power of the vapour, and the marshes can then, too, be partially traversed, for there is no channel for a boat. But the moment anything be moved, whether it be a bush, or a willow, even a flag, if the ice be broken, the pestilence rises yet stronger. Besides which, there are portions which never freeze, and which may be approached unawares, or a turn of the wind may drift the gas towards the explorer.

In the midst of the summer, after long heat, the vapour rises, and is in a degree dissipated into the sky, and then by following devious ways an entrance may be effected, but always at the cost of illness. If the explorer be unable to quit the spot before night, whether in summer or winter, his death is certain. In the earlier times some bold and adventurous men did indeed succeed in getting a few jewels, but since then the marsh has become more dangerous, and its pestilent character, indeed, increases year by year, as the stagnant water penetrates deeper. So that now for very many years no such attempts have been made.

The extent of these foul swamps is not known with certainty, but it is generally believed that they are, at the widest, twenty miles across, and that they reach in a winding line for nearly forty. But the outside parts are much less fatal; it is only the interior which is avoided.

Towards the Lake the sand thrown up by the waves has long since formed a partial barrier between the sweet water and the stagnant, rising up to within a few feet of the surface. This barrier is overgrown with flags and reeds, where it is shallow. Here it is possible to sail along the sweet water within an arrow-shot of the swamp. Nor, indeed, would the stagnant mingle with the sweet, as is evident at other parts of the swamp, where streams flow side by side with the dark or reddish water; and there are pools, upon one side of which the deer drink, while the other is not frequented even by rats.

The common people aver that demons reside in these swamps; and, indeed, at night fiery shapes are seen, which, to the ignorant, are sufficient confirmation of such tales. The vapour, where it is most dense, takes fire, like the blue flame of spirits, and these flaming clouds float to and fro, and yet do not burn the reeds. The superstitious trace in them the forms of demons and winged fiery serpents, and say that white spectres haunt the margin of the marsh after dusk. In a lesser degree, the same thing has taken place with other ancient cities. It is true that there are not always swamps, but the sites are uninhabitable because of the emanations from the ruins. Therefore they are avoided. Even the spot where a single house has been known to have existed, is avoided by the hunters in the woods.

They say when they are stricken with ague or fever, that they must have unwittingly slept on the site of an ancient habitation. Nor can the ground be cultivated near the ancient towns, because it causes fever; and thus it is that, as I have already stated, the present places of the same name are often miles distant from the former locality. No sooner does the plough or the spade turn up an ancient site than those who work there are attacked with illness. And thus the cities of the old world, and their houses and habitations, are deserted and lost in the forest. If the hunters, about to pitch their camp for the night, should stumble on so much as a crumbling brick or a fragment of hewn stone, they at once remove at least a bowshot away.

The eastward flow of the Thames being at first checked, and finally almost or quite stopped by the formation of these banks, the water turned backwards as it were, and began to cover the hitherto dry land. And this, with the other lesser rivers and brooks that no longer had any ultimate outlet, accounts for the Lake, so far as this side of the country is concerned.

At the western extremity the waters also contract between the steep cliffs called the Red Rocks, near to which once existed the city of Bristol. Now the Welsh say, and the tradition of those who dwell in that part of the country bears them out, that in the time of the old world the river Severn flowed past the same spot, but not between these cliffs. The great river Severn coming down from the north, with England on one bank and Wales upon the other, entered the sea, widening out as it did so. Just before it reached the sea, another lesser river, called the Avon, the upper part of which is still there, joined it passing through this cleft in the rocks.

But when the days of the old world ended in the twilight of the ancients, as the salt ocean fell back and its level became lower, vast sandbanks were disclosed, which presently extended across the most part of the river Severn. Others, indeed, think that the salt ocean did not sink, but that the land was lifted higher. Then they say that the waves threw up an immense quantity of shingle and sand, and that thus these banks were formed. All that we know with certainty, however, is, that across the estuary of the Severn there rose a broad barrier of beach, which grew wider with the years, and still increases westwards. It is as if the ocean churned up its floor and cast it forth upon the strand.

Now when the Severn was thus stayed yet more effectually than the Thames, in the first place it also flowed backwards as it were, till its overflow and that of the lesser rivers which ran into it met and mingled with the reflux of the Thames. Thus the inland sea of fresh water was formed; though Silvester hints (what is most improbable) that the level of the land sank and formed a basin. After a time, when the waters had risen high enough, since all water must have an outlet somewhere, the Lake, passing over the green country behind the Red Rocks, came pouring through the channel of the Avon.

Then, farther down, it rose over the banks which were lowest there, and thus found its way over a dam into the sea. Now when the tide of the ocean is at its ebb, the waters of the Lake rush over these banks with so furious a current that no vessel can either go down or come up. If they attempted to go down, they would be swamped by the meeting of the waves; if they attempted to come up, the strongest gale that blows could not force them against the stream. As the tide gradually returns, however, the level of the ocean rises to the level of the Lake, the outward flow of the water ceases, and there is even a partial inward flow of the tide which, at its highest, reaches to the Red Rocks. At this state of the tide, which happens twice in a day and night, vessels can enter or go forth.

The Irish ships, of which I have spoken, thus come into the Lake, waiting outside the bar till the tide lifts them over. The Irish ships, being built to traverse the ocean from their country, are large and stout and well manned, carrying from thirty to fifty men. The Welsh ships, which come down from that inlet of the Lake which follows the ancient course of the Severn, are much smaller and lighter, as not being required to withstand the heavy seas. They carry but fifteen or twenty men each, but then they are more numerous. The Irish ships, on account of their size and draught, in sailing about the sweet waters, cannot always haul on shore at night, nor follow the course of the ships of burden between the fringe of islands and the strand.

They have often to stay in the outer and deeper waters; but the Welsh boats come in easily at all parts of the coast, so that no place is safe against them. The Welsh have ever been most jealous as to that part of the Lake which we suppose to follow the course of the Severn, and will on no account permit so much as a canoe to enter it. So that whether it be a narrow creek, or whether there be wide reaches, or what the shores may be like, we are ignorant. And this is all that is with certainty known concerning the origin of the inland sea of sweet water, excluding all that superstition and speculation have advanced, and setting down nothing but ascertained facts.

A beautiful sea it is, clear as crystal, exquisite to drink, abounding with fishes of every kind, and adorned with green islands. There is nothing more lovely in the world than when, upon a calm evening, the sun goes down across the level and gleaming water, where it is so wide that the eye can but just distinguish a low and dark cloud, as it were, resting upon the horizon, or perhaps, looking lengthways, cannot distinguish any ending to the expanse. Sometimes it is blue, reflecting the noonday sky; sometimes white from the clouds; again green and dark as the wind rises and the waves roll.

Storms, indeed, come up with extraordinary swiftness, for which reason the ships, whenever possible, follow the trade route, as it is called, behind the islands, which shelter them like a protecting reef. They drop equally quickly, and thus it is not uncommon for the morning to be calm, the midday raging in waves dashing resistlessly upon the beach, and the evening still again. The Irish, who are accustomed to the salt ocean, say, in the suddenness of its storms and the shifting winds, it is more dangerous than the sea itself. But then there are almost always islands, behind which a vessel can be sheltered.

Beneath the surface of the Lake there must be concealed very many ancient towns and cities, of which the names are lost. Sometimes the anchors bring up even now fragments of rusty iron and old metal, or black beams of timber. It is said, and with probability, that when the remnant of the ancients found the water gradually encroaching (for it rose very slowly), as they were driven back year by year, they considered that in time they would be all swept away and drowned. But after extending to its present limits the Lake rose no farther, not even in the wettest seasons, but always remains the same. From the position of certain quays we know that it has thus remained for the last hundred years at least.

Never, as I observed before, was there so beautiful an expanse of water. How much must we sorrow that it has so often proved only the easiest mode of bringing the miseries of war to the doors of the unoffending. Yet men are never weary of sailing to and fro upon it, and most of the cities of the present time are upon its shore. And in the evening we walk by the beach, and from the rising grounds look over the waters, as if to gaze upon their loveliness were reward to us for the labour of the day.

Part II
Wild England

CHAPTER I

SIR FELIX

ON a bright May morning, the sunlight, at five o'clock, was pouring into a room which faced the east at the ancestral home of the Aquilas. In this room Felix, the eldest of the three sons of the Baron, was sleeping. The beams passed over his head, and lit up a square space on the opposite whitewashed wall, where, in the midst of the brilliant light, hung an ivory cross. There were only two panes of glass in the window, each no more than two or three inches square, the rest of the window being closed by strong oaken shutters, thick enough to withstand the stroke of an arrow.

In the daytime one of these at least would have been thrown open to admit air and light. They did not quite meet, and a streak of sunshine, in addition to that which came through the tiny panes, entered at the chink. Only one window in the house contained more than two such panes (it was in the Baroness's sitting-room), and most of them had none at all. The glass left by the ancients in their dwellings had long since been used up or broken, and the fragments that remained were too precious to be put in ordinary rooms. When larger pieces were discovered, they were taken for the palaces of the princes, and even these were but sparingly supplied, so that the saying 'he has glass in his window' was equivalent to 'he belongs to the upper ranks'.

On the recess of the window was an inkstand, which had been recently in use, for a quill lay beside it, and a sheet of parchment partly covered with writing. The ink was thick and very dark, made of powdered charcoal, leaving a slightly raised writing, which could be perceived by the finger on rubbing it lightly over. Beneath the window on the bare floor was an open chest, in which were several similar parchments and books, and from which the sheet on the recess had evidently been taken. This chest, though small, was extremely heavy and strong, being dug out with the chisel and gouge from a solid block of oak. Except a few parallel grooves, there was no attempt at ornamentation upon it. The lid, which had no hinges, but lifted completely off, was tilted against the wall. It was, too, of oak some inches thick, and fitted upon the chest by a kind of dovetailing at the edges.

Instead of a lock, the chest was fastened by a lengthy thong of oxhide, which now lay in a coil on the floor. Bound round and round, twisted and intertangled, and finally tied with a special and secret knot (the ends being concealed), the thong of leather secured the contents of the chest from prying eyes or thievish hands. With axe or knife, of course, the knot might easily have been severed, but no one could obtain access to the room except the retainers of the house, and which of them, even if unfaithful, would dare to employ such means in view of the certain punishment that must follow? It would occupy hours to undo the knot, and then it could not be tied again in exactly the same fashion, so that the real use of the thong was to assure the owner that his treasures had not been interfered with in his absence. Such locks as were made were of the clumsiest construction. They were not so difficult to pick as the thong to untie, and their expense, or rather the difficulty of getting a workman who could manufacture them, confined their use to the heads of great houses. The Baron's chest was locked, and his alone, in the dwelling.

Besides the parchments which were nearest the top, as most in use, there were three books, much worn and decayed, which had been preserved, more by accident than by care, from the libraries of the ancients. One was an abridged history of Rome, the other a similar account of English history, the third a primer of science or knowledge; all three, indeed, being books which, among the ancients, were used for teaching children, and which, by the men of those days, would have been cast aside with contempt.

Exposed for years in decaying houses, rain and mildew had spotted and stained their pages; the covers had rotted away these hundred years, and were now supplied by a broad sheet of limp leather with wide margins far overlapping the edges; many of the pages were quite gone, and others torn by careless handling. The abridgment of Roman history had been scorched by a forest fire, and the charred edges of the leaves had dropped away in semi-circular holes. Yet, by pondering over these, Felix had, as it were, reconstructed much of the knowledge which was the common (and therefore unvalued) possession of all when they were printed.

The parchments contained his annotations, and the result of his thought; they were also full of extracts from decaying volumes lying totally neglected in the houses of other nobles. Most of these were of extreme antiquity, for when the ancients departed, the modern books which they had composed being left in the decaying houses at the

mercy of the weather, rotted, or were destroyed by the frequent grass
fires. But those that had been preserved by the ancients in museums
escaped for a while, and some of these yet remained in lumber-rooms
and corners, whence they were occasionally dragged forth by the servants for greater convenience in lighting the fires. The young nobles,
entirely devoted to the chase, to love intrigues, and war, overwhelmed
Felix Aquila with ridicule when they found him poring over these
relics, and being of a proud and susceptible spirit, they so far succeeded
that he abandoned the open pursuit of such studies, and stole his
knowledge by fitful glances when there was no one near. As among the
ancients learning was esteemed above all things, so now, by a species of
contrast, it was of all things the most despised.

Under the books, in one corner of the chest, was a leather bag
containing four golden sovereigns, such as were used by the ancients,
and eighteen pieces of modern silver money, the debased shillings of
the day, not much more than half of which was silver and the rest
alloy. The gold coins had been found while digging holes for the posts
of a new stockade, and by the law should have been delivered to the
Prince's treasury. All the gold discovered, whether in the form of coin
or jewellery, was the property of the Prince, who was supposed to pay
for its value in currency.

As the actual value of the currency was only half of its nominal
value (and sometimes less), the transaction was greatly in favour of
the treasury. Such was the scarcity of gold that the law was strictly
enforced, and had there been the least suspicion of the fact, the house
would have been ransacked from the cellars to the roof. Imprisonment
and fine would have been the inevitable fate of Felix, and the family
would very probably have suffered for the fault of one of its members.
But independent and determined to the last degree, Felix ran any risk
rather than surrender that which he had found, and which he deemed
his own. This unbending independence and pride of spirit, together
with scarce concealed contempt for others, had resulted in almost isolating him from the youth of his own age, and had caused him to be
regarded with dislike by the elders. He was rarely, if ever, asked to join
the chase, and still more rarely invited to the festivities and amuse-
ments provided in adjacent houses, or to the grander entertainments
of the higher nobles. Too quick to take offence where none was really
intended, he fancied that many bore him ill-will who had scarcely given
him a passing thought. He could not forgive the coarse jokes uttered
upon his personal appearance by men of heavier build, who despised
so slender a stripling.

He would rather be alone than join their company, and would not compete with them in any of their sports, so that, when his absence from the arena was noticed, it was attributed to weakness or coward-ice. These imputations stung him deeply, driving him to brood within himself. He was never seen in the courtyards or ante-rooms at the palace, nor following in the train of the Prince, as was the custom with the youthful nobles. The servility of the court angered and disgusted him; the eagerness of strong men to carry a cushion or fetch a dog annoyed him.

There were those who observed this absence from the crowd in the ante-rooms. In the midst of so much intrigue and continual striving for power, designing men, on the one hand, were ever on the alert for what they imagined would prove willing instruments; and on the other, the Prince's councillors kept a watchful eye on the dispositions of every one of the least consequence; so that, although but twenty-five, Felix was already down in two lists, the one, at the palace, of persons whose views, if not treasonable, were doubtful, and the other, in the hands of a possible pretender, as a discontented and therefore useful man. Felix was entirely ignorant that he had attracted so much observation. He supposed himself simply despised and ignored; he cherished no trea-son, had not the slightest sympathy with any pretender, held totally aloof from intrigue, and his reveries, if they were ambitious, concerned only himself.

But the most precious of the treasures in the chest were eight or ten small sheets of parchment, each daintily rolled and fastened with a ribbon, letters from Aurora Thyma, who had also given him the ivory cross on the wall. It was of ancient workmanship, a relic of the old world. A compass, a few small tools (valuable because preserved for so many years, and not now to be obtained for any consideration), and a magnifying glass, a relic also of the ancients, completed the contents of the chest.

Upon a low table by the bedstead was a flint and steel and tinder, and an earthenware oil lamp, not intended to be carried about. There, too, lay his knife, with buckhorn hilt, worn by every one in the belt, and his forester's axe, a small tool, but extremely useful in the woods, without which, indeed, progress was often impossible. These were in the belt, which, as he undressed, he had cast upon the table, together with his purse, in which were about a dozen copper coins, not very regular in shape, and stamped on one side only. The table was formed of two short hewn planks, scarcely smoothed, raised on similar planks (on edge) at each end, in fact, a larger form.

From a peg driven into the wall hung a disc of brass by a thin leath-ern lace; this disc, polished to the last degree, answered as a mirror.

The only other piece of furniture, if so it could be called, was a block of wood at the side of the table, used as a chair. In the corner, between the table and the window, stood a long yew bow, and a quiver full of arrows ready for immediate use, besides which three or four sheaves lay on the floor. A crossbow hung on a wooden peg; the bow was of wood, and, therefore, not very powerful; bolts and squareheaded quarrels were scattered carelessly on the floor under it.

Six or seven slender darts used for casting, as javelins, with the hand, stood in another corner by the door, and two stouter boar spears. By the wall a heap of nets lay in apparent confusion, some used for partridges, some of coarse twine for bush hens, another, lying a little apart, for fishes. Near these the component parts of two turkeytraps were strewn about, together with a small round shield or targe, such as are used by swordsmen, snares of wire, and, in an open box, several chisels, gouges, and other tools.

A blowtube was fastened to three pegs, so that it might not warp, a hunter's horn hung from another, and on the floor were a number of arrows in various stages of manufacture, some tied to the straightening rod, some with the feathers already attached, and some hardly shaped from the elder or aspen log. A heap of skins filled the third corner, and beside them were numerous stag's horns, and two of the white cow, but none yet of the much dreaded and much desired white bull. A few peacock's feathers were there also, rare and difficult to get, and intended for Aurora. Round one footpost of the bed was a long coil of thin hide, a lasso, and on another was suspended an iron cap, or visorless helmet.

There was no sword or lance. Indeed, of all these weapons and implements, none seemed in use, to judge by the dust that had gathered upon them, and the rusted edges, except the bow and crossbow and one of the boar spears. The bed itself was very low, framed of wood, thick and solid; the clothes were of the coarsest linen and wool; there were furs for warmth in winter, but these were not required in May. There was no carpet, nor any substitute for it; the walls were whitewashed, ceiling there was none, the worm-eaten rafters were visible, and the roof tree. But on the table was a large earthenware bowl, full of meadow orchis, bluebells, and a bunch of may in flower.

His hat, wide in the brim, lay on the floor; his doublet was on the wooden block or seat, with the long tight-fitting trousers, which showed every muscle of the limb, and by them high shoes of tanned but unblacked leather. His short cloak hung on a wooden peg against the door, which was fastened with a broad bolt of oak. The parchment in the recess of the window at which he had been working just before retiring, was covered with rough sketches, evidently sections of a design for a ship or galley propelled by oars.

The square spot of light upon the wall slowly moved as the sun rose higher, till the ivory cross was left in shadow, but still the slumberer slept on, heedless, too, of the twittering of the swallows under the eaves, and the call of the cuckoo not far distant.

CHAPTER II

THE HOUSE OF AQUILA

PRESENTLY there came the sound of a creaking axle, which grew louder and louder as the waggon drew nearer, till it approached to a shriek. The sleeper moved uneasily, but recognising the noise even in his dreams, did not wake. The horrible sounds stopped; there was the sound of voices, as if two persons, one without and one within the wall, were hailing each other; a gate swung open, and the waggon came past under the very window of the bedroom. Even habit could not enable Felix to entirely withstand so piercing a noise when almost in his ears. He sat up a minute, and glanced at the square of light on the wall to guess the time by its position.

In another minute or two the squeaking of the axle ceased, as the waggon reached the storehouses, and he immediately returned to the pillow. Without, and just beneath the window, there ran a road or way, which in part divided the enclosure into two portions; the dwelling-house and its offices being on one side, the granaries and storehouses on the other. But a few yards to the left of his room, a strong gate in the enclosing wall gave entrance to this roadway. It was called the Maple Gate, because a small maple tree grew near outside. The wall, which surrounded the whole place at a distance of eight or ten yards from the buildings, was of brick, and about nine feet high, with a ditch without.

It was partly embattled, and partly loopholed, and a banquette* of earth rammed hard ran all round inside, so that the defenders might discharge darts or arrows through the embrasures, and step down out of sight to prepare a fresh supply. At each corner there was a large platform, where a considerable number of men could stand and command the approaches; there were, however, no bastions or flanking towers. On the roof of the dwelling-house a similar platform had been prepared, protected by a parapet; from which height the entire enclosure could be overlooked.

Another platform, though at a less height, was on the roof of the

---

* A raised walkway below a palisade wall or parapet, used as a platform for defensive soldiers. Throughout the text Jefferies uses archaic and medieval terms in his depiction of the debased feudal society of the future.

retainers' lodgings, so placed as especially to command the second gate. Entering by the Maple Gate, the dwelling-house was on the right hand, and the granaries and general storehouses on the left, the latter built on three sides of a square. Farther on, on the same side, were the stables, and near them the forge and workshops. Beyond these, again, were the lodgings of the retainers and labourers, near which, in the corner, was the South Gate, from which the South Road led to the cattle-pens and farms, and out to the south.

Upon the right hand, after the dwellinghouse, and connected with it, came the steward's stores, where the iron tools and similar valuable articles of metal were kept. Then, after a covered passage-way, the kitchen and general hall, under one roof with the house. The house fronted in the opposite direction to the roadway; there was a narrow green lawn between it and the enceinte,* or wall, and before the general hall and kitchens a gravelled court. This was parted from the lawn by palings, so that the house folk enjoyed privacy, and yet were close to their servitors. The place was called the Old House, for it dated back to the time of the ancients, and the Aquilas were proud of the simple designation of their fortified residence.

Felix's window was almost exactly opposite the entrance to the storehouse or granary yard, so that the waggon, after passing it, had to go but a little distance, and then, turning to the left, was drawn up before the doors of the warehouse. This waggon was low, built for the carriage of goods only, of hewn plank scarcely smooth, and the wheels were solid; cut, in fact, from the butt of an elm tree. Unless continually greased the squeaking of such wheels is terrible, and the carters frequently forgot their grease-horns.

Much of the work of the farm, such as the carting of hay and corn in harvest-time, was done upon sleds; the waggons (there were but few of them) being reserved for longer journeys on the rough roads. This waggon, laden with wool, some of the season's clip, had come in four or five miles from an out-lying cot, or sheep-pen, at the foot of the hills. In the buildings round the granary yard there were stored not only the corn and flour required for the retainers (who might at any moment become a besieged garrison), but the most valuable products of the estate, the wool, hides, and tanned leather from the tan-pits, besides a great quantity of bacon and salt beef; indeed, every possible article that could be needed.

These buildings were put together with wooden pins, on account of the scarcity of iron, and were all (dwelling-house included) roofed with

---

* Usually the main defensive wall at a fortified site or castle.

red tile. Lesser houses, cottages, and sheds at a distance were thatched, but in an enclosure tiles were necessary, lest, in case of an attack, fire should be thrown.

Half an hour later, at six o'clock, the watchman blew his horn as loudly as possible for some two or three minutes, the hollow sound echoing through the place. He took the time by the sundial on the wall, it being a summer morning; in winter he was guided by the position of the stars, and often, when sun or stars were obscured, went by guess. The house horn was blown thrice a day; at six in the morning, as a signal that the day had begun, at noon as a signal for dinner, at six in the afternoon as a signal that the day (except in harvest-time) was over. The watchmen went their round about the enclosure all night long, relieved every three hours, armed with spears, and attended by mastiffs. By day one sufficed, and his station was then usually (though not always) on the highest part of the roof.

The horn re-awoke Felix; it was the note by which he had been accustomed to rise for years. He threw open the oaken shutters, and the sunlight and the fresh breeze of the May morning came freely into the room. There was now the buzz of voices without, men unloading the wool, men at the workshops and in the granaries, and others waiting at the door of the steward's store for the tools, which he handed out to them. Iron being so scarce, tools were a temptation, and were carefully locked up each night, and given out again in the morning.

Felix went to the ivory cross and kissed it in affectionate recollection of Aurora, and then looked towards the open window, in the pride and joy of youth turning to the East, the morning, and the light. Before he had half dressed there came a knock and then an impatient kick at the door. He unbarred it, and his brother Oliver entered. Oliver had been for his swim in the river. He excelled in swimming, as, indeed, in every manly exercise, being as active and energetic as Felix was outwardly languid.

His room was only across the landing, his door just opposite. It also was strewn with implements and weapons. But there was a far greater number of tools; he was an expert and artistic workman, and his table and his seat, unlike the rude blocks in Felix's room, were tastefully carved. His seat, too, had a back, and he had even a couch of his own construction. By his bedhead hung his sword, his most valued and most valuable possession. It was one which had escaped the dispersion of the ancients; it had been ancient even in their days, and of far better work than they themselves produced.

Broad, long, straight, and well-balanced, it appeared capable of cutting through helmet and mail, when wielded by Oliver's sturdy arm. Such a sword could not have been purchased for money; money, indeed, had often been offered for it in vain; persuasion, and even covert threats from those higher in authority who coveted it, were alike wasted. The sword had been in the family for generations, and when the Baron grew too old, or rather when he turned away from active life, the second son claimed it as the fittest to use it. The claim was tacitly allowed; at all events, he had it, and meant to keep it.

In a corner stood his lance, long and sharp, for use on horseback, and by it his saddle and accoutrements. The helmet and the shirt of mail, the iron greaves and spurs, the short iron mace to hang at the saddle-bow, spoke of the knight, the man of horses and war.

Oliver's whole delight was in exercise and sport. The boldest rider, the best swimmer, the best at leaping, at hurling the dart or the heavy hammer, ever ready for tilt or tournament, his whole life was spent with horse, sword, and lance. A year younger than Felix, he was at least ten years physically older. He measured several inches more round the chest; his massive shoulders and immense arms, brown and hairy, his powerful limbs, tower-like neck, and somewhat square jaw were the natural concomitants of enormous physical strength.

All the blood and bone and thew and sinew of the house seemed to have fallen to his share; all the fiery, restless spirit and defiant temper; all the utter recklessness and warrior's instinct. He stood every inch a man, with dark, curling, short-cut hair, brown cheek and Roman chin, trimmed moustache, brown eye, shaded by long eyelashes and well-marked brows; every inch a natural king of men. That very physical preponderance and animal beauty was perhaps his bane, for his comrades were so many, and his love adventures so innumerable, that they left him no time for serious ambition.

Between the brothers there was the strangest mixture of affection and repulsion. The elder smiled at the excitement and energy of the younger; the younger openly despised the studious habits and solitary life of the elder. In time of real trouble and difficulty they would have been drawn together; as it was, there was little communion; the one went his way, and the other his. There was perhaps rather an inclination to detract from each other's achievements than to praise them, a species of jealousy or envy without personal dislike, if that can be understood. They were good friends, and yet kept apart.

Oliver made friends of all, and thwacked and banged his enemies into respectful silence. Felix made friends of none, and was equally despised by nominal friends and actual enemies. Oliver was open and jovial; Felix reserved and contemptuous, or sarcastic in manner. His

slender frame, too tall for his width, was against him; he could neither lift the weights nor undergo the muscular strain readily borne by
Oliver. It was easy to see that Felix, although nominally the eldest, had
not yet reached his full development. A light complexion, fair hair and
eyes, were also against him; where Oliver made conquests, Felix was
unregarded. He laughed, but perhaps his secret pride was hurt.

There was but one thing Felix could do in the way of exercise and
sport. He could shoot with the bow in a manner till then entirely
unapproached. His arrows fell unerringly in the centre of the target,
the swift deer and the hare were struck down with ease, and even
the wood-pigeon in full flight. Nothing was safe from those terrible
arrows. For this, and this only, his fame had gone forth; and even this
was made a source of bitterness to him.

The nobles thought no arms worthy of men of descent but the sword
and lance; missile weapons, as the dart and arrow, were the arms
of retainers. His degradation was completed when, at a tournament,
where he had mingled with the crowd, the Prince sent for him to shoot
at the butt, and display his skill among the soldiery, instead of with the
knights in the tilting ring. Felix shot, indeed, but shut his eyes that his
arrow might go wide, and was jeered at as a failure even in that ignoble
competition. Only by an iron self-control did he refrain that day from
planting one of the despised shafts in the Prince's eye.

But when Oliver joked him about his failure, Felix asked him
to hang up his breastplate at two hundred yards. He did so, and
in an instant a shaft was sent through it. After that Oliver held his
peace, and in his heart began to think that the bow was a dangerous
weapon.

'So you are late again this morning,' said Oliver, leaning against
the recess of the window, and placing his arms on it. The sunshine fell
on his curly dark hair, still wet from the river. 'Studying last night, I
suppose?' turning over the parchment. 'Why didn't you ride into town
with me?'

'The water must have been cold this morning?' said Felix, ignoring
the question.

'Yes; there was a slight frost, or something like it, very early, and a
mist on the surface; but it was splendid in the pool. Why don't you get
up and come? You used to.'

'I can swim,' said Felix, laconically, implying that, having learnt the
art, it no more tempted him. 'You were late last night; I heard you put
Night in.'

'We came home in style; it was rather dusky, but Night galloped the
Green Miles.'

ie doesn't put her hoof in a rabbit's hole, some night.'

it. She can see like a cat. I believe we got over the twelve

s than an hour. Sharp work, considering the hills. You don't

the news.'

the news to me?'

'Well, there was a quarrel at the palace yesterday afternoon. The Prince told Louis he was a double-faced traitor, and Louis told the Prince he was a suspicious fool. It nearly came to blows, and Louis is banished.'

'For the fiftieth time.'

'This time it's more serious.'

'Don't believe it. He will be sent for again this morning; cannot you see why?'

'No.'

'If the Prince is really suspicious, he will never send his brother into the country, where he might be resorted to by discontented people. He will keep him close at hand.'

'I wish the quarrelling would cease; it spoils half the fun; one's obliged to creep about the court and speak in whispers, and you can't tell whom you are talking to; they may turn on you if you say too much. There is no dancing either. I hate this moody state. I wish they would either dance or fight.'

'Fight! Who?'

'Anybody. There's some more news, but you don't care.'

'No. I do not.'

'Why don't you go and live in the woods all by yourself?' said Oliver, in some heat.

Felix laughed.

'Tell me your news. I am listening.'

'The Irish landed at Blacklands the day before yesterday, and burnt Robert's place; they tried Letburn, but the people there had been warned, and were ready. And there's an envoy from Sypolis arrived; some think the Assembly has broken up; they were all at daggers drawn. So much for the Holy League.'

'So much for the Holy League,' repeated Felix.

'What are you going to do to-day?' asked Oliver, after awhile.

'I am going down to my canoe,' said Felix.

'I will go with you; the trout are rising. Have you got any hooks?'

'There's some in the box there, I think; take the tools out.'

Oliver searched among the tools in the open box, all rusty and covered with dust, while Felix finished dressing, put away his parchment, and knotted the thong round his chest. He found some hooks at the bottom, and after breakfast they walked out together, Oliver carrying his rod, and a boarspear, and Felix a boar-spear also, in addition to a small flag basket with some chisels and gouges.

CHAPTER III

THE STOCKADE

WHEN Oliver and Felix started, they left Philip, the third and youngest of the three brothers, still at breakfast. They turned to the left, on getting out of doors, and again to the left, through the covered passage between the steward's store and the kitchens. Then crossing the waggon yard, they paused a moment to glance in at the forge, where two men were repairing part of a plough.

Oliver must also look for a moment at his mare, after which they directed their steps to the South Gate. The massive oaken door was open, the bolts having been drawn back at hornblow. There was a guard-room on one side of the gate under the platform in the corner, where there was always supposed to be a watch.

But in times of peace, and when there were no apprehensions of attack, the men whose turn it was to watch there were often called away for a time to assist in some labour going forward, and at that moment were helping to move the woolpacks farther into the warehouse. Still they were close at hand, and had the day watchman or warder, who was now on the roof, blown his horn, would have rushed direct to the gate. Felix did not like this relaxation of discipline. His precise ideas were upset at the absence of the guard; method, organisation, and precision, were the characteristics of his mind, and this kind of uncertainty irritated him.

'I wish Sir Constans would insist on the guard being kept,' he remarked. Children, in speaking of their parents, invariably gave them their titles. Now their father's title was properly 'my lord', as he was a baron, and one of the most ancient. But he had so long abnegated the exercise of his rights and privileges, sinking the noble in the mechanician, that men had forgotten the proper style in which they should address him. 'Sir' was applied to all nobles, whether they possessed estates or not. The brothers were invariably addressed as Sir Felix or Sir Oliver. It marked, therefore, the low estimation in which the Baron was held when even his own sons spoke of him by that title.

Oliver, though a military man by profession, laughed at Felix's strict view of the guards' duties. Familiarity with danger, and natural carelessness, had rendered him contemptuous of it.

'There's no risk,' said he, 'that I can see. Who could attack us? The Bushmen would never dream of it; the Romany would be seen coming days beforehand; we are too far from the Lake for the pirates; and as we are not great people, as we might have been, we need dread no private enmity. Besides which, any assailants must pass the stockades first.'

'Quite true. Still I don't like it; it is a loose way of doing things.'

Outside the gate they followed the waggon track, or South Road, for about half a mile. It crossed meadows parted by low hedges, and they remarked, as they went, on the shortness of the grass, which, for want of rain, was not nearly fit for mowing. Last year there had been a bad wheat crop; this year there was at present scarcely any grass. These matters were of the highest importance; peace or war, famine or plenty, might depend upon the weather of the next few months.

The meadows, besides being divided by the hedges, kept purposely cropped low, were surrounded, like all the cultivated lands, by high and strong stockades. Half a mile down the South Road they left the track, and following a footpath some few hundred yards, came to the pool where Oliver had bathed that morning. The river, which ran through the enclosed grounds, was very shallow, for they were near its source in the hills, but just there it widened, and filled a depression fifty or sixty yards across, which was deep enough for swimming. Beyond the pool the stream curved and left the enclosure; the stockade, or at least an open work of poles, was continued across it. This work permitted the stream to flow freely, but was sufficiently close to exclude any one who might attempt to enter by creeping up the bed of the river.

They crossed the river just above the pool by some stepping-stones, large blocks rolled in for the purpose, and approached the stockade. It was formed of small but entire trees, young elms, firs, or very thick ash-poles, driven in a double row into the earth, the first or inner row side by side, the outer row filling the interstices, and the whole bound together at the bottom by split willow woven in and out. This inter-weaving extended only about three feet up, and was intended first to bind the structure together, and secondly to exclude small animals which might creep in between the stakes. The reason it was not carried all up was that it should not afford a footing to human thieves desirous of climbing over.

The smooth poles by themselves afforded no notch or foothold for a Bushman's naked foot. They rose nine or ten feet above the willow, so that the total height of the palisade was about twelve feet, and the tops of the stakes were sharpened. The construction of such palisades required great labour, and could be carried out only by those who could command the services of numbers of men, so that a small proprietor was impossible, unless within the walls of a town. This particular stockade was by no means an extensive one, in comparison with the estates of more prominent nobles.

The enclosure immediately surrounding the Old House was of an irregular oval shape, perhaps a mile long, and not quite three-quarters of a mile wide, the house being situate towards the northern and higher end of the oval. The river crossed it, entering on the west and leaving on the eastern side. The enclosure was for the greater part meadow and pasture, for here the cattle were kept which supplied the house with milk, cheese, and butter, while others intended for slaughter were driven in here for the last month of fattening.

The horses in actual use for riding, or for the waggons, were also turned out here temporarily. There were two pens and rickyards within it, one beside the river, one farther down. The South Road ran almost down the centre, passing both rickyards, and leaving the stockade at the southern end by a gate, called the barrier. At the northern extremity of the oval the palisade passed within three hundred yards of the house, and there was another barrier, to which the road led from the Maple Gate, which has been mentioned. From thence it went across the hills to the town of Ponze. Thus, any one approaching the Old House had first to pass the barrier and get inside the palisade.

At each barrier there was a cottage and a guard-room, though, as a matter of fact, the watch was kept in peaceful times even more carelessly than at the inner gates of the wall about the house itself. Much the same plan, with local variations, was pursued on the other estates of the province, though the stockade at the Old House was remarkable for the care and skill with which it had been constructed. Part of the duty of the watchman on the roof was to keep an eye on the barriers, which he could see from his elevated position.

In case of an incursion of gipsies or any danger, the guard at the barrier was supposed to at once close the gate, blow a horn, and exhibit a flag. Upon hearing the horn or observing the flag, the warder on the roof raised the alarm, and assistance was sent. Such was the system, but as no attack had taken place for some years the discipline had grown lax.

After crossing on the stepping-stones Oliver and Felix were soon under the stockade which ran high above them, and was apparently as difficult to get out of as to get into. By the strict law of the estate, any person who left the stockade except by the public barrier rendered himself liable to the lash or imprisonment. Any person, even a retainer, endeavouring to enter from without by pole, ladder, or rope, might be killed with an arrow or dart, putting himself into the position of an outlaw. In practice, of course, this law was frequently evaded. It did not apply to the family of the owner.

Under some bushes by the palisade was a ladder of rope, the rungs, however, of wood. Putting his fishing-tackle and boar-spear down, Oliver took the ladder and threw the end over the stockade. He then picked up a pole with a fork at the end from the bushes, left there of course for the purpose, and with the fork pushed the rungs over till the ladder was adjusted, half within and half without the palisade. It hung by the wooden rungs which caught the tops of the stakes. He then went up, and when at the top, leant over and drew up the outer part of the ladder one rung, which he put the inner side of the palisade, so that on transferring his weight to the outer side it might uphold him. Otherwise the ladder, when he got over the points of the stakes, must have slipped the distance between one rung and a second.

Having adjusted this, he got over, and Felix carrying up the spears and tackle handed them to him. Felix followed, and thus in three minutes they were on the outer side of the stockade. Originally the ground for twenty yards, all round outside the stockade, had been cleared of trees and bushes that they might not harbour vermin, or thorn-hogs, or facilitate the approach of human enemies. Part of the weekly work of the bailiffs was to walk round the entire circumference of the stockade to see that it was in order, and to have any bushes removed that began to grow up. As with other matters, however, in the lapse of time the bailiffs became remiss, and under the easy, and perhaps too merciful rule of Sir Constans, were not recalled to their duties with sufficient sharpness.

Brambles and thorns and other underwood had begun to cover the space that should have been open, and young sapling oaks had risen from dropped acorns. Felix pointed this out to Oliver, who seldom accompanied him; he was indeed rather glad of the opportunity to do so, as Oliver had more interest with Sir Constans than himself. Oliver admitted it showed great negligence, but added that after all it really did not matter. 'What I wish,' said he, 'is that Sir Constans would go to Court, and take his proper position.'

Upon this they were well agreed; it was, in fact, almost the only point upon which all three brothers did agree. They sometimes talked about it till they separated in a furious temper, not with each other but with him. There was a distinct track of footsteps through the narrow band of low brambles and underwood between the stockade and the forest. This had been made by Felix in his daily visits to his canoe.

The forest there consisted principally of hawthorn trees and thorn thickets, with some scattered oaks and ashes; the timber was sparse, but the fern was now fast rising up so thick, that in the height of the summer it would be difficult to walk through it. The tips of the fronds unrolling were now not up to the knee; then the brake would reach to the shoulder. The path wound round the thickets (the blackthorn being quite impenetrable except with the axe) and came again to the river some four or five hundred yards from the stockade. The stream, which ran from west to east through the enclosure, here turned and went due south.

On the bank Felix had found a fine black poplar, the largest and straightest and best grown of that sort for some distance round, and this he had selected for his canoe. Stones broke the current here into eddies, below which there were deep holes and gullies where alders hung over, and an ever-rustling aspen spread the shadow of its boughs across the water. The light-coloured mud, formed of disintegrated chalk, on the farther and shallower side was only partly hidden by flags and sedges, which like a richer and more alluvial earth. Nor did the bushes grow very densely on this soil over the chalk, so that there was more room for casting the fly than is usually the case where a stream runs through a forest. Oliver, after getting his tackle in order, at once began to cast, while Felix, hanging his doublet on an oft-used branch, and leaning his spear against a tree, took his chisels and gouge from the flag basket.

He had chosen the black poplar for the canoe because it was the lightest wood, and would float best. To fell so large a tree had been a great labour, for the axes were of poor quality, cut badly, and often required sharpening. He could easily have ordered half-a-dozen men to throw the tree, and they would have obeyed immediately; but then the individuality and interest of the work would have been lost. Unless he did it himself its importance and value to him would have been diminished. It had now been down some weeks, had been hewn into outward shape, and the larger part of the interior slowly dug away with chisel and gouge.

He had commenced while the hawthorn was just putting forth its first spray, when the thickets and the trees were yet bare. Now the May bloom scented the air, the forest was green, and his work approached completion. There remained, indeed, but some final shaping and rounding off, and the construction or rather cutting out of a secret locker in the stern. This locker was nothing more than a square aperture chiselled out like a mortice, entering not from above but parallel with the bottom, and was to be closed with a tight-fitting piece of wood driven in by force of mallet.

A little paint would then conceal the slight chinks, and the boat might be examined in every possible way without any trace of this hiding-place being observed. The canoe was some eleven feet long, and nearly three feet in the beam; it tapered at either end, so that it might be propelled backwards or forwards without turning, and stem and stern (interchangeable definitions in this case) each rose a few inches higher than the general gunwale. The sides were about two inches thick, the bottom three, so that although dug out from light wood the canoe was rather heavy.

At first Felix constructed a light shed of fir poles roofed with spruce fir branches over the log, so that he might work sheltered from the bitter winds of the early spring. As the warmth increased he had taken the shed down, and now as the sun rose higher was glad of the shade of an adjacent beech.

CHAPTER IV

THE CANOE

FELIX had scarcely worked half an hour before Oliver returned and threw himself on the ground at full length. He had wearied of fishing, the delicate adjustment of the tackle and the care necessary to keep the hook and line from catching in the branches had quickly proved too much for his patience. He lay on the grass, his feet towards the stream which ran and bubbled beneath, and watched Felix chipping out the block intended to fit into the secret opening or locker.

'It is nearly finished, then?' he said presently. 'What a time you have been at it!'

'Nearly three months.'

'Why did you make it so big? It is too big.'

'Is it really? Perhaps I want to put some things in it.'

'Oh, I see; cargo. But where are you going to launch it?'

'Below the stones there.'

'Well, you won't be able to go far; there's an old fir across the river down yonder, and a hollow willow has fallen in. Besides, the stream's too shallow; you'll take ground before you get half a mile.'

'Shall I?'

'Of course you will. That boat will float six inches deep by herself, and I'm sure there's not six inches by the Thorns.'

'Very awkward.'

'Why didn't you have a hide boat made, with a willow framework and leather cover? Then you might perhaps get down the river by hauling it past the shallows and the fallen trees. In two days' time you would be in the hands of the gipsies.'

'And you would be Sir Constans' heir!'

'Now, come, I say; that's too bad. You know I didn't mean that. Besides, I think I'm as much his heir as you now' (looking at his sinewy arm); 'at least, he doesn't listen much to you. I mean, the river runs into the gipsies' country as straight as it can go.'

'Just so.'

'Well, you seem very cool about it!'

'I am not going down the river.'

'Then, where are you going?'

'On the Lake.'

'Whew! (whistling). Pooh! Why, the Lake's – let me see, to Heron Bay it's quite fifteen miles. You can't paddle across the land.'

'But I can put the canoe on a cart.'

'Aha! Why didn't you tell me before?'

'Because I did not wish any one to know. Don't say anything.'

'Not I. But what on earth, or rather, on water, are you driving at? Where are you going? What's the canoe for?'

'I am going a voyage. But I will tell you all when it is ready. Meantime, I rely on you to keep silence. The rest think the boat is for the river.'

'I will not say a word. But why did you not have a hide boat?'

'They are not strong enough. They can't stand knocking about.'

'If you want to go a voyage (where to, I can't imagine), why not take a passage on board a ship?'

'I want to go my own way. They will only go theirs. Nor do I like the company.'

'Well, certainly the sailors are the roughest lot I know. Still, that would not have hurt you. You are rather dainty, Sir Felix!'

'My daintiness does not hurt you.'

'Can't I speak?' (sharply).

'Please yourself.'

A silence. A cuckoo sang in the forest, and was answered from a tree within the distant palisade. Felix chopped away slowly and deliberately; he was not a good workman. Oliver watched his progress with contempt; he could have put it into shape in half the time. Felix could draw, and design; he could invent, but he was not a practical workman, to give speedy and accurate effect to his ideas.

'My opinion is,' said Oliver, 'that that canoe will not float upright. It's one-sided.'

Felix, usually so self-controlled, could not refrain from casting his chisel down angrily. But he picked it up again, and said nothing. This silence had more influence upon Oliver, whose nature was very generous, than the bitterest retort. He sat up on the sward.

'I will help launch it,' he said. 'We could manage it between us, if you don't want a lot of the fellows down here.'

'Thank you. I should like that best.'

'And I will help you with the cart when you start.'

Oliver rolled over on his back, and looked up idly at the white flecks of cloud sailing at a great height.

'Old Mouse is a wretch not to give me a command,' he said presently.

Felix looked round involuntarily, lest any one should have heard; Mouse was the nick-name for the Prince. Like all who rule with irresponsible power, the Prince had spies everywhere. He was not a cruel man, nor a benevolent, neither clever nor foolish, neither strong nor weak; simply an ordinary, a very ordinary being, who chanced to sit upon a throne because his ancestors did, and not from any personal superiority.

He was at times much influenced by those around him; at others he took his own course, right or wrong; at another he let matters drift. There was never any telling in the morning what he might do towards night, for there was no vein of will or bias running through his character. In fact, he lacked character; he was all uncertainty, except in jealousy of his supremacy. Possibly some faint perception of his own incapacity, of the feeble grasp he had upon the State, that seemed outwardly so completely his, occasionally crossed his mind.

Hence the furious scenes with his brother; hence the sudden imprisonments and equally sudden pardons; the spies and eavesdroppers, the sequestration of estates for no apparent cause. And, following these erratic severities to the suspected nobles, proclamations giving privileges to the people, and removing taxes. But in a few days these were imposed again, and men who dared to murmur were beaten by the soldiers, or cast into the dungeons. Yet Prince Louis (the family were all of the same name) was not an ill-meaning man; he often meant well, but had no stability or firmness of purpose.

This was why Felix dreaded lest some chance listener should hear Oliver abuse him. Oliver had been in the army for some time; his excellence in all arms, and especially with lance and sword, his acknowledged courage, and his noble birth, entitled him to a command, however lowly it might be. But he was still in the ranks, and not the slightest recognition had ever been taken of his feats, except, indeed, if whispers were true, by some sweet smiles from a certain lady of the palace, who admired knightly prowess. Oliver chafed under this neglect. 'I would not say those kind of things,' remarked Felix. 'Certainly it is annoying.'

'Annoying! that is a mild expression. Of course, everyone knows the reason. If we had any money, or influence, it would be very different. But Sir Constans has neither gold nor power, and he might have had both.'

'There was a clerk from the notary's at the house yesterday evening,' said Felix.

'About the debts, no doubt. Some day the cunning old scoundrel, when he can squeeze no more interest out of us, will find a legal quibble and take the lot.'

'Or put us in the Blue Chamber, the first time the Prince goes to war and wants money. The Blue Chamber will say, "Where can we get it? Who's weakest?" "Why, Sir Constans!" "Then away with him."'

'Yes, that will be it. Yet I wish a war would happen; there would be some chance for me. I would go with you in your canoe, but you are going you don't know where. What's your object? Nothing. You don't know yourself.'

'Indeed!'

'No, you don't; you're a dreamer.'

'I am afraid it is true.'

'I hate dreams.' After a pause, in a lower voice, 'Have you any money?'

Felix took out his purse and showed him the copper pieces.

'The eldest son of Constans Aquila with ten copper pieces,' growled Oliver, rising, but taking them all the same. 'Lend them to me. I'll try them on the board to-night. Fancy me putting down copper! It's intolerable' (working himself into a rage). 'I'll turn bandit, and rob on the roads. I'll go to King Yeo and fight the Welsh. Confusion!'

He rushed into the forest, leaving his spear on the sward.

Felix quietly chipped away at the block he was shaping, but his temper, too, was inwardly rising. The same talk, varied in detail, but the same in point, took place every time the brothers were together, and always with the same result of anger. In earlier days Sir Constans had been as forward in all warlike exercises as Oliver was now, and being possessed of extraordinary physical strength, took a leading part among men. Wielding his battle-axe with irresistible force, he distinguished himself in several battles and sieges.

He had a singular talent for mechanical construction (the wheel by which water was drawn from the well at the palace was designed by him), but this very ingenuity was the beginning of his difficulties. During a long siege, he invented a machine for casting large stones against the walls, or rather put it together from the fragmentary descriptions he had seen in authors, whose works had almost perished before the dispersion of the ancients; for he, too, had been studious in youth.

The old Prince was highly pleased with this engine, which promised him speedy conquest over his enemies, and the destruction of their strongholds. But the nobles who had the hereditary command of the siege artillery, which consisted mainly of battering-rams, could not endure to see their prestige vanishing. They caballed, traduced the Baron, and he fell into disgrace. This disgrace, as he was assured by secret messages from the Prince, was but policy; he would be recalled so soon as the Prince felt himself able to withstand the pressure of the nobles. But it happened that the old Prince died at that juncture, and the present Prince succeeded.

The enemies of the Baron, having access to him, obtained his confidence; the Baron was arrested and amerced* in a heavy fine, the payment of which laid the foundation of those debts which had since been constantly increasing. He was then released, but was not for some two years permitted to approach the Court. Meantime, men of not half his descent, but with an unblushing brow and unctuous tongue, had become the favourites at the palace of the Prince, who, as said before, was not bad, but the mere puppet of circumstances.

Into competition with these vulgar flatterers Aquila could not enter. It was indeed pride, and nothing but pride, that had kept him from the palace. By slow degrees he had sunk out of sight, occupying himself more and more with mechanical inventions, and with gardening, till at last he had come to be regarded as no more than an agriculturist. Yet in this obscure condition he had not escaped danger.

The common people were notoriously attached to him. Whether this was due to his natural kindliness, his real strength of intellect, and charm of manner, or whether it was on account of the uprightness with which he judged between them, or whether it was owing to all these things combined, certain it is that there was not a man on the estate that would not have died for him. Certain it is, too, that he was beloved by the people of the entire district, and more especially by the shepherds of the hills, who were freer and less under the control of the patrician caste. Instead of carrying disputes to the town, to be adjudged by the Prince's authority, many were privately brought to him.

This, by degrees becoming known, excited the jealousy and anger of the Prince, an anger cunningly inflamed by the notary Francis, and by other nobles. But they hesitated to execute anything against him lest the people should rise, and it was doubtful, indeed, if the very retainers of the nobles would attack the Old House, if ordered. Thus the Baron's weakness was his defence. The Prince, to do him justice, soon forgot the matter, and laughed at his own folly, that he should be jealous of a man who was no more than an agriculturist.

The rest were not so appeased; they desired the Baron's destruction if only from hatred of his popularity, and they lost no opportunity of casting discredit upon him, or of endeavouring to alienate the affec-

---

* Amercement (of Anglo-Norman origin) was in medieval English law a financial penalty imposed by a court or a gathering of peers. Unlike a fine, an amercement was of an arbitrary, rather than a fixed, amount. To be amerced literally means 'to be at the mercy of', and is an appropriate term given Jefferies's wider depiction of arbitrary court rule.

tions of the people by representing him as a magician, a thing clearly proved by his machines and engines, which must have been designed by some supernatural assistance. But the chief, as the most immediate and pressing danger, was the debt to Francis the notary, which might at any moment be brought before the Court.

Thus it was that the three sons found themselves without money or position, with nothing but a bare patent of nobility. The third and youngest alone had made any progress, if such it could be called. By dint of his own persistent efforts, and by enduring insults and rebuffs with indifference, he had at last obtained an appointment in that section of the Treasury which received the dues upon merchandise, and regulated the imposts. He was but a messenger at every man's call; his pay was not sufficient to obtain his food, still it was an advance, and he was in a government office. He could but just exist in the town, sleeping in a garret, where he stored the provisions he took in with him every Monday morning from Old House. He came home on the Saturday and returned to his work on the Monday. Even his patience was almost worn out.

The whole place was thus falling to decay, while at the same time it seemed to be flowing with milk and honey, for under the Baron's personal attention the estate, though so carelessly guarded, had become a very garden. The cattle had increased, and were of the best kind, the horses were celebrated and sought for, the sheep valued, the crops the wonder of the province. Yet there was no money; the product went to the notary. This extraordinary fertility was the cause of the covetous longing of the Court favourites to divide the spoil.

CHAPTER V

BARON AQUILA

FELIX'S own position was bitter in the extreme. He felt he had talent. He loved deeply, he knew that he was in turn as deeply beloved; but he was utterly powerless. On the confines of the estate, indeed, the men would run gladly to do his bidding. Beyond, and on his own account, he was helpless. Manual labour (to plough, to sow, to work on ship-board) could produce nothing in a time when almost all work was done by bondsmen or family retainers. The life of a hunter in the woods was free, but produced nothing.

The furs he sold simply maintained him; it was barter for existence, not profit. The shepherds on the hills roamed in comparative freedom, but they had no wealth except of sheep. He could not start as a mer-chant without money; he could not enclose an estate and build a house or castle fit for the nuptials of a noble's daughter without money, or that personal influence which answers the same purpose; he could not even hope to succeed to the hereditary estate, so deeply was it encum-bered; they might, indeed, at any time be turned forth.

Slowly the iron entered into his soul. This hopelessness, helplessness, embittered every moment. His love increasing with the passage of time rendered his position hateful in the extreme. The feeling within that he had talent which only required opportunity stung him like a scor-pion. The days went by, and everything remained the same. Continual brooding and bitterness of spirit went near to drive him mad.

At last the resolution was taken, he would go forth into the world. That involved separation from Aurora, long separation, and without communication, since letters could be sent only by special messenger, and how should he pay a messenger? It was this terrible thought of separation which had so long kept him inactive. In the end the bit-terness of hopelessness forced him to face it. He began the canoe, but kept his purpose secret, especially from her, lest tears should melt his resolution.

There were but two ways of travelling open to him, on foot, as the hunters did, or by the merchant vessels. The latter, of course, required payment, and their ways were notoriously coarse. If on foot he could not cross the Lake, nor visit the countries on either shore nor the islands; therefore he cut down the poplar and commenced the canoe. Whither he should go, and what he should do, was entirely at the mercy of circumstances. He had no plan, no route.

He had a dim idea of offering his services to some distant king or prince, of unfolding to him the inventions he had made. He tried to conceal from himself that he would probably be repulsed and laughed at. Without money, without a retinue, how could he expect to be received or listened to? Still, he must go; he could not help himself, go he must.

As he chopped and chipped through the long weeks of early spring, while the easterly winds bent the trees above him, till the buds unfolded and the leaves expanded, while his hands were thus employed, the whole map, as it were, of the known countries seemed to pass without volition before his mind. He saw the cities along the shores of the great Lake; he saw their internal condition, the weakness of the social fabric, the misery of the bondsmen. The uncertain action of the League, the only thread which bound the world together; the threatening aspect of the Cymry and the Irish; the dread north, the vast northern forests, from which at any time invading hosts might descend on the fertile south; it all went before his eyes.

What was there behind the immense and untraversed belt of forest which extended to the south, to the east, and west? Where did the great Lake end? Were the stories of the gold and silver mines of Devon and Cornwall true? And where were the iron mines, from which the ancients drew their stores of metal?

Led by these thoughts he twice or thrice left his labour, and walking some twenty miles through the forests, and over the hills, reached the summit of White Horse. From thence, resting on the sward, he watched the vessels making slow progress by oars, and some drawn with ropes by gangs of men or horses on the shore, through the narrow straits. North and South there nearly met. There was but a furlong of water between them. If ever the North came down *there* the armies would cross. *There* was the key of the world. Excepting the few cottages where the owners of the horses lived, there was neither castle nor town within twenty miles.

Forced on by these thoughts, he broke the long silence which had existed between him and his father. He spoke of the value and importance of this spot; could not the Baron send forth his retainers and enclose a new estate there? There was nothing to prevent him. The forest was free to all, provided that they rendered due service to the Prince. Might not a house or castle built there become the beginning of a city? The Baron listened, and then said he must go and see that a new hatch was put in the brook to irrigate the water-meadow. That was all.

Felix next wrote an anonymous letter to the Prince pointing out the value of the place. The Prince should seize it, and add to his power. He knew that the letter was delivered, but there was no sign. It had, indeed, been read and laughed at. Why make further efforts when they already had what they desired? One only, the deep and designing Valentine, gave it serious thought in secret. It seemed to him that something might come of it, another day, when he was himself in power; if that should happen. But he, too, forgot it in a week. Some secret effort was made to discover the writer, for the council was very jealous of political opinion, but it soon ended. The idea, not being supported by money or influence, fell into oblivion.

Felix worked on chipping out the canoe. The days passed, and the boat was nearly finished. In a day or two now it would be launched, and soon afterwards he should commence his voyage. He should see Aurora once more only. He should see her, but he should not say farewell; she would not know that he was going till he had actually departed. As he thought thus a dimness came before his eyes; his hand trembled, and he could not work. He put down the chisel, and paused to steady himself.

Upon the other side of the stream, somewhat lower down, a yellow wood-dog had been lapping the water to quench its thirst, watching the man the while. So long as Felix was intent upon his work, the wild animal had no fear; the moment he looked up, the creature sprang back into the underwood. A dove was cooing in the forest not far distant, but as he was about to resume work the cooing ceased. Then a wood-pigeon rose from the ashes with a loud clapping of wings. Felix listened. His hunter instinct told him that something was moving there. A rustling of the bushes followed, and he took his spear which had been leant against the adjacent tree. But, peering into the wood, in a moment he recognised Oliver, who, having walked off his rage, was returning.

'I thought it might have been a Bushman,' said Felix, replacing his spear; 'only they are noiseless.'

'Any of them might have cut me down,' said Oliver; 'for I forgot my weapon. It is nearly noon; are you coming home to dinner?'

'Yes; I must bring my tools.'

He put them in the basket, and together they returned to the rope ladder. As they passed the Pen by the river they caught sight of the Baron in the adjacent gardens, which were irrigated by his contrivances from the stream, and went towards him. A retainer held two horses, one gaily caparisoned, outside the garden; his master was talking with Sir Constans.

'It is Lord John,' said Oliver. They approached slowly under the fruit-trees, not to intrude. Sir Constans was showing the courtier an early cherry-tree, whose fruit was already set. The dry hot weather had caused it to set even earlier than usual. A suit of black velvet, an extremely expensive and almost unprocurable material, brought the courtier's pale features into relief. It was only by the very oldest families that any velvet or satin or similar materials were still preserved; if these were in pecuniary difficulties they might sell some part of their store, but such things were not to be got for money in the ordinary way.

Two small silver bars across his left shoulder showed that he was a lord-in-waiting. He was a handsome man, with clear-cut features, somewhat rakish from late hours and dissipation, but not the less interesting on that account. But his natural advantages were so over-run with the affectation of the Court that you did not see the man at all, being absorbed by the studied gesture to display the jewelled ring, and the peculiarly low tone of voice in which it was the fashion to speak.

Beside the old warrior he looked a mere stripling. The Baron's arm was bare, his sleeve rolled up; and as he pointed to the tree above, the muscles, as the limb moved, displayed themselves in knots, at which the courtier himself could not refrain from glancing. Those mighty arms, had they clasped him about the waist, could have crushed his bending ribs. The heaviest blow that he could have struck upon that broad chest would have produced no more effect than a hollow sound; it would not even have shaken that powerful frame.

He felt the steel blue eye, bright as the sky of midsummer, glance into his very mind. The high forehead bare, for the Baron had his hat in his hand, mocked at him in its humility. The Baron bared his head in honour of the courtier's office and the Prince who had sent him. The beard, though streaked with white, spoke little of age; it rather indicated an abundant, a luxuriant vitality.

Lord John was not at ease. He shifted from foot to foot, and occasionally puffed a large cigar of Devon tobacco. His errand was simple enough. Some of the ladies at the Court had a fancy for fruit, especially strawberries, but there were none in the market, nor to be obtained from the gardens about the town. It was recollected that Sir Constans was famous for his gardens, and the Prince despatched Lord John to Old House with a gracious message and request for a basket of strawberries. Sir Constans was much pleased; but he regretted that the hot, dry weather had not permitted the fruit to come to any size or perfection. Still there were some.

The courtier accompanied him to the gardens, and saw the water-wheel which, turned by a horse, forced water from the stream into a small pond or elevated reservoir, from which it irrigated the ground. This supply of water had brought on the fruit, and Sir Constans was able to gather a small basket. He then looked round to see what other early product he could send to the palace. There was no other fruit; the cherries, though set, were not ripe; but there was some asparagus, which had not yet been served, said Lord John, at the Prince's table.

Sir Constans set men to hastily collect all that was ready, and while this was done took the courtier over the gardens. Lord John felt no interest whatever in such matters, but he could not choose but admire the extraordinary fertility of the enclosure, and the variety of the products. There was everything, fruit of all kinds, herbs of every species, plots specially devoted to those possessing medicinal virtue. This was only one part of the gardens; the orchards proper were farther down, and the flowers nearer the house. Sir Constans had sent a man to the flower-garden, who now returned with two fine bouquets, which were presented to Lord John: the one for the Princess, the Prince's sister; the other for any lady to whom he might choose to present it.

The fruit had already been handed to the retainer who had charge of the horses. Though interested, in spite of himself, Lord John, acknowledging the flowers, turned to go with a sense of relief. This simplicity of manners seemed discordant to him. He felt out of place, and in some way lowered in his own esteem, and yet he despised the rural retirement and beauty about him.

Felix and Oliver, a few yards distant, were waiting with rising tempers. The spectacle of the Baron in his native might of physique, humbly standing, hat in hand, before this Court messenger, discoursing on cherries, and offering flowers and fruit, filled them with anger and disgust. The affected gesture and subdued voice of the courtier, on the other hand, roused an equal contempt.

As Lord John turned, he saw them. He did not quite guess their relationship, but supposed they were cadets of the house, it being customary for those in any way connected to serve the head of the family. He noted the flag basket in Felix's hand, and naturally imagined that he had been at work.

'You have been to – to plough, eh?' he said, intending to be very gracious and condescending. 'Very healthy employment. The land requires some rain, does it not? Still I trust it will not rain till I am home, for my plume's sake,' tossing his head. 'Allow me,' and as he passed he offered Oliver a couple of cigars. 'One each,' he added, 'the best Devon.'

Oliver took the cigars mechanically, holding them as if they had been vipers, at arm's length, till the courtier had left the garden, and the hedge interposed. Then he threw them into the water carrier. The best tobacco, indeed the only real tobacco, came from the warm Devon land, but little of it reached so far, on account of the distance, the difficulties of intercourse, the rare occasions on which the merchant succeeded in escaping the vexatious interference, the downright robbery of the way. Intercourse was often entirely closed by war.

These cigars, therefore, were worth their weight in silver, and such tobacco could be obtained only by those about the Court, as a matter of favour, too, rather than by purchase. Lord John would, indeed, have stared aghast had he seen the rustic to whom he had given so valuable a present cast them into a ditch. He rode towards the Maple Gate, excusing his haste volubly to Sir Constans, who was on foot, and walked beside him a little way, pressing him to take some refreshment.

His sons overtook the Baron as he walked towards home, and walked by his side in silence. Sir Constans was full of his fruit.

'The wall cherry,' said he, 'will soon have a few ripe.'

Oliver swore a deep but soundless oath in his chest. Sir Constans continued talking about his fruit and flowers, entirely oblivious of the silent anger of the pair beside him. As they approached the house, the warder blew his horn thrice for noon. It was also the signal for dinner.

CHAPTER VI

THE FOREST TRACK

WHEN the canoe was finished, Oliver came to help Felix launch it, and they rolled it on logs down to the place where the stream formed a pool. But when it was afloat, as Oliver had foretold, it did not swim upright in the water. It had not been shaped accurately, and one side was higher out of the water than the other.

Felix was so disgusted at this failure that he would not listen to anything Oliver could suggest. He walked back to the spot where he had worked so many weeks, and sat down with his face turned from the pool. It was not so much the actual circumstance which depressed him, as the long train of untoward incidents which had preceded it for years past. These seemed to have accumulated, till now this comparatively little annoyance was like the last straw.

Oliver followed him, and said that the defect could be remedied by placing ballast on the more buoyant side of the canoe to bring it down to the level of the other; or, perhaps, if some more wood were cut away on the heavier side, that would cause it to rise. He offered to do the work himself, but Felix, in his gloomy mood, would not answer him. Oliver returned to the pool, and getting into the canoe, poled it up and down the stream. It answered perfectly, and could be easily managed; the defect was more apparent than real, for when a person sat in the canoe, his weight seemed to bring it nearly level.

It was only when empty that it canted to one side. He came back again to Felix, and pointed this out to him. The attempt was useless; the boat might answer the purpose perfectly well, but it was not the boat Felix had intended it to be. It did not come up to his ideal. Oliver was now somewhat annoyed at Felix's sullen silence, so he drew the canoe partly on shore, to prevent it from floating away, and then left him to himself.

Nothing more was said about it for a day or two. Felix did not go near the spot where he had worked so hard and so long, but on the Saturday Philip came home as usual, and, as there was now no secret about the canoe, went down to look at it with Oliver. They pushed it off, and floated two or three miles down the stream, hauling it on the shore past the fallen fir tree, and then, with a cord, towed it back again.

The canoe, with the exception of the trifling deficiency alluded to, was a good one, and thoroughly serviceable.

They endeavoured again to restore Felix's opinion of it, and an idea occurring to Philip, he said a capital plan would be to add an outrigger, and so balance it perfectly. But though usually quick to adopt ideas when they were good, in this case Felix was too much out of conceit with himself. He would listen to nothing. Still, he could not banish it from his mind, though now ashamed to return to it after so obstinately refusing all suggestions. He wandered aimlessly about in the woods, till one day he found himself in the path that led to Heron Bay.

Strolling to the shore of the great Lake, he sat down and watched a vessel sailing afar off slowly before the west wind. The thought presently occurred to him, that the addition of an outrigger in the manner Philip had mentioned would enable him to carry a sail. The canoe could not otherwise support a sail (unless a very small one merely for going before the breeze), but with such a sail as the outrigger would bear, he could venture much farther away from land, his voyage might be much more extended, and his labour with the paddle lessened.

This filled him with fresh energy; he returned, and at once recommenced work. Oliver, finding that he was again busy at it, came and insisted upon assisting. With his help, the work progressed rapidly. He used the tools so deftly as to accomplish more in an hour than Felix could in a day. The outrigger consisted of a beam of poplar, sharpened at both ends, and held at some six or seven feet from the canoe by two strong cross pieces.

A mast, about the same height as the canoe was long, was then set up; it was made from a young fir tree. Another smaller fir supplied the yard, which extended fore and aft, nearly the length of the boat. The sail, of coarse canvas, was not very high, but long, and rather broader at each end where the rope attached it to the prow and stern, or, rather, the two prows. Thus arranged, it was not so well suited for running straight before the wind, as for working into it, a feat never attempted by the ships of the time.

Oliver was delighted with the appearance of the boat, so much so that now and then he announced his intention of accompanying Felix on his voyage. But after a visit to the town, and a glance at the Princess Lucia, his resolution changed. Yet he wavered, one time openly reproaching himself for enduring such a life of inaction and ignominy, and at another deriding Felix and his visionary schemes. The canoe was now completed; it was tried on the pool and found to float exactly as it should. It had now to be conveyed to Heron Bay.

The original intention was to put it on a cart, but the rude carts used on the estate could not very well carry it, and a sledge was substituted. Several times, during the journey through the forest, the sledge had to be halted while the underwood was cut away to permit of its passing; and once a slough had to be filled up with branches hewn from fir trees, and bundles of fern. These delays made it evening before the shore of the creek was reached.

It was but a little inlet, scarce a bowshot wide at the entrance and coming to a point inland. Here the canoe was left in charge of three serfs, who were ordered to build a hut and stay beside it. Some provisions were sent next day on the backs of other serfs, and in the afternoon (it was Saturday) all three brothers arrived; the canoe was launched, and they started for a trial sail. With a south wind they ran to the eastward at a rapid pace, keeping close to the shore till within a mile of White Horse.

There they brought to by steering the canoe dead against the wind; then transferring the steering-paddle (a rather larger one, made for the purpose) to the other end, and readjusting the sail, the outrigger being still to leeward, they ran back at an equal speed. The canoe answered perfectly, and Felix was satisfied. He now despatched his tools and various weapons to the hut to be put on board. His own peculiar yew bow he kept to the last at home; it and his chest bound with hide would go with him on the last day.

Although, in his original scheme, Felix had designed to go forth without any one being aware of his intention, the circumstances which had arisen, and the necessary employment of so many men, had let out the secret to some degree. The removal of the tools and weapons, the crossbow, darts, and spear, still more attracted attention. But little or nothing was said about it, though the Baron and Baroness could not help but observe these preparations. The Baron deliberately shut his eyes and went about his gardening; he was now, too, busy with the first mowing. In his heart, perhaps, he felt that he had not done altogether right in so entirely retiring from the world.

By doing so he had condemned his children to loneliness, and to be regarded with contempt. Too late now, he could only obstinately persist in his course. The Baroness, inured for so many, many years to disappointment, had contracted her view of life till it scarcely extended beyond mere physical comfort. Nor could she realise the idea of Felix's approaching departure; when he was actually gone, it would, perhaps, come home to her.

All was now ready, and Felix was only waiting for the Feast of St. James to pay a last visit to Aurora at Thyma Castle. The morning before the day of the Feast, Felix and Oliver set out together. They had not lived altogether in harmony, but now, at this approaching change, Oliver felt that he must bear Felix company. Oliver rode his beautiful Night, he wore his plumed hat and precious sword, and carried his horseman's lance. Felix rode a smaller horse, useful, but far from handsome. He carried his yew bow and hunting knife.

Thyma Castle was situated fifteen miles to the south; it was the last outpost of civilization; beyond it there was nothing but forest, and the wild open plains, the home of the gipsies. This circumstance of position had given Baron Thyma, in times past, a certain importance, more than was due to the size of his estate or the number of his retainers. During an invasion of the gipsies, his castle bore the brunt of the war, and its gallant defence, indeed, broke their onward progress. So many fell in endeavouring to take it, that the rest were disheartened, and only scattered bands penetrated beyond.

For this service the Baron received the grant of various privileges; he was looked on as a pillar of the State, and was welcome at the court. But it proved an injury to him in the end. His honours, and the high society they led him into, were too great for the comparative small-ness of his income. Rich in flocks and herds, he had but little coin. High-spirited, and rather fond of display, he could not hold back; he launched forth, with the usual result of impoverishment, mortgage, and debt.

He had hoped to obtain the command of an army in the wars that broke out from time to time; it was, indeed, universally admitted that he was in every respect qualified for such a post. The courtiers and others, however, jealous, as is ever the case, of ability and real talent, debarred him by their intrigues from attaining his object. Pride pre-vented him from acquiescing in this defeat; he strove by display and extravagance to keep himself well to the front, flaunting himself before the eyes of all. This course could not last long; he was obliged to retire to his estate, which narrowly escaped forfeiture to his creditors.

So ignominious an end after such worthy service was, however, prevented by the personal interference of the old Prince, who, from his private resources, paid off the most pressing creditors. To the last, the old Prince received him as a friend, and listened to his counsel. Thyma was ever in hopes that some change in the balance of parties would give him his opportunity. When the young Prince succeeded, he was clever enough to see that the presence of such men about his Court gave it a stability, and he, too, invited Thyma to tender his advice. The Baron's hopes now rose higher than ever, but again he was disappointed.

The new Prince, himself incapable, disliked and distrusted talent.

The years passed, and the Baron obtained no appointment. Still he strained his resources to the utmost to visit the Court as often as possible; still he believed that sooner or later a turn of the wheel would elevate him.

There had existed between the houses of Thyma and Aquila the bond of hearth-friendship; the gauntlets, hoofs, and rings were preserved by both, and the usual presents passed thrice a year, at midsummer, Christmas, and lady-day. Not much personal intercourse had taken place, however, for some years, until Felix was attracted by the beauty of the Lady Aurora. Proud, showy, and pushing, Thyma could not understand the feelings which led his hearth-friend to retire from the arena and busy himself with cherries and water-wheels. On the other hand, Constans rather looked with quiet derision on the ostentation of the other. Thus there was a certain distance, as it were, between them.

Baron Thyma could not, of course, be ignorant of the attachment between his daughter and Felix; yet as much as possible he ignored it. He never referred to Felix; if his name was incidentally mentioned, he remained silent. The truth was, he looked higher for Lady Aurora. He could not in courtesy discourage even in the faintest manner the visits of his friend's son; the knightly laws of honour would have forbidden so mean a course. Nor would his conscience permit him to do so, remembering the old days when he and the Baron were glad companions together, and how the Baron Aquila was the first to lead troops to his assistance in the gipsy war. Still, he tacitly disapproved; he did not encourage.

Felix felt that he was not altogether welcome; he recognised the sense of restraint that prevailed when he was present. It deeply hurt his pride, and nothing but his love for Aurora could have enabled him to bear up against it. The galling part of it was that he could not in his secret heart condemn the father for evidently desiring a better alliance for his child. This was the strongest of the motives that had determined him to seek the unknown.

If anything, the Baron would have preferred Oliver as a suitor for his daughter; he sympathised with Oliver's fiery spirit, and admired his feats of strength and dexterity with sword and spear. He always welcomed Oliver heartily, and paid him every attention. This, to do Oliver justice, was one reason why he determined to accompany his brother, thinking that if he was there he could occupy attention, and thus enable Felix to have more opportunity to speak with Aurora.

The two rode forth from the courtyard early in the morning, and passing through the whole length of the enclosure within the stockade, issued at the South Barrier and almost immediately entered the forest.

They rather checked their horses' haste, fresh as the animals were from the stable, but could not quite control their spirits, for the walk of a horse is even half as fast again while he is full of vigour. The turn of the track soon shut out the stockade; they were alone in the woods.

Long since, early as they were, the sun had dried the dew, for his beams warm the atmosphere quickly as the spring advances towards summer. But it was still fresh and sweet among the trees, and even Felix, though bound on so gloomy an errand, could not choose but feel the joyous influence of the morning. Oliver sang aloud in his rich deep voice, and the thud thud of the horses' hoofs kept time to the ballad.

The thrushes flew but a little way back from the path as they passed, and began to sing again directly they were by. The whistling of black-birds came from afar where there were open glades or a running stream; the notes of the cuckoo became fainter and fainter as they advanced farther from the stockade, for the cuckoo likes the wood-lands that immediately border on cultivation. For some miles the track was broad, passing through thickets of thorn and low hawthorn trees with immense masses of tangled underwood between, brambles and woodbine twisted and matted together, impervious above but hollow beneath; under these they could hear the bush hens running to and fro and scratching at the dead leaves which strewed the ground. Sounds of clucking deeper in betrayed the situation of their nests.

Rushes, and the dead sedges of last year up through which the green fresh leaves were thrusting themselves, in some places stood beside the way, fringing the thorns where the hollow ground often held the water from rainstorms. Out from these bushes a rabbit occasionally started and bounded across to the other side. Here, where there were so few trees, and the forest chiefly consisted of bush, they could see some distance on either hand, and also a wide breadth of the sky. After a time the thorn bushes were succeeded by ash wood, where the trees stood closer to the path, contracting the view; it was moister here, the hoofs cut into the grass, which was coarse and rank. The trees growing so close together destroyed themselves, their lower branches rubbed together and were killed, so that in many spots the riders could see a long way between the trunks.

Every time the wind blew they could hear a distant cracking of branches as the dead boughs, broken by the swaying of the trees, fell off and came down. Had any one attempted to walk into the forest there they would have sunk above the ankle in soft decaying wood, hidden from sight by thick vegetation. Wood-pigeons rose every minute from these ash trees with a loud clatter of wings; their calls resounded con-tinually, now deep in the forest, and now close at hand. It was evident that a large flock of them had their nesting-place here, and indeed their nests of twigs could be frequently seen from the path. There seemed no other birds.

Again the forest changed, and the track, passing on higher ground, entered among firs. These, too, had killed each other by growing so thickly; the lower branches of many were dead, and there was nothing but a little green at the tops, while in many places there was an open space where they had decayed away altogether. Brambles covered the ground in these open places, brambles and furze now bright with golden blossom. The jays screeched loudly, startled as the riders passed under them, and fluttered away; rabbits, which they saw again here, dived into their burrows. Between the firs the track was very narrow, and they could not conveniently ride side by side; Oliver took the lead, and Felix followed.

CHAPTER VII

THE FOREST TRACK CONTINUED

ONCE as they trotted by a pheasant rose screaming from the furze and flew before them down the track. Just afterwards Felix, who had been previously looking very carefully into the firs upon his right hand, suddenly stopped, and Oliver, finding this, pulled up as quickly as he could, thinking that Felix wished to tighten his girth.

'What is it?' he asked, turning round in his saddle.

'Hush!' said Felix, dismounting; his horse, trained to hunting, stood perfectly still, and would have remained within a few yards of the spot by the hour together. Oliver reined back, seeing Felix about to bend and string his bow.

'Bushmen,' whispered Felix, as he, having fitted the loop to the horn notch, drew forth an arrow from his girdle, where he carried two or three more ready to hand than in the quiver on his shoulder. 'I thought I saw signs of them some time since, and now I am nearly sure. Stay here a moment.'

He stepped aside from the track in among the firs, which just there were far apart, and went to a willow bush standing by some furze. He had noticed that one small branch on the outer part of the bush was snapped off, though green, and only hung by the bark. The wood cattle, had they browsed upon it, would have nibbled the tenderest leaves at the end of the bough; nor did they usually touch willow, for the shoots are bitter and astringent. Nor would the deer touch it in the spring, when they had so wide a choice of food.

Nothing could have broken the branch in that manner unless it was the hand of a man, or a blow with a heavy stick wielded by a human hand. On coming to the bush he saw that the fracture was very recent, for the bough was perfectly green; it had not turned brown, and the bark was still soft with sap. It had not been cut with a knife or any sharp instrument; it had been broken by rude violence, and not divided. The next thing to catch his eye was the appearance of a larger branch farther inside the bush.

This was not broken, but a part of the bark was abraded, and even torn up from the wood as if by the impact of some hard substance as a stone thrown with great force. He examined the ground, but there was no stone visible, and on again looking at the bark he concluded that it had not been done with a stone at all, because the abraded portion was not cut. The blow had been delivered by something without edges or projections. He had now no longer any doubt that the lesser branch outside had been broken, and the large inside branch bruised, by the passage of a Bushman's throw-club.

These, their only missile weapons, are usually made of crab-tree, and consist of a very thin short handle, with a large, heavy, and smooth knob. With these they can bring down small game, as rabbits or hares, or a fawn (even breaking the legs of deer), or the large birds, as the wood-turkeys. Stealing up noiselessly within ten yards, the Bushman throws his club with great force, and rarely misses his aim. If not killed at once, the game is certain to be stunned, and is much more easily secured than if wounded with an arrow, for with an arrow in its wing a large bird will flutter along the ground, and perhaps creep into sedges or under impenetrable bushes.

Deprived of motion by the blow of the club, it can, on the other hand, be picked up without trouble and without the aid of a dog, and if not dead is despatched by a twist of the Bushman's fingers or a thrust from his spud. The spud is at once his dagger, his knife and fork, his chisel, his grub-axe, and his gouge. It is a piece of iron (rarely or never of steel, for he does not know how to harden it) about ten inches long, an inch and a half wide at the top or broadest end, where it is shaped and sharpened like a chisel, only with the edge not straight but sloping, and from thence tapering to a point at the other, the pointed part being four-sided, like a nail.

It has, indeed, been supposed that the original spud was formed from a large wrought-iron nail, such as the ancients used, sharpened on a stone at one end, and beaten out flat at the other. This instrument has a handle in the middle, half-way between the chisel end and the point. The handle is of horn or bone (the spud being put through the hollow of the bone), smoothed to fit the hand. With the chisel end he cuts up his game and his food; the edge, being sloping, is drawn across the meat and divides it. With this end, too, he fashions his club and his traps, and digs up the roots he uses. The other end he runs into his meat as a fork, or thrusts it into the neck of his game to kill it and let out the blood, or with it stabs a sleeping enemy.

The stab delivered by the Bushman can always be distinguished, because the wound is invariably square, and thus a clue only too certain has often been afforded to the assassin of many an unfortunate hunter. Whatever the Bushman in this case had hurled his club at, the club had gone into the willow bush, snapping the light branch and leaving its mark upon the bark of the larger. A moment's reflection convinced Felix that the Bushman had been in chase of a pheasant. Only a few moments previously a pheasant had flown before them down the track, and where there was one pheasant there were generally several more in the immediate neighbourhood.

The Bushmen were known to be peculiarly fond of the pheasant, pursuing them all the year round without reference to the breeding season, and so continuously, that it was believed they caused these birds to be much less numerous, notwithstanding the vast extent of the forests, than they would otherwise have been. From the fresh appearance of the snapped bough, the Bushman must have passed but a few hours previously, probably at the dawn, and was very likely concealed at that moment near at hand in the forest, perhaps within a hundred yards.

Felix looked carefully round, but could see nothing; there were the trees, not one of them large enough to hide a man behind it, the furze branches were small and scattered, and there was not sufficient fern to conceal anything. The keenest glance could discern nothing more. There were no footmarks on the ground, indeed, the dry, dead leaves and fir needles could hardly have received any impression, and up in the firs the branches were thin, and the sky could be seen through them. Whether the Bushman was lying in some slight depression of the ground, or whether he had covered himself with dead leaves and fir needles, or whether he had gone on and was miles away, there was nothing to show. But of the fact that he had been there Felix was perfectly certain.

He returned towards Oliver, thoughtful and not without some anxiety, for he did not like the idea (though there was really little or no danger) of these human wild beasts being so near Aurora, while he should so soon be far away. Thus occupied he did not heed his steps, and suddenly felt something soft under his feet, which struggled. Instantaneously he sprang as far as he could, shuddering, for he had crushed an adder, and but just escaped, by his involuntary and mechanical leap, from its venom.

In the warm sunshine the viper, in its gravid state, had not cared to move as usual on hearing his approach; he had stepped full upon it. He hastened from the spot, and rejoined Oliver in a somewhat shaken state of mind. Common as such an incident was in the woods, where sandy soil warned the hunter to be careful, it seemed ominous that particular morning, and, joined with the discovery of Bushman traces, quite destroyed his sense of the beauty of the day.

On hearing the condition of the willow boughs Oliver agreed as to

the cause, and said that they must remember to warn the Baron's shepherds that the Bushmen, who had not been seen for some time, were
about. Soon afterwards they emerged from the sombre firs and crossed
a wide and sloping ground, almost bare of trees, where a forest fire last
year had swept away the underwood. A verdant growth of grass was
now springing up. Here they could canter side by side. The sunshine
poured down, and birds were singing joyously. But they soon passed
it, and checked their speed on entering the trees again.

Tall beeches, with round smooth trunks, stood thick and close upon
the dry and rising ground; their boughs met overhead, forming a green
continuous arch for miles. The space between was filled with brake
fern, now fast growing up, and the track itself was green with moss. As
they came into this beautiful place a red stag, startled from his brows-
ing, bounded down the track, his swift leaps carried him away like
the wind; in another moment he left the path and sprang among the
fern, and was seen only in glimpses as he passed between the beeches.
Squirrels ran up the trunks as they approached; they could see many
on the ground in among the trees, and passed under others on the
branches high above them. Woodpeckers flashed across the avenue.

Once Oliver pointed out the long, lean flank of a grey pig, or fern-
hog, as the animal rushed away among the brake. There were several
glades, from one of which they startled a few deer, whose tails only
were seen as they bounded into the underwood, but after the glades
came the beeches again. Beeches always form the most beautiful forest,
beeches and oak; and though nearing the end of their journey, they
regretted when they emerged from these trees and saw the castle before
them.

The ground suddenly sloped down into a valley, beyond which rose
the Downs; the castle stood on a green isolated low hill, about half-way
across the vale. To the left a river wound past; to the right the beech
forest extended as far as the eye could see. The slope at their feet had
been cleared of all but a few hawthorn bushes. It was not enclosed, but
a neatherd* was there with his cattle half a mile away, sitting himself at
the foot of a beech, while the cattle grazed below him.

Down in the valley the stockade began; it was not wide but long.
The enclosure extended on the left to the bank of the river, and two
fields on the other side of it. On the right it reached a mile and a half
or nearly, the whole of which was overlooked from the spot where they
had passed. Within the enclosure the corn crops were green and flour-
ishing; horses and cattle, ricks and various buildings, were scattered

* Middle English variant of cowherd or cattleherd.

about it. The town or cottages of the serfs were on the bank of the river immediately beyond the castle. On the Downs, which rose a mile or more on the other side of the castle, sheep were feeding; part of the ridge was wooded and part open. Thus the cultivated and enclosed valley was everywhere shut in with woods and hills.

The isolated round hill on which the castle stood was itself enclosed with a second stockade; the edge of the brow above that again was defended by a stout high wall of flints and mortar, crenellated at the top. There were no towers or bastions. An old and ivy-grown building stood inside the wall; it dated from the time of the ancients; it had several gables, and was roofed with tiles. This was the dwelling-house. The gardens were situated on the slope between the wall and the inner stockade. Peaceful as the scene appeared, it had been the site of furious fighting not many years ago. The Downs trended to the south, where the Romany and the Zingari resided, and a keen watch was kept both from the wall and from the hills beyond.

They now rode slowly down the slope, and in a few minutes reached the barrier or gateway in the outer stockade. They had been observed, and the guard called by the warden, but as they approached were recognised, and the gate swang open before them. Walking their horses they crossed to the hill, and were as easily admitted to the second enclosure. At the gate of the wall they dismounted, and waited while the warden carried the intelligence of their arrival to the family. A moment later, and the Baron's son advanced from the porch, and from the open window the Baroness and Aurora beckoned to them.

CHAPTER VIII

THYMA CASTLE

SOON afterwards the hollow sound of the warden's horn, from the watch over the gate of the wall, proclaimed the hour of noon, and they all assembled for dinner in the banqueting chamber. This apartment was on the ground floor, and separated from the larger hall only by an internal wall. The house, erected in the time of the ancients, was not designed for our present style of life; it possessed, indeed, many comforts and conveniences which are scarcely now to be found in the finest palaces, but it lacked the breadth of construction which our architects have now in view.

In the front there were originally only two rooms, extensive for those old days, but not sufficiently so for ours. One of these had therefore been enlarged, by throwing into it a back room and part of the entrance, and even then it was not long enough for the Baron's retainers, and at feast-time a wooden shed was built opposite and up to the window, to continue, as it were, the apartment out of doors. Workmen were busy putting up this shed when they arrived.

The second apartment retained its ancient form, and was used as the dining-room on ordinary days. It was lighted by a large window, now thrown wide open that the sweet spring air might enter, which window was the pride of the Baroness, for it contained more true glass than any window in the palace of the Prince. The glass made now is not transparent, but merely translucent; it indeed admits light after a fashion, but it is thick and cannot be seen through. These panes were almost all (the central casement wholly) of ancient glass, preserved with the greatest care through the long years past.

Three tables were arranged in an open square; the Baron and Baroness's chairs of oak faced the window, the guests sat at the other tables sideways to them, the servants moved on the outer side, and thus placed the food before them without pushing against or incommoding them. A fourth table was placed in a corner between the fireplace and the window. At it sat the old nurse, the housekeeper (frequently arising to order the servants), and the Baron's henchman, who had taught him to ride, but now, grey and aged, could not mount himself without assistance, and had long ceased from active service.

Already eight or nine guests had arrived besides Felix and Oliver. Some had ridden a great distance to be present at the House Day. They were all nobles, richly dressed; one or two of the eldest were wealthy and powerful men, and the youngest was the son and heir of the Earl of Essiton, who was then the favourite at Court. Each had come with his personal attendants; the young Lord Durand brought with him twenty-five retainers, and six gentlemen friends, all of whom were lodged in the town, the gentlemen taking their meals at the castle at the same time as the Baron, but, owing to lack of room, in another apartment by themselves. Durand was placed, or rather, quietly helped himself to a seat, next the Lady Aurora, and of all the men there present, certainly there was none more gallant and noble than he.

His dark eyes, his curling hair short but brought in a thick curl over his forehead, his lips well shaped, his chin round and somewhat prominent, the slight moustache (no other hair on the face), formed the very ideal of what many women look for in a man. But it was his bright, lively conversation, the way in which his slightly swarthy complexion flushed with animation, the impudent assurance and yet generous warmth of his manner, and, indeed, of his feelings, which had given him the merited reputation of being the very flower of the nobles.

With such a reputation, backed with the great wealth and power of his father, gentlemen competed with each other to swell his train; he could not, indeed, entertain all that came, and was often besieged with almost as large a crowd as the Prince himself. He took as his right the chair next Aurora, to whom, indeed, he had been paying unremitting attention all the morning. She was laughing heartily as she sat down at some sally of his upon a beauty at the Court.

The elder men were placed highest up the tables, and nearest the host, but to the astonishment of all, and not the least of himself, Oliver was invited by the Baron to sit by his side. Oliver could not understand this special mark of favour; the others, though far too proud for a moment to resent what they might have deemed a slight upon them, at once began to search their minds for a reason. They knew the Baron as an old intriguer; they attached a meaning, whether intended or not, to his smallest action.

Felix, crowded out, as it were, and unnoticed, was forced to take his seat at the end of the table nearest that set apart in the corner for the aged and honoured servitors of the family. Only a few feet intervened between him and the ancient henchmen; and he could not but overhear their talk among themselves, whispered as it was. He had merely shaken hands with Aurora; the crowd in the drawing-room and the marked attentions of Durand had prevented the exchange of a single word between them. As usual, the sense of neglect and injury over which he had so long brooded with little or no real cause (considering, of course, his position, and that the world can only see our coats and not our hearts), under these entirely accidental circumstances rose up again within him, and blinded him to the actual state of things.

His seat, the lowest, and the nearest to the servitors, was in itself a mark of the low estimation in which he was held. The Lord Durand had been placed next to Aurora, as a direct encouragement to him, and a direct hint to himself not to presume. Doubtless, Durand had been at the castle many times, not improbably had already been accepted by the Baron, and not altogether refused by Aurora. As a fact, though delighted with her beauty and conversation, Durand's presence was entirely due to the will of his father, the Earl, who wished to maintain friendly relations with Baron Thyma, and even then he would not have come had not the lovely weather invited him to ride into the forest.

It was, however, so far true, that though his presence was accidental, yet he was fast becoming fascinated by one who, girl though she was, was stronger in mind than he. Now Aurora, knowing that her father's eye was on her, dared not look towards Felix, lest by an open and pro- nounced conduct she should be the cause of his being informed that his presence was not desirable. She knew that the Baron only needed a pretext to interfere, and was anxious to avoid affording him a chance.

Felix, seeing her glance bent downwards or towards her companion, and never all the time turned to him, not unnaturally, but too hastily, concluded that she had been dazzled by Durand and the possibility of an alliance with his powerful family. He was discarded, worthless, and of no account; he had nothing but his sword; nay, he had not a sword, he was only an archer, a footman. Angry, jealous, and burning with inward annoyance, despising himself since all others despised him, scarce able to remain at the table, Felix was almost beside himself, and did not answer nor heed the remarks of the gentlemen sitting by him, who put him down as an ill-bred churl.

For the form's sake, indeed, he put his lips to the double-handled cup of fine ale, which continually circulated round the table, and was never allowed to be put down; one servant had nothing else to do but to see that its progress never stopped. But he drank nothing, and ate nothing; he could not swallow. How visionary, how weak and feeble now seemed the wild scheme of the canoe and the proposed voyage! Even should it succeed, years must elapse before he could accomplish anything substantial; while here were men who really had what he could only think of or imagine.

The silver chain or sword-belt of Durand (the sword and the dagger were not worn at the banquet, nor in the house, they were received by the marshal, and deposited in his care, a precaution against quarrelling), solid silver links passing over his shoulder, were real actual things. All the magnificence that he could call up by the exercise of his imagination, was but imagination; a dream no more to be seen by others than the air itself.

The dinner went on, and the talk became more noisy. The trout, the chicken, the thyme lamb (trapped on the hills by the shepherds), the plover eggs, the sirloin, the pastry (the Baroness superintended the making of it herself), all the profusion of the table, rather set him against food than tempted him. Nor could he drink the tiny drop, as it were, of ancient brandy, sent round to each guest at the conclusion, precious as liquid gold, for it had been handed down from the ancients, and when once the cask was empty it could not be re-filled.

The dessert, the strawberries, the nuts and walnuts, carefully preserved with a little salt, and shaken in the basket from time to time that they might not become mouldy, the apples, the honey in the comb with slices of white bread, nothing pleased him. Nor did he drink, otherwise than the sip demanded by courtesy, of the thin wine of Gloucester, costly as it was, grown in the vineyard there, and shipped across the Lake, and rendered still more expensive by risk of pirates. This was poured into flagons of maple wood, which, like the earthenware cup of ale, were never allowed to touch the board till the dinner was over.

Wearily the time went on; Felix glanced more and more often at the sky seen through the casement, eagerly desiring to escape, and at least to be alone. At last (how long it seemed!) the Baron rose, and immediately the rest did the same, and they drank the health of the Prince. Then a servitor brought in a pile of cigars upon a carved wooden tray, like a large platter, but with a rim. 'These,' said the Baron, again rising (the signal to all to cease conversing and to listen), 'are a present from my gracious and noble friend the Earl of Essiton' (he looked towards Durand), 'not less kindly carried by Lord Durand. I could have provided only our own coarse tobacco; but these are the best Devon.'

The ladies now left the table, Aurora escorted by Durand, the Baroness by Oliver. Oliver, indeed, was in the highest spirits; he had eaten heartily of all, especially the sweet thyme lamb, and drunk as freely. He was in his element, his laugh the loudest, his talk the liveliest. Directly Durand returned (he had gone even a part of the way upstairs towards the drawing-room with Aurora, a thing a little against etiquette) he took his chair (formality being now at an end) and placed it by Oliver. They seemed to become friends at once by sympathy of mind and taste.

Round them the rest gradually grouped themselves, so that presently Felix, who did not move, found himself sitting alone at the extreme end of the table; quite apart, for the old retainers, who dined at the separate table, had quitted the apartment when the wine was brought in. Freed from the restraint of the ladies, the talk now became extremely noisy, the blue smoke from the long cigars filled the great apartment; one only remained untouched, that placed before Felix. Suddenly it struck him that thus sitting alone and apart, he should attract attention; he, therefore, drew his chair to the verge of the group, but remained silent, and as far off as ever. Presently the arrival of five more guests caused a stir and confusion, in the midst of which he escaped into the open air.

He wandered towards the gate of the wall, passing the wooden shed where the clink of hammers resounded, glanced at the sun-dial, which showed the hour of three (three weary hours had they feasted), and went out into the gardens. Still going on, he descended the slope, and not much heeding whither he was going, took the road that led into the town. It consisted of some hundred or more houses, built of wood and thatched, placed without plan or arrangement on the bank of the stream. Only one long street ran through it, the rest were mere by-ways.

All these were inhabited by the Baron's retainers, but the number and apparently small extent of the houses did not afford correct data for the actual amount of the population. In these days the people (as is well known) find much difficulty in marrying; it seems only possible for a certain proportion to marry, and hence there are always a great number of young or single men out of all ratio to the houses. At the sound of the bugle the Baron could reckon on at least three hundred men flocking without a minute's delay to man the wall; in an hour more would arrive from the outer places, and by nightfall, if the summons went forth in the morning, his shepherds and swineherds would arrive, and these together would add some hundred and fifty to the garrison.

Next must be reckoned the armed servants of the house, the Baron's personal attendants, the gentlemen who formed his train, his sons and the male relations of the family; these certainly were not less than fifty. Altogether over five hundred men, well armed and accustomed to the use of their weapons, would range themselves beneath his banner. Two of the buildings in the town were of brick (the material carried hither, for there was no clay or stone thereabouts); they were not far apart. The one was the Toll House, where all merchants or traders paid the charges in corn or kind due to the Baron; the other was the Court House, where he sat to administer justice and decide causes, or to send the criminal to the gibbet.

These alone of the buildings were of any age, for the wooden houses were extremely subject to destruction by fire, and twice in the Baron's time half the town had been laid in ashes, only to arise again in a few weeks. Timber was so abundant and so ready of access, it seemed a loss of labour to fetch stone or brick, or to use the flints of the hills. About the doors of the two inns there were gathered groups of people; among them the liveries of the nobles visiting the castle were conspicuous; the place was full of them, the stables were filled, and their horses were picketed under the trees and even in the street.

Every minute the numbers increased as others arrived; men, too (who had obtained permission of their lords), came in on foot, ten or twelve travelling together for mutual protection, for the feuds of their masters exposed them to frequent attack. All (except the nobles) were disarmed at the barrier by the warden and guard, that peace might be preserved in the enclosure. The folk at the moment he passed were watching the descent of three covered waggons from the forest track, in which were travelling the ladies of as many noble families.

Some, indeed, of the youngest and boldest ride on horseback, but ladies chiefly move in these waggons, which are fitted up with considerable comfort, and are necessary to sleep in when the camp is formed by the wayside at night. None noticed him as he went by, except a group of three cottage girls, and a serving-woman an attendant of a lady visitor at the castle. He heard them allude to him; he quickened his pace, but heard one say, 'He's nobody; he hasn't even got a horse.'

'Yes, he is,' replied the serving-woman; 'he's Oliver's brother; and I can *tell* you my lord Oliver is somebody; the Princess Lucia——' and she made the motion of kissing with her lips. Felix, ashamed and annoyed to the last degree, stepped rapidly from the spot. The serving-woman, however, was right in a measure; the real or supposed favour shown Oliver by the Prince's sister, the Duchess of Deverell, had begun to be bruited abroad, and this was the secret reason why the Baron had shown Oliver so much and so marked an attention, even more than he had paid to Lord Durand.

Full well he knew the extraordinary influence possessed by ladies of rank and position. From what we can learn out of the scanty records of the past, it was so even in the days of the ancients; it is a hundredfold more so in these times, when, although every noble must of necessity be taught to read and write, as a matter of fact the men do neither, but all the correspondence of kings and princes, and the diplomatic documents, and notices, and so forth, are one and all, almost without a single exception, drawn up by women. They know the secret and hidden motives of courts, and have this great advantage, that they can use their knowledge without personal fear, since women are never seriously interfered with, but are protected by all.

The one terrible and utterly shameful instance to the contrary had not occurred at the time of which we are now speaking, and it was and is still repudiated by every man, from the knight to the boys who gather the acorns for the swine. Oliver himself had no idea whatever that he was regarded as a favourite lover of the Duchess; he took the welcome that was held out to him as perfectly honest. Plain, straightforward, and honest, Oliver, had he been openly singled out by a queen, would have scorned to give himself an air for such a reason. But the Baron, deep in intrigue this many a year, looked more profoundly into the possibilities of the future when he kept the young knight at his side.

CHAPTER IX

SUPERSTITIONS

FELIX was now outside the town and alone in the meadow which bordered the stream; he knelt, and drank from it with the hollow of his hand. He was going to ascend the hill beyond, and had already reached the barrier upon that side, when he recollected that etiquette demanded the presence of the guests at meal-times, and it was now the hour for tea. He hastened back, and found the courtyard of the castle crowded. Within, the staircase leading to the Baroness's chamber (where tea was served) could scarcely be ascended, what with the ladies and their courtiers, the long trains of the serving-women, the pages winding their way in and out, the servants endeavouring to pass, the slender pet greyhounds, the inseparable companions of their mistresses.

By degrees, and exercising patience, he gained the upper floor, and entered the drawing-room. The Baroness alone sat at the table, the guests wheresoever they chose, or chance carried them; for the most part they stood, or leaned against the recess of the open window. Of tea itself there was none; there has been no tea to be had for love or money these fifty years past, and, indeed, its use would have been forgotten, and the name only survived, had not some small quantities been yet preserved and brought out on rare occasions at the palaces. Instead, there was chiccory prepared from the root of the plant, grown for the purpose; fresh milk; fine ale and mead; and wine of Gloucester. Butter, honey, and cake, were also upon the table.

The guests helped themselves, or waited till the servants came to them with wooden carved trays. The particular characteristic of tea is the freedom from restraint; it is not considered necessary to sit as at dinner or supper, nor to do as others do; each pleases himself, and there is no ceremony. Yet, although so near Aurora, Felix did not succeed in speaking to her; Durand still engaged her attention whenever other ladies were not talking with her. Felix found himself, exactly as at dinner-time, quite outside the circle. There was a buzz of conversation around, but not a word of it was addressed to him. Dresses brushed against him, but the fair owners were not concerned even to acknowledge his existence.

Pushed by the jostling crowd aside from the centre of the floor, Felix presently sat down, glad to rest at last, behind the open door. Forgotten, he forgot; and, looking as it were out of the present in a bitter reverie, scarcely knew where he was, except at moments when he heard the well-known and loved voice of Aurora. A servant after a while came to him with a tray; he took some honey and bread. Almost immediately afterwards another servant came and presented him with a plate, on which was a cup of wine, saying, 'With my lady's loving wishes.'

As in duty bound, he rose and bowed to the Baroness; she smiled and nodded; the circle which had looked to see who was thus honoured, turned aside again, not recognising him. To send a guest a plate with wine or food is the highest mark of esteem, and this plate in especial was of almost priceless value, as Felix saw when his confusion had abated. It was of the ancient china, now not to be found in even the houses of the great.

In all that kingdom but five perfect plates were known to exist, and two of these were at the palace. They are treasured as heirlooms, and, if ever broken, can never be replaced. The very fragments are rare; they are often set in panels, and highly prized. The Baroness, glancing round her court, had noticed at last the young man sitting in the obscure corner behind the door; she remembered, not without some twinge of conscience, that his house was their ancient ally and sworn hearthfriend.

She knew, far better than the Baron, how deeply her daughter loved him; better, perhaps, even than Aurora herself. She, too, naturally hoped a higher alliance for Aurora; yet she was a true woman, and her heart was stronger than her ambition. The trifle of the wine was, of course, nothing; but it was open and marked recognition. She expected that Felix (after his wont in former times, before love or marriage was thought of for Aurora) would have come upon this distinct invitation, and taken his stand behind her, after the custom. But as he did not come, fresh guests and the duties of hospitality distracted her attention, and she again forgot him.

He was, indeed, more hurt than pleased with the favour that had been shown him; it seemed to him (though really prompted by the kindest feeling) like a bone cast at a dog. He desired to be so regarded that no special mark of favour should be needed. It simply increased his discontent. The evening wore on, the supper began; how weary it seemed to him, that long and jovial supper, with the ale that ran in a continual stream, the wine that ceaselessly circled round, the jokes, and bustle, and laughter, the welcome to guests arriving; the cards, and chess, and games that succeeded it, the drinking, and drinking, and drinking, till the ladies again left; then drinking yet more freely.

He slipped away at the first opportunity, and having first strolled to and fro on the bowling green, wet with dew, at the rear of the castle, asked for his bedroom. It was some time before he could get attended to; he stood alone at the foot of the staircase while others went first (their small coins bought them attention), till at last a lamp was brought to him, and his chamber named. That chamber, such as it was, was the only pleasure, and that a melancholy one, he had had that day.

Though overflowing with guests, so that the most honoured visitors could not be accommodated within the castle, and only the ladies could find sleeping room there, yet the sacred law of honour, the pledge of the hearth-friend passed three generations ago, secured him this privilege. The hearth-friend must sleep within, if a king were sent without. Oliver, of course, would occupy the same room, but he was drinking and shouting a song below, so that for a while Felix had the chamber to himself.

It pleased him, because it was the room in which he had always slept when he visited the place from a boy, when, half afraid and yet determined to venture, he had first come through the lonely forest alone. How well he remembered the first time! the autumn sunshine on the stubble at Old House, and the red and brown leaves of the forest as he entered; how he entered on foot, and twice turned back, and twice adventured again, till he got so deep into the forest that it seemed as far to return as to advance. How he started at the sudden bellow of two stags, and the clatter of their horns as they fought in the brake close by, and how beautiful the castle looked when presently he emerged from the bushes and looked down upon it!

This was the very room he slept in; the Baroness, mother-like, came to see that he was comfortable. Here he had slept every time since; here he had listened in the early morning for Aurora's footfall as she passed his door, for the ladies rose earlier than did the men. He now sat down by the open window; it was a brilliant moonlight night, warm and delicious, and the long-drawn note of the nightingale came across the gardens from the hawthorn bushes without the inner stockade. To the left he could see the line of the hills, to the right the forest; all was quiet there, but every now and then the sound of a ballad came round the castle, a sound without recognisable words, inarticulate merriment.

If he started upon the hazardous voyage he contemplated, and for which he had been so long preparing, should he ever sleep there again, so near the one he loved? Was it not better to be poor and despised, but near her, than to attempt such an expedition, especially as the chances (as his common sense told him) were all against him? Yet he could not stay; he must do it, and he tried to stifle the doubt which insisted upon arising in his mind. Then he recurred to Durand; he remembered that not once on that day had he exchanged one single word, beyond the first and ordinary salutation, with Aurora.

Might she not, had she chosen, have arranged a moment's interview? Might she not easily have given him an opportunity? Was it not clear that she was ashamed of her girlish fancy for a portionless and despised youth? If so, was it worth while to go upon so strange an enterprise for her sake? But if so, also, was life worth living, and might he not as well go and seek destruction?

While this conflict of feeling was proceeding, he chanced to look towards the table upon which he had carelessly placed his lamp, and observed, what in his agitated state of mind he had previously overlooked, a small roll of manuscript tied round with silk. Curious in books, he undid the fastening, and opened the volume. There was not much writing, but many singular diagrams, and signs arranged in circles. It was, in fact, a book of magic, written at the dictation, as the preface stated, of one who had been for seven years a slave among the Romany.

He had been captured, and forced to work for the tent to which his owners belonged. He had witnessed their worship and their sorceries; he had seen the sacrifice to the full moon, their chief goddess, and the wild extravagances with which it was accompanied. He had learnt some few of their signs, and, upon escaping, had reproduced them from memory. Some were engraved on the stones set in their rings; some were carved on wooden tablets, some drawn with ink on parchment; but, with all, their procedure seemed to be the repetition of certain verses, and then a steady gaze upon the picture. Presently they became filled with rapture, uttered what sounded as the wildest ravings, and (their women especially) prophesied of the future.

A few of the signs he understood the meaning of, but the others he owned were unknown to him. At the end of the book were several pages of commentary, describing the demons believed in and worshipped by the Romany, demons which haunted the woods and hills, and against which it was best to be provided with amulets blessed by the holy fathers of St. Augustine. Such demons stole on the hunter at noonday, and, alarmed at the sudden appearance, upon turning his head (for demons invariably approach from behind, and their presence is indicated by a shudder in the back), he toppled into pits hidden by fern, and was killed.

Or, in the shape of a dog, they ran between the traveller's legs; or as women, with tempting caresses, lured him from the way at nightfall into the leafy recesses, and then instantaneously changing into vast bat-like forms, fastened on his throat and sucked his blood. The terrible screams of such victims had often been heard by the warders at the outposts. Some were invisible, and yet slew the unwary by descending unseen upon him, and choking him with a pressure as if the air had suddenly become heavy.

But none of these were, perhaps, so much to be dreaded as the sweetly-formed and graceful ladies of the fern. These were creatures, not of flesh and blood, and yet not incorporeal like the demons, nor were they dangerous to the physical man, doing no bodily injury. The harm they did was by fascinating the soul, so that it revolted from all religion and all the rites of the Church. Once resigned to the caress of the fern-woman, the unfortunate was lured farther and farther from the haunts of men, until at last he wandered into the unknown forest, and was never seen again. These creatures were usually found among the brake fern, nude, but the lower limbs and body hidden by the green fronds, their white arms and shoulders alone visible, and their golden hair aglow with the summer sunshine.

Demons there were, too, of the streams, and demons dwelling in the midst of the hills; demons that could travel only in the moonbeams, and others that floated before the stormy winds and hurled the wretched wanderer to destruction, or crushed him with the overthrown trees. In proof of this the monk asked the reader if he had not heard of huge boughs falling from trees without visible cause, suddenly and without warning, and even of trees themselves in full foliage, in calm weather, toppling with a crash, to the imminent danger or the death of those who happened to be passing. Let all these purchase the amulets of St. Augustine, concluded the writer, who it appeared was a monk in whose monastery the escaped prisoner had taken refuge, and who had written down his relation and copied his rude sketches.

Felix pored over the strange diagrams, striving to understand the hidden meaning; some of them he thought were alchemical signs, and related to the making of gold, especially as the prisoner stated the Romany possessed much more of that metal in their tents than he had seen in the palaces of our kings. Whether they had a gold mine from whence they drew it, or whether they had the art of transmutation, he knew not, but he had heard allusions to the wealth in the mountain of the apple trees, which he supposed to be a mystical phrase.

When Felix at last looked up, the lamp was low, the moonbeams had entered and fell upon the polished floor, and from the window he could see a long white ghostly line of mist where a streamlet ran at the base of the slope by the forest. The songs were silent; there was no sound save the distant neigh of a horse and the heavy tramp of a guest coming along the gallery. Half bewildered by poring over the magic scroll full of the signs and the demons, and still with a sense of injury and jealousy cankering his heart, Felix retired to his couch, and, weary beyond measure, instantly fell asleep.

In his unsettled state of mind it did not once occur to him to ask himself how the manuscript came to be upon his table. Rare as they were, books were not usually put upon the tables of guests, and at an ordinary time he would certainly have thought it peculiar. The fact was, that Aurora, whom all day he had inwardly accused of forgetting him, had placed it there for him with her own hands. She, too, was curious in books and fond of study. She had very recently bought the volume from a merchant who had come thus far, and who valued it the least of all his wares.

She knew that Felix had read and re-read every other scrap of writing there was in the castle, and thought that this strange book might interest him, giving, as it did, details of those powers of the air in which almost all fully believed. Unconscious of this attention, Felix, fell asleep, angry and bitter against her. When, half an hour afterwards, Oliver blundered into the room, a little unsteady on his legs, notwithstanding his mighty strength, he picked up the roll, glanced at it, flung it down with contempt, and without a minute's delay sought and obtained slumber.

CHAPTER X

THE FEAST

AT ten in the morning next day the feast began with a drama from Sophocles, which was performed in the open air. The theatre was in the gardens between the wall and the inner stockade; the spectators sat on the slope, tier above tier; the actors appeared upon a green terrace below, issuing from an arbour and passing off behind a thick box hedge on the other side of the terrace. There was no scenery whatever.

Aurora had selected the Antigone. There were not many dramatists from whom to choose, for so many English writers, once famous, had dropped out of knowledge and disappeared. Yet some of the far more ancient Greek and Roman classics remained because they contained depth and originality of ideas in small compass. They had been copied in MS. by thoughtful men from the old printed books before they mouldered away, and their MSS. being copied again, these works were handed down. The books which came into existence with printing had never been copied by the pen, and had consequently nearly disappeared. Extremely long and diffuse, it was found, too, that so many of them were but enlargements of ideas or sentiments which had been expressed in a few words by the classics. It is so much easier to copy an epigram of two lines than a printed book of hundreds of pages, and hence it was that Sophocles had survived while much more recent writers had been lost.

From a translation Aurora had arranged several of his dramas. Antigone was her favourite, and she wished Felix to see it. In some indefinable manner the spirit of the ancient Greeks seemed to her in accord with the times, for men had or appeared to have so little control over their own lives that they might well imagine themselves overruled by destiny. Communication between one place and another was difficult, the division of society into castes, and the iron tyranny of arms, prevented the individual from making any progress in lifting himself out of the groove in which he was born, except by the rarest opportunity, unless specially favoured by fortune. As men were born so they lived; they could not advance, and when this is the case the idea of Fate is always predominant. The workings of destiny, the Irresistible overpowering both the good and the evil-disposed, such as were traced in the Greek drama, were paralleled in the lives of many a miserable slave at that day. They were forced to endure, for there was no possibility of effort.

Aurora saw this and felt it deeply; ever anxious as she was for the good of all, she saw the sadness that reigned even in the midst of the fresh foliage of spring and among the flowers. It was Fate; it was Sophocles.

She took the part of the heroine herself, clad in Greek costume; Felix listened and watched, absorbed in his love. Never had that ancient drama appeared so beautiful as then, in the sunlight; the actors stepped upon the daisied sward, and the song of birds was all their music.

While the play was still proceeding, those who were to form the usual procession had already been assembling in the court before the castle, and just after noon, to the sound of the trumpet, the Baron, with his youngest son beside him (the eldest was at Court), left the porch, wearing his fur-lined short mantle, his collar, and golden spurs, and the decoration won so many years before; all the insignia of his rank. He walked; his war-horse, fully caparisoned, with axe at the saddle-bow, was led at his right side, and upon the other came a knight carrying the banneret* of the house.

The gentlemen of the house followed closely, duly marshalled in ranks, and wearing the gayest dress; the leading retainers fully armed, brought up the rear. Immediately upon issuing from the gate of the wall, the procession was met and surrounded by the crowd, carrying large branches of may in bloom, flowers, and green willow boughs. The flowers they flung before him on the ground; the branches they bore with them, chaunting old verses in honour of the family. The route was through the town, where the Baron stopped at the door of the Court House, and proclaimed a free pardon to all serfs (who were released within a few minutes) not guilty of the heavier crimes.

Thence he went to the pasture just beyond, carefully mown close and swept for the purpose, where the May-pole stood, wreathed with flowers and green branches. Beneath it he deposited a bag of money for distribution upon a carved butt placed there, the signal that the games were open. Instantly the fiddles began to play, and the feast really commenced. At the inns ale was served out freely (at the Baron's charge), carts, too, came down from the castle laden with ale and cooked provisions. Wishing them joy, the Baron returned by the same road to the

---

* A knight-at-arms permitted to lead a troop of soldiers under his own banner. Jefferies appears to have used the term incorrectly to mean a banner.

castle, where dinner was already served in the hall and the sheds that had been erected to enlarge the accommodation.

In the afternoon there were foot-races, horseraces, and leaping competitions, and the dances about the May-pole were prolonged far into the night. The second day, early in the morning, the barriers were opened, and trials of skill with the blunt sword, jousting with the blunt lance at the quintain, and wrestling began, and continued almost till sunset. Tournament with sharpened lance or sword, when the combatants fight with risk of serious wounds, can take place only in the presence of the Prince or his deputy. But in these conflicts sufficiently severe blows were given to disable the competitors.

On the third day there was a set battle in the morning between fifteen men on each side, armed with the usual buckler or small shield, and stout single sticks instead of swords. This combat excited more interest than all the duels that had preceded it; the crowd almost broke down the barriers, and the cheering and cries of encouragement could be heard upon the hills. Thrice the combatants rested from the engagement, and thrice at the trumpet call started again to meet each other, at least those who had sustained the first onslaught.

Blood, indeed, was not shed (for the iron morions* saved their skulls), but nearly half of the number required assistance to reach the tents pitched for their use. Then came more feasting, the final dinner prolonged till six in the evening, when the company, constantly rising from their seats, cheered the Baron, and drank to the prosperity of the house. After the horn blew at six, the guests who had come from a distance rapidly dispersed (their horses were already waiting), for they were anxious to pass the fifteen miles of forest before nightfall. Those on foot, and those ladies who had come in covered waggons, stayed till next morning, as they could not travel so speedily. By seven or eight the castle courtyard was comparatively empty, and the Baron, weary from the mere bodily efforts of saying farewell to so many, had flung himself at full length on a couch in the drawing-room.

During the whole of this time Felix had not obtained a single moment with Aurora; her time, when not occupied in attending to the guests, was always claimed by Lord Durand. Felix, after the short-lived but pure pleasure he had enjoyed in watching her upon the grass-grown stage, had endured three days of misery. He was among the crowd, he was in the castle itself, he sat at table with the most honoured visitors,

---

* An open helmet worn by soldiers. Morions have a long history, being mentioned in Homer's *The Iliad* (book 10), and being still in occasional use by the Vatican Swiss Guard, but the helmet is most commonly associated with Spanish conquistadores and the parliamentary foot-soldiers of the English Civil War.

yet he was distinct from all. There was no sympathy between them and him. The games, the dancing, the feasting and laughter, the ceaseless singing and shouting, and jovial jostling, jarred upon him.

The boundless interest the people took in the combats, and especially that of the thirty, seemed to him a strange and inexplicable phenomenon. It did not excite him in the least; he could turn his back upon it without hesitation. He would, indeed, have left the crowd, and spent the day in the forest, or on the hills, but he could not leave Aurora. He must be near her; he must see her, though he was miserable. Now he feared that the last moment would come, and that he should not exchange a word with her.

He could not, with any show of pretext, prolong his stay beyond the sunset; all were already gone, with the exceptions mentioned. It would be against etiquette to remain longer, unless specially invited, and he was not specially invited. Yet he lingered, and lingered. His horse was ready below; the groom, weary of holding the bridle, had thrown it over an iron hook in the yard, and gone about other business. The sun perceptibly declined, and the shadow of the beeches of the forest began to descend the grassy slope. Still he stayed, restlessly moving, now in the dining chamber, now in the hall, now at the foot of the staircase, with an unpleasant feeling that the servants looked at him curiously, and were watching him.

Oliver had gone long since, riding with his new friend Lord Durand; they must by now be halfway through the forest. Forced by the inexorable flight of time, he put his foot upon the staircase to go up to the drawing-room and bid farewell to the Baroness. He ascended it, step by step, as a condemned person goes to his doom. He stayed to look out of the open windows as he went by; anything to excuse delay to himself. He reached the landing at last, and had taken two steps towards the door, when Aurora's maid, who had been waiting there an hour or more for the opportunity, brushed past him, and whispered, 'The Rose arbour.'

Without a word he turned, hastened down the stairs, ran through the castle yard, out at the gate, and, entering the gardens between the wall and the inner stockade, made for the arbour on the terrace where the drama had been enacted. Aurora was not there; but as he looked round, disappointed, she came from the Filbert walk, and, taking his arm, led him to the arbour. They sat down without a word. In a moment she placed her head upon his shoulder; he did not respond. She put her arm (how warm it felt!) about his neck; he yielded stiffly and ungraciously to the pressure; she drew down his head, and kissed him. His lips touched but did not press hers; they met, but did not join.

In his sullen and angry silence he would not look. She drew still nearer, and whispered his name.

Then he broke out: he pushed her away; his petty jealousy and injured self-esteem poured out upon her. 'I am not the heir to an earl-dom,' he said; 'I do not ride with a score of gentlemen at my back. They have some wonderful diamonds, have they not——*Countess*?'

'Felix!'

'It is no use. Yes, your voice is sweet, I know. But you, all of you, despise me. I am nothing, no one!'

'You are all, *everything*, to me.'

'You were with—with Durand the whole time.'

'I could not help myself.'

'Not help yourself! Do you think I believe that?'

'Felix, dear. I tell you I could not help myself; I could not, indeed. You do not know all——'

'No, probably not. I do not know the terms of the marriage contract.'

'Felix, there is no such thing. Why, what has come to you? How pale you look! Sit down!' for he had risen.

'I cannot, Aurora, dear; I cannot! Oh, what shall I do? I love you so!'

CHAPTER XI

AURORA

FELIX fell on the seat beside her, burying his face in the folds of her dress; he sobbed, not with tears, but choking passion. She held him to her heart as if he had been a child, stroking his hair and kissing it, whispering to him, assuring him that her love was his, that she was unchanged. She told him that it was not her fault. A little while before the feast the Baron had suddenly broken out into a fit of temper, such as she had never seen him indulge in previously; the cause was pressure put upon him by his creditors. Unpleasant truths had escaped him; amongst the rest, his dislike, his positive disapproval of the tacit engagement they had entered into.

He declared that if the least outward sign of it appeared before the guests that were expected, he would order Felix to leave the place, and cancel the hearth-friendship, no matter what the consequence. It was clear that he was set upon a wealthy and powerful alliance for her; that the Earl was either coming, or would send his son, he knew; and he knew that nothing so repels a possible suitor as the rumour that the lady has a previous engagement. In short, he made it a condition of Felix's presence being tolerated at all, that Aurora should carefully abstain from showing the slightest attention to him; that she should ignore his existence.

Nor could she prevent Durand following her without a marked refusal to listen to his conversation, a refusal which would most certainly at once have brought about the dreaded explosion. She thought it better, under the circumstances, to preserve peace, lest intercourse between her and Felix should be entirely broken off for ever. This was the secret history of the apparent indifference and neglect which had so deeply hurt him. The explanation, accompanied as it was with so many tender expressions and caresses, soothed him; he returned her kisses and became calmer. He could not doubt her, for in his heart he had suspected something of the kind long since.

Yet it was not so much the explanation itself, nor even the love she poured upon him, as the mere fact of her presence so near that brought him to himself. The influence of her steadfast nature, of her clear, broad, straightforward view of things, the decision of her character, the high unselfish motives which animated her, all together supplied that which was wanting in himself. His indecision, his too impressionable disposition, which checked and stayed the force of his talent, and counteracted the determination of a naturally iron will; these, as it were, were relieved; in a word, with her he became himself.

How many times he had told her as much! How many times she had replied that it was not herself, but that in which she believed, that was the real cause of this feeling! It was that ancient and true religion; the religion of the primitive church, as she found it in the fragments of the Scriptures that had come down from the ancients.

Aurora had learnt this faith from childhood; it was, indeed, a tradition of the house preserved unbroken these hundred years in the midst of the jarring creeds, whose disciples threatened and destroyed each other. On the one hand, the gorgeous rite of the Vice-Pope, with the priests and the monks, claimed dominion, and really held a large share, both over the body and the soul; on the other, the Leaguers, with their bold, harsh, and flowerless creed, were equally over-bearing and equally bigoted. Around them the Bushmen wandered without a god; the Romany called upon the full moon. Within courts and cities the gay and the learned alike mocked at all faith, and believed in gold alone.

Cruelty reigned everywhere; mercy, except in the name of honour, there was none; humanity was unknown. A few, a very few only, had knowledge of or held to the leading tenets, which, in the time of the ancients, were assented to by every one, such as the duty of humanity to all, the duty of saving and protecting life, of kindness and gentleness. These few, with their pastors, simple and unassuming, had no power or influence; yet they existed here and there, a living protest against the lawlessness and brutality of the time.

Among these the house of Thyma had in former days been conspicuous, but of late years the barons of Thyma had, more from policy than aught else, rather ignored their ancestral faith, leaning towards the League, which was then powerful in that kingdom. To have acted otherwise would have been to exclude himself from all appointments. But Aurora, learning the old faith at her mother's knee, had become too deeply imbued with its moral beauty to consent to this course. By degrees, as she grew up, it became in her a passion; more than a faith, a passion; the object of her life.

A girl, indeed, can do but little in our iron days, but that little she did. The chapel beside the castle, long since fallen to decay, was, at her earnest request, repaired; a pastor came and remained as chaplain, and services, of the simplest kind, but serious and full of meaning, took place twice a week. To these she drew as many as possible of the inhabitants of the enclosure; some even came from afar once now and then to attend them. Correspondence was carried on with the remnant of the faith.

That no one might plead ignorance (for there was up to that date no written record) Aurora set herself the task of reducing the traditions which had been handed down to writing. When the manuscript was at last completed it occupied her months to transcribe copies of it for circulation; and she still continued to make copies, which were sent by messengers and by the travelling merchants to the markets, and even across the sea. Apart from its intrinsically elevating character, the mere mental labour expended on this work had undoubtedly strengthened a naturally fine intellect. As she said, it was the faith, the hope that that faith would one day be recognised, which gave her so much influence over others.

Upon this one thing only they differed; Felix did not oppose, did not even argue, he was simply untouched. It was not that he believed in anything else, nor that he doubted; he was merely indifferent. He had too great a natural aptitude for the physical sciences, and too clear a mind, to accept that which was taught by the one or the other of the two chief opposing parties. Nor could he join in the ridicule and derision of the gay courtiers, for the mystery of existence had impressed him deeply while wandering alone in the forest. But he stood aloof; he smiled and listened, unconvinced; like the wild creatures of the forest, he had no ears for these matters. He loved Aurora, that was all.

But he felt the influence just the same; with all his power of mind and contempt of superstitions in others, he could not at times shake off the apprehensions aroused by untoward omens, as when he stepped upon the adder in the woods. Aurora knew nothing of such things; her faith was clear and bright like a star; nothing could alarm her, or bring uneasiness of mind. This beautiful calm, not cold, but glowing with hope and love, soothed him.

That evening, with her hope and love, with her message of trust, she almost persuaded him. He almost turned to what she had so long taught. He almost repented of that hardness of heart, that unutterable distance, as it were, between him and other men, which lay at the bottom of his proposed expedition. He opened his lips to confess to her his purpose, and had he done so assuredly she would have persuaded him from it. But in the very act to speak, he hesitated. It was characteristic of him to do so. Whether she instinctively felt that there was something concealed from her, or guessed that the discontent she knew he had so long endured was coming to a point, or feared lest what she had told him might drive him to some ill-considered act, she begged him with all the power of her love to do nothing hasty, or in despair, nothing that would separate them. He threw his arms around her, he pressed her closely to him, he trembled with the passion and the struggle within him.

'My lady calls for you, Mademoiselle,' said a voice; it was Aurora's maid who had kept watch. 'She has asked for you some time since. Some one is coming into the garden!'

There was no help for it; Aurora kissed him, and was gone before he could come to himself. How long the interview had lasted (time flies swiftly in such sweet intercourse), or how long he sat there after she left, he could not tell; but when he went out already the dusk was gathering, the sun had gone down, and in the east the as yet pale orb of the moon was rising over the hills. As if in a dream he walked with unsteady steps to the castle stable; his horse had been put back, and the grooms suggested to him that it was better not to attempt the forest at night. But he was determined; he gave them all the coin he had about him, it was not much, but more than they had expected.

They ran beside him to the barrier; advising him as they ran, as he would go, to string his bow and loosen an arrow in his girdle, and above all not to loiter, or let his horse walk, but to keep him at as sharp a trot as he could. The fact that so many wealthy persons had assembled at the castle for the feast would be sure to be known to the banditti (the outlaws of the cities and the escaped serfs). They were certain to be on the look-out for travellers; let him beware.

His ears tingled and his head felt hot, as if the blood had rushed into it (it was the violence of the emotion that he had felt), as he rode from the barrier, hearing, and yet without conscious knowledge of what they said. They watched him up the slope, and saw him disappear from sight under the dark beeches of the forest.

CHAPTER XII

NIGHT IN THE FOREST

AT first Felix rode quickly, but his horse stumbling, though accustomed to the woods, warned him to be more careful. The passage of so many horsemen in the last few days had cut up and destroyed the track, which was nothing but a green path, and the covered waggons had of course assisted in rendering it rough and broken. He therefore rode slowly, and giving his horse his head, he picked his way of his own accord at the side of the road, often brushing against the underwood.

Still, indeed, absorbed by the feelings which had almost mastered him in the arbour, and thinking of Aurora, he forgot where he was, till the dismal howling of wood-dogs deep in the forest woke him. It was almost pitch dark under the tall beeches, the highest of the trees preventing the beams of the moon from illuminating the path till later in the night. Like a curtain the thick foliage above shut out the sky, so that no star was visible. When the wood-dogs ceased there was no sound beyond the light fall of the horse's hoofs as he walked upon the grass. Darkness and silence prevailed; he could see nothing. He spoke to his horse and patted his neck; he stepped a little faster and lifted his head, which he had held low as if making his way by scent.

The gloom weighed upon him, unhappy as he was. Often as he had voluntarily sought the loneliness of the woods, now in this state of mind it oppressed him; he remembered that beyond the beeches the ground was open and cleared by a forest fire, and began to be anxious to reach it. It seemed an hour, but it really was only a few minutes, when the beeches became thinner and wider apart, the foliage above ceased, and the stars shone. Before him was the open space he had desired, sloping to the right hand, the tall grass grey-green in the moonlight, and near at hand sparkling with dew.

Amongst it stood the crooked and charred stems of furze with which it had been covered before the fire passed. A white owl floated rather than flew by, following the edge of the forest; from far down the slope came the chattering notes of a brooksparrow, showing that there was water in the hollow. Some large animal moved into the white mist that hung there and immediately concealed it, like a cloud upon the ground. He was not certain in the dim light, and with so momentary and distant a view, but supposed from its size that it must have been a white or dun wood-cow.

Ahead, across the open, rose the dark top of the fir trees through which the route ran. Instead of the relief which he had anticipated as he rode towards them, the space clear of trees around seemed to expose him to the full view of all that might be lurking in the forest. As he approached the firs and saw how dark it was beneath them, the shadowy depths suggested uncertain shapes hiding therein, and his memory immediately reverted to the book of magic he had read at the castle.

There could not be such things, and yet no one in his heart doubted their existence; deny it as they might with their tongues as they sat at the supper-table and handed round the ale, out of doors in the night, the haste to pass the haunted spot, the bated breath, and the fearful glances cast around, told another tale. He endeavoured to call philosophy to his aid; he remembered, too, how many nights he had spent in the deepest forest without seeing anything, and without even thinking of such matters. He reproved himself for his folly, and asked himself if ever he could hope to be a successful leader of men who started at a shadow. In vain: the tone of his mind had been weakened by the strain it had undergone.

Instead of strengthening him, the teachings of philosophy now seemed cold and feeble, and it occurred to him that possibly the belief of the common people (fully shared by their religious instructors) was just as much entitled to credence as these mere suppositions and theories. The details of the volume recurred to his mind; the accurate description of the demons of the forest and the hill, and especially the horrible vampires enfolding the victim with outstretched wings. In spite of himself, incredulous, yet excited, he pressed his horse to greater speed, though the track was narrow and very much broken under the firs. He obeyed, and trotted, but reluctantly, and needed continual urging.

The yellow spark of a glowworm shining by a bush made him set his teeth; trifling and well known as it was, the light suddenly seen thrilled him with the terror of the unexpected. Strange rushings sounded among the fern, as if the wings of a demon brushed it as he travelled. Felix knew that they were caused by rabbits hastening off, or a boar bounding away, yet they increased the feverish excitement with which he was burdened. Though dark beneath the firs, it was not like the darkness of the beeches; these trees did not form a perfect canopy overhead everywhere. In places he could see where a streak of moonlight came aslant through an opening and reached the ground. One such streak fell upon the track ahead; the trees there had decayed and fallen, and a broad band of light lit up the way.

As he approached it and had almost entered, suddenly something shot towards him in the air, a flash, as it were, as if some object had crossed the streak, and was rendered visible for the tenth of a second, like a mote in the sunbeams. At the same instant of time, the horse, which he had pressed to go faster, put his foot into a rut or hole, and stumbled, and Felix was flung so far forward that he only saved himself from being thrown by clinging to his neck. A slight whizzing sound passed over his head, followed immediately by a sharp tap against a tree in his rear.

The thing happened in the twinkling of an eye, but he recognised the sound; it was the whizz of a crossbow bolt, which had missed his head, and buried its point in a fir. The stumble saved him; the bolt would have struck the head or chest had not the horse gone nearly on his knee. The robber had so planned his ambush that his prey should be well seen distinct in the moonlight, so that his aim might be sure. Recovering himself, the horse, without needing the spur, as if he recognised the danger to his rider, started forward at full speed, and raced, regardless of ruts, along the track. Felix, who had hardly got into his seat again, could for awhile but barely restrain it, so wildly he fled. He must have been carried within a few yards of the bandit, but saw nothing, neither did a second bolt follow him; the crossbow takes time to bend, and if the robber had companions they were differently armed.

He was a furlong or more from the spot before he quite realised the danger he had escaped. His bow was unstrung in his hand, his arrows were all in the quiver; thus, had the bolt struck him, even if the wound had not been mortal (as it most likely would have been) he could have made no resistance. How foolish to disregard the warnings of the grooms at the castle! It was now too late; all he could do was to ride. Dreading every moment to be thrown, he pushed on as fast as the horse would go. There was no pursuit, and after a mile or so, as he left the firs and entered the ash woods, he slackened somewhat. It was, indeed, necessary, for here the hoofs of preceding horsemen had poached the turf (always damp under ash) into mud. It was less dark, for the boughs of the ashes did not meet above.

As he passed, wood-pigeons rose with loud clatterings from their roosting-places, and once or twice he saw in the gloom the fiery phosphoric eyeballs of the grey wood-cats. How gladly he recognised presently the change from trees to bushes, when he rode out from the thick ashes among the low hawthorns, and knew that he was within a mile or so of the South Barrier at home! Already he heard the song of the nightingale, the long note which at night penetrates so far; the nightingale, which loves the hawthorn and the neighbourhood of man.

Imperceptibly he increased the speed again; the horse, too, knew that he was nearing home, and responded willingly.

The track was much broader and fairly good, but he knew that at one spot where it was marshy it must be cut up. There he went at the side, almost brushing a projecting maple bush. Something struck the horse, he fancied the rebound of a bough; he jumped, literally jumped, like a buck, and tore along the road. With one foot out of the stirrup, it was with the utmost difficulty he stuck to his seat; he was not riding, but holding on for a moment or two. Presently recovering from the jolt, he endeavoured to check him, but the bit was of no avail; the animal was beside himself with terror, and raced headlong till they reached the barrier. It was, of course, closed, and the warder was asleep; so that, until he dismounted, and kicked and shouted, no one challenged him.

Then the warder, spear in hand, appeared with his lantern, but, recognising the voice, ran to the gate. Within the gate a few yards there were the embers of a fire, and round it a bivouac of footmen who had been to the feast, and had returned thus far before nightfall. Hearing the noise, some of them arose, and came round him, when one immediately exclaimed and asked if he was wounded. Felix replied that he was not, but looking at his foot where the man pointed, saw that it was covered with blood. But, upon close examination, there was no cut or incision; he was not hurt. The warder now called to them, and showed a long deep scratch on the near flank of the horse, from which the blood was dripping.

It was such a scratch as might have been made with an iron nail, and, without hesitation, they all put it down to a Bushman's spud. Without doubt, the Bushman, hearing Felix approach, had hidden in the maple bush, and, as he passed, struck with his nail-like dagger; but, miscalculating the speed at which the horse was going, instead of piercing the thigh of the rider, the blow fell on the horse, and the sharp point was dragged along the side. The horse trembled as they touched him.

'Sir,' said one of the retainers, their headman, 'if you will pardon me, you had best string your bow and send a shaft through his heart, for he will die in misery before morning.'

The Bushman's spud, the one he uses for assassination or to despatch his prey, is poisoned. It is a lingering poison, and takes several hours to produce its effect; but no remedy is known, and many who have escaped from the cowardly blow have crawled to the path only to expire in torture. There was no denying that what the retainer proposed was the only thing that could be done. The warder had meantime brought a bucket of water, of which the poor creature drank eagerly. Felix could not do it; he could not slay the creature which had carried him so long, and which twice that night had saved him, and was now to die, as it were, in his place. He could not consent to it; he led the horse towards home, but he was weak or weary, and could not be got beyond the Pen.

There the group assembled around him. Felix ordered the scratch to be cleansed, while he ran over in his mind every possible remedy. He gave strict orders that he should not be despatched, and then hastened to the house. He undid with trembling hands the thongs that bound his chest, and took out his manuscripts, hoping against hope that among the many notes he had made there might be something. But there was nothing, or in his excitement he overlooked it. Remembering that Oliver was a great authority upon horses, he went into his room and tried to wake him. Oliver, weary with his ride, and not as yet having slept off the effects of the feast, could not be roused.

Felix left him and hurried back to the Pen. Weary as he was, he watched by the horse till the larks began to sing and the dawn was at hand. As yet he had not shown any severe symptoms except twitching of the limbs, and a constant thirst, which water could not quench. But suddenly he fell, and the old retainer warned them all to stand away, for he would bite anything that was near. His words were instantly fulfilled; he rolled, and kicked, and bit at everything within reach. Seeing this agony, Felix could no longer delay. He strung his bow, but he could not fit the arrow to the string, he missed the notch, so much did his hands shake. He motioned to the retainers who had gathered around, and one of them thrust his spear into the horse behind his shoulder.

When Felix at last returned to his chamber he could not but reflect, as the sun rose and the beams entered, that every omen had been against him: the adder under foot, the bandit's bolt, the Bushman's poisoned point. He slept till noon, and, upon going out, unrefreshed and still weary, he found that they had already buried the horse, and ordered a mound to be raised above his grave. The day passed slowly; he wandered about the castle and the enclosed grounds, seeking comfort and finding none. His mind vacillated; he recalled all that Aurora had said, persuading him not to do anything in haste or despair. Yet he could not continue in his present condition. Another day went by, and still undecided and doubting, he remained at home.

Oliver began to jest at him; had he abandoned the expedition? Oliver could not understand indecision; perhaps he did not see so many sides to the question, his mind was always quickly made up. Action was his forte, not thought. The night came, and still Felix lingered hesitating.

CHAPTER XIII

SAILING AWAY

BUT the next morning Felix arose straight from his sleep resolved to carry out his plan. Without staying to think a moment, without further examination of the various sides of the problem, he started up the instant his eyes unclosed, fully determined upon his voyage. The breath of the bright June morn as he threw open the window-shutter filled him with hope; his heart responded to its joyous influence. The excitement which had disturbed his mind had had time to subside. In the still slumber of the night the strong undercurrent of his thought resumed its course, and he awoke with his will firmly bent in one direction.

When he had dressed, he took his bow and the chest bound with the leathern thongs, and went down. It was early, but the Baron had already finished breakfast and gone out to his gardens; the Baroness had not yet appeared. While he was making a hurried breakfast (for having now made up his mind he was eager to put his resolve into execution), Oliver came in, and seeing the chest and the bow, understood that the hour had arrived. He immediately said he should accompany him to Heron Bay, and assist him to start, and went out to order their horses. There were always plenty of riding horses at Old House (as at every fortified mansion), and there was not the least difficulty in getting another for Felix in place of his favourite.

Oliver insisted upon taking the wooden chest, which was rather heavy, before him on the saddle, so that Felix had nothing to carry but his favourite bow. Oliver was surprised that Felix did not first go to the gardens and say good-bye to the Baron, or at least knock at the Baroness's door and bid her farewell. But he made no remark, knowing Felix's proud and occasionally hard temper. Without a word Felix left the old place.

He rode forth from the North Barrier, and did not even so much as look behind him. Neither he nor Oliver thought of the events that might happen before they should again meet in the old familiar house! When the circle is once broken up it is often years before it is reformed. Often, indeed, the members of it never meet again, at least, not in the same manner, which, perhaps, they detested then, and ever afterwards regretted. Without one word of farewell, without a glance, Felix rode out into the forest.

There was not much conversation on the trail to Heron Bay. The serfs were still there in charge of the canoe, and were glad enough to see their approach, and thus to be relieved from their lonely watch. They launched the canoe with ease, the provisions were put on board, the chest lashed to the mast that it might not be lost, the favourite bow was also fastened upright to the mast for safety, and simply shaking hands with Oliver, Felix pushed out into the creek. He paddled the canoe to the entrance and out into the Lake till he arrived where the south-west breeze coming over the forest touched and rippled the water, which by the shore was perfectly calm.

Then hoisting the sail, he put out the larger paddle which answered as a rudder, took his seat, and, waving his hand to Oliver, began his voyage. The wind was but light, and almost too favourable, for he had determined to sail to the eastward; not for any specific reason, but because there the sun rose, and that was the quarter of light and hope. His canoe, with a long fore-and-aft sail and so well adapted for working into the wind, was not well rigged for drifting before a breeze, which was what he was now doing. He had merely to keep the canoe before the wind, steering so as to clear the bold headland of White Horse which rose blue from the water's edge far in front of him. Though the wind was light, the canoe being so taper and sharp at the prow, and the sail so large in comparison, slipped from the shore faster than he at first imagined.

As he steered aslant from the little bay outwards into the great Lake, the ripples rolling before the wind gradually enlarged into wavelets, these again increased, and in half an hour, as the wind now played upon them over a mile of surface, they seemed in his canoe, with its low freeboard, to be considerable waves. He had purposefully refrained from looking back till now, lest they should think he regretted leaving, and in his heart desired to return. But now, feeling that he had really started, he glanced behind. He could see no one.

He had forgotten that the spot where they had launched the canoe was at the end of an inlet, and as he sailed away the creek was shut off from view by the shore of the Lake. Unable to get to the mouth of the bay because of the underwood and the swampy soil, Oliver had remained gazing in the direction the canoe had taken for a minute or two, absorbed in thought (almost the longest period he had ever wasted in such an occupation), and then with a whistle turned to go. The serfs, understanding that they were no longer required, gathered their things together, and were shortly on their way home. Oliver, holding Felix's horse by the bridle, had already ridden that way, but he presently halted, and waited till the three men overtook him. He then gave the horse into their charge, and turning to the right, along a forest path which branched off there, went to Ponze. Felix could therefore see no one when he looked back, and they were indeed already on their way from the place.

He now felt that he was alone. He had parted from the shore, and from all the old associations; he was fast passing not only out upon the water, but out into the unknown future. But his spirit no longer vacillated; now that he was really in the beginning of his long contemplated enterprise his natural strength of mind returned. The weakness and irresolution, the hesitation, left him. He became full of his adventure, and thought of nothing else.

The south-west breeze, blowing as a man breathes, with alternate rise and fall, now driving him along rapidly till the water bubbled under the prow, now sinking, came over his right shoulder and cooled his cheek, for it was now noon, and the June sun was unchecked by clouds. He could no longer distinguish the shape of the trees on shore, all the boughs were blended together in one great wood, stretching as far as he could see. On his left there was a chain of islands, some covered with firs, and others only with brushwood, while others again were so low and flat that the waves in stormy weather broke almost over them.

As he drew near White Horse, five white terns, or sea-swallows, flew over; he did not welcome their appearance, as they usually preceded rough gales. The headland, wooded to its ridge, now rose high against the sky; ash and nut-tree and hawthorn had concealed the ancient graven figure of the horse upon its side, but the tradition was not forgotten, and the site retained its name. He had been steering so as just to clear the promontory, but he now remembered that when he had visited the summit of the hill, he had observed that banks and shoals extended far out from the shore, and were nearly on a level with the surface of the Lake. In a calm they were visible, but waves concealed them, and unless the helmsman recognised the swirl sufficiently early to change his course, they were extremely dangerous.

Felix bore more out from the land, and passing fully a mile to the north, left the shoals on his right. On his other hand there was a sandy and barren island barely a quarter of a mile distant, upon which he thought he saw the timbers of a wreck. It was quite probable, for the island lay in the track of vessels coasting along the shore. Beyond White Horse, the land fell away in a series of indentations, curving inwards to the south; an inhospitable coast, for the hills came down to the strand, ending abruptly in low, but steep, chalk cliffs. Many islands of large size stood out on the left, but Felix, not knowing the shape of the Lake beyond White Horse, thought it best to follow the trend of the land. He thus found, after about three hours, that he had gone far out of his course, for the gulf-like curve of the coast now began to return to the northward, and looking in that direction he saw a merchant vessel under her one square sail of great size, standing across the bay.

She was about five miles distant, and was evidently steering so as to keep just inside the line of the islands. Felix, with some difficulty, steered in a direction to interrupt her. The south-west wind being then immediately aft, his sail did not answer well; presently he lowered it, and paddled till he had turned the course so that the outrigger was now on the eastern side. Then hoisting the sail again, he sat at what had before been the prow, and steered a point or so nearer the wind. This improved her sailing, but as the merchant ship had at least five miles start, it would take some hours to overtake her. Nor on reflection was he at all anxious to come up with her, for mariners were dreaded for their lawless conduct, being, when on a voyage, beyond all jurisdiction.

On the one hand, if they saw an opportunity, they did not hesitate to land and pillage a house, or even a hamlet. On the other, those who dwelt anywhere near the shore considered it good sport to light a fire and lure a vessel to her destruction, or if she was becalmed to sally out in boats, attack, and perhaps destroy both ship and crew. Hence the many wrecks, and losses, and the risks of navigation, not so much from natural obstacles, since the innumerable islands, and the creeks and inlets of the mainland, almost always offered shelter, no matter which way the storm blew, but from the animosity of the coast people. If there was an important harbour and a town where provisions could be obtained, or repairs effected, the right of entrance was jealously guarded, and no ship, however pressed by the gale, was permitted to leave, if she had anchored, without payment of a fine. So that vessels as much as possible avoided the harbours and towns and the mainland altogether, sailing along beside the islands, which were, for the most part, uninhabited, and anchoring under their lee at night.

Felix, remembering the character of the mariners, resolved to keep well away from them, but to watch their course as a guide to himself. The mainland now ran abruptly to the north, and the canoe, as he brought her more into the wind, sprang forward at a rapid pace. The outrigger prevented her from making any leeway, or heeling over, and the large spread of sail forced her swiftly through the water. He had lost sight of the ship behind some islands, and as he approached these, began to ask himself if he had not better haul down his sail there, as he must now be getting near her, when to his surprise, on coming close, he saw her great square sail in the middle, as it seemed, of the land. The shore there was flat, the hills which had hitherto bounded it suddenly ceasing; it was overgrown with reeds and flags, and about two miles away the dark sail of the merchantman drifted over these, the hull being hidden. He at once knew that he had reached the western mouth of the straits which divide the southern and northern mainland. When he went to see the channel on foot through the forest, he must have struck it a mile or two more to the east, where it wound under the hills.

In another half hour he arrived at the opening of the strait; it was about a mile wide, and either shore was quite flat, that on the right for a short distance, the range of downs approaching within two miles; that on the left, or north, was level as far as he could see. He had now again to lower his sail, to get the outrigger on his lee as he turned to the right and steered due east into the channel. So long as the shore was level, he had no difficulty, for the wind drew over it, but when the hills gradually came near and almost overhung the channel, they shut off much of the breeze, and his progress was slow. When it turned and ran narrowing every moment to the south, the wind failed him altogether.

On the right shore, wooded hills rose from the water like a wall; on the left, it was a perfect plain. He could see nothing of the merchantman, although he knew that she could not sail here, but must be working through with her sweeps. Her heavy hull and bluff bow must make the rowing a slow and laborious process; therefore she could not be far ahead, but was concealed by the winding of the strait. He lowered the sail, as it was now useless, and began to paddle; in a very short time he found the heat under the hills oppressive when thus working. He had now been afloat between six and seven hours, and must have come fully thirty miles, perhaps rather more than twenty in a straight line, and he felt somewhat weary and cramped from sitting so long in the canoe.

Though he paddled hard he did not seem to make much progress, and at length he recognised that there was a distinct current, which opposed his advance, flowing through the channel from east to west. If he ceased paddling, he found he drifted slowly back; the long aquatic weeds, too, which he passed, all extended their floating streamers westward. We did not know of this current till Felix Aquila observed and recorded it.

Tired and hungry (for, full of his voyage, he had taken no refreshment since he started), he resolved to land, rest a little while, and then ascend the hill, and see what he could of the channel. He soon reached the shore, the strait having narrowed to less than a mile in width, and ran the canoe on the ground by a bush, to which, on getting out, he attached the painter. The relief of stretching his limbs was so great that it seemed to endow him with fresh strength, and without waiting to eat, he at once climbed the hill. From the top, the remainder of the strait could be easily distinguished. But a short distance from where he stood, it bent again, and proceeded due east.

CHAPTER XIV

THE STRAITS

THE passage contracted there to little over half a mile, but these narrows did not continue far; the shores, having approached thus near each other, quickly receded, till presently they were at least two miles apart. The merchant vessel had passed the narrows with the aid of her sweeps, but she moved slowly, and, as it seemed to him, with difficulty. She was about a mile and a half distant, and near the eastern mouth of the strait. As Felix watched he saw her square sail again raised, showing that she had reached a spot where the hills ceased to shut off the wind. Entering the open Lake she altered her course and sailed away to the north-north-east, following the course of the northern mainland.

Looking now eastwards, across the Lake, he saw a vast and beautiful expanse of water, without island or break of any kind, reaching to the horizon. Northwards and southwards the land fell rapidly away, skirted as usual with islets and shoals, between which and the shore vessels usually voyaged. He had heard of this open water, and it was his intention to sail out into and explore it, but as the sun now began to decline towards the west, he considered that he had better wait till morning, and so have a whole day before him. Meantime, he would paddle through the channel, beach the canoe on the islet that stood farthest out, and so start clear on the morrow.

Turning now to look back the other way, westward, he was surprised to see a second channel, which came almost to the foot of the hill on which he stood, but there ended and did not connect with the first. The entrance to it was concealed, as he now saw, by an island, past which he must have sailed that afternoon. This second or blind channel seemed more familiar to him than the flat and reedy shore at the mouth of the true strait, and he now recognised it as the one to which he had journeyed on foot through the forest. He had not then struck the true strait at all; he had sat down and pondered beside this deceptive inlet thinking that it divided the mainlands. From this discovery he saw how easy it was to be misled in such matters.

But it even more fully convinced him of the importance of this uninhabited and neglected place. It seemed like a canal cut on purpose to supply a fort from the Lake in the rear with provisions and material, supposing access in front prevented by hostile fleets and armies. A castle, if built near where he stood, would command the channel; arrows, indeed, could not be shot across, but vessels under the protection of the castle could dispute the passage, obstructed as it could be with floating booms. An invader coming from the north must cross here; for many years past there had been a general feeling that some day such an attempt would be made. Fortifications would be of incalculable value in repelling the hostile hordes and preventing their landing.

Who held this strait would possess the key of the Lake, and would be the master of, or would at least hold the balance between, the kings and republics dotted along the coasts on either hand. No vessel could pass without his permission. It was the most patent illustration of the extremely local horizon, the contracted mental view of the petty kings and their statesmen, who were so concerned about the frontiers of their provinces, and frequently interfered and fought for a single palisaded estate or barony, yet were quite oblivious of the opportunity of empire open here to any who could seize it.

If the governor of such a castle as he imagined built upon the strait, had also vessels of war, they could lie in this second channel sheltered from all winds, and ready to sally forth and take an attacking force upon the flank. While he pondered upon these advantages he could not conceal from himself that he had once sat down and dreamed beside this second inlet, thinking it to be the channel. The doubt arose whether, if he was so easily misled in such a large, tangible, and purely physical matter, he might not be deceived also in his ideas; whether, if tested, they might not fail; whether the world was not right and he wrong.

The very clearness and many-sided character of his mind often hindered and even checked altogether the best founded of his impressions, the more especially when he, as it were, stood still and thought. In reverie, the subtlety of his mind entangled him; in action, he was almost always right. Action prompted his decision. Descending from the hill he now took some refreshment, and then pushed out again in the canoe. So powerful was the current in the narrowest part of the strait that it occupied him two hours in paddling as many miles.

When he was free of the channel, he hoisted sail and directed his course straight out for an island which stood almost opposite the entrance. But as he approached, driven along at a good pace, suddenly the canoe seemed to be seized from beneath. He knew in a moment that he had grounded on soft mud, and sprang up to lower the sail, but before he could do so the canoe came to a standstill on the mud-bank,

and the waves following behind, directly she stopped, broke over the
stern. Fortunately they were but small, having only a mile or so to roll
from the shore, but they flung enough water on board in a few minutes
to spoil part of his provisions, and to set everything afloat that was
loose on the bottom of the vessel.

He was apprehensive lest she should fill, for he now perceived that
he had forgotten to provide anything with which to bale her out.
Something is always forgotten. Having got the sail down (lest the wind
should snap the mast), he tried hard to force the canoe back with his
longer paddle, used as a movable rudder. His weight and the resistance
of the adhesive mud on which she had driven with much force were too
great; he could not shove her off. When he pushed, the paddle sank
into the soft bottom, and gave him nothing to press against. After
struggling for some time he paused, beginning to fear that his voyage
had already reached an end.

A minute's thought, more potent than the strength of ten men,
showed him that the canoe required lightening. There was no cargo to
throw overboard, nor ballast. He was the only weight. He immediately
undressed, and let himself overboard at the prow, retaining hold of the
stem. His feet sank deep into the ooze; he felt as if, had he let go, he
should have gradually gone down into this quicksand of fine mud. By
rapidly moving his feet he managed, however, to push the canoe; she
rose considerably so soon as he was out of her, and, although he had
hold of the prow, still his body was lighter in the water. Pushing, struggling, and pressing forward, he, by sheer impact, as it were, for his feet
found no hold in the mud, forced her back by slow degrees.

The blows of the waves drove her forward almost as much as he
pushed her back. Still, in time, and when his strength was fast decreas-
ing, she did move, and he had the satisfaction of feeling the water
deeper beneath him. But when he endeavoured to pull himself into
the canoe over the prow, directly his motive power ceased, the waves
undid the advance he had achieved, and he had to resume his labour.
This time, thinking again, before he attempted to get into the canoe he
turned her sideways to the wind, with the outrigger to leeward. When
her sharp prow and rounded keel struck the mud-bank end on she ran
easily along it. But, turned sideways, her length found more resistance,
and though the waves sent her some way upon it, she soon came to a
standstill. He clambered in as quickly as he could (it is not easy to get
into a boat out of the water, the body feels so heavy), and, taking the
paddle, without waiting to dress, worked away from the spot.

Not till he had got some quarter of a mile back towards the mainland did he pause to dry himself and resume part of his clothing:

the canoe being still partly full of water, it was no use to put on all. Resting awhile after his severe exertions, he looked back, and now supposed, from the colour of the water and the general indications, that these shallows extended a long distance, surrounding the islands at the mouth of the channel, so that no vessel could enter or pass out in a direct line, but must steer to the north or south until the obstacle was rounded. Afraid to attempt to land on another island, his only course, as the sun was now going down, was to return to the mainland, which he reached without much trouble, as the current favoured him.

He drew the canoe upon the ground as far as he could. It was not a good place to land, as the bottom was chalk, washed into holes by the waves, and studded with angular flints. As the wind was off the shore it did not matter; if it had blown from the east, his canoe might very likely have been much damaged. The shore was overgrown with hazel to within twenty yards of the water, then the ground rose and was clothed with low ash trees, whose boughs seemed much stunted by tempest, showing how exposed the spot was to the easterly gales of spring. The south-west wind was shut off by the hills behind. Felix was so weary that for some time he did nothing save rest upon the ground, which was but scantily covered with grass. An hour's rest, however, restored him to himself.

He gathered some dry sticks (there were plenty under the ashes), struck his flint against the steel, ignited the tinder, and soon had a fire. It was not necessary for warmth, the June evening was soft and warm, but it was the hunter's instinct. Upon camping for the night the hunter, unless Bushmen are suspected to be in the neighbourhood, invariably lights a fire, first to cook his supper, and secondly, and often principally, to make the spot his home. The hearth is home, whether there be walls round it or not. Directly there are glowing embers the place is no longer wild, it becomes human. Felix had nothing that needed cooking. He took his cowhide from the canoe and spread it on the ground.

A well-seasoned cowhide is the first possession of every hunter; it keeps him from the damp; and with a second, supported on three short poles stuck in the earth (two crossed at the top in front, forming a fork, and fastened with a thong, the third resting on these), he protects himself from the heaviest rain. This little tent is always built with the back to windward. Felix did not erect a second hide, the evening was so warm and beautiful he did not need it, his cloak would be ample for covering. The fire crackled and blazed at intervals, just far enough from him that he might feel no inconvenience from its heat.

Thrushes sang in the ash wood all around him, the cuckoo called, and the chiff-chaff never ceased for a moment. Before him stretched the expanse of waters; he could even here see over the low islands. In the sky a streak of cloud was tinted by the sunset, slowly becoming paler as the light departed. He reclined in that idle, thoughtless state which succeeds unusual effort, till the deepening shadow and the sinking fire, and the appearance of a star, warned him that the night was really here. Then he arose, threw on more fuel, and fetched his cloak, his chest, and his boar-spear from the canoe. The chest he covered with a corner of the hide, wrapped himself in the cloak, bringing it well over his face on account of the dew; then, drawing the lower corners of the hide over his feet and limbs, he stretched himself at full length and fell asleep, with the spear beside him.

There was the possibility of Bushmen, but not much probability. There would be far more danger near the forest path, where they might expect a traveller and watch to waylay him, but they could not tell beforehand where he would rest that night. If any had seen the movements of his canoe, if any lighted upon his bivouac by chance, his fate was certain. He knew this, but trusted to the extreme improbability of Bushmen frequenting a place where there was nothing to plunder. Besides, he had no choice, as he could not reach the islands. If there was risk, it was forgotten in the extremity of his weariness.

CHAPTER XV

SAILING ONWARDS

WHEN Felix awoke, he knew at once by the height of the sun that the morning was far advanced. Throwing off the cloak, he stood up, but immediately crouched again, for a vessel was passing but a short distance from the shore, and nearly opposite his encampment. She had two masts, and from the flags flying, the numerous bannerets, and the movements of so many men on board, he knew her to be a ship of war. He was anxious that he should not be seen, and regretted that his canoe was so much exposed, for the bush by which he had landed hid it only from one side. As the shore was so bare and open, if they looked that way the men on board could hardly fail to see it, and might even distinguish him. But whether they were too much engaged with their own affairs, or kept a careless look-out, no notice appeared to be taken, no boat was lowered.

He watched the war ship for nearly an hour before he ventured to move. Her course was to the eastward inside the fringe of islands. That she was neither Irish nor Welsh he was certain from her build, and from her flags; they were too distant for the exact designs upon them to be seen, but near enough for him to know that they were not those displayed by the foreigners. She sailed fast, having the wind nearly aft, which suited her two square sails.

The wind had risen high during the night, and now blew almost a gale, so that he saw he must abandon for the present his project of sailing out upon the open water. The waves there would be too high for his canoe, which floated low in the water, and had but about six inches freeboard. They would wash over and possibly swamp her. Only two courses were open to him: either to sail inside the islands under shelter of the land, or to remain where he was till the breeze moderated. If he sailed inside the islands following the northward course of the merchant vessel he had observed the previous evening, that would carry him past Eaststock, the eastern port of Sypolis, which city, itself inland, had two harbours, with the western of which (Weststock) it had communication by water.

Should he continue to sail on, he would soon reach that part of the northern continent which was occupied by the Irish outposts. On the other hand, to follow the war ship, east by south, would, he knew, bring him by the great city of Aisi, famous for its commerce, its riches, and the warlike disposition of its king, Isembard. He was the acknowledged head of the forces of the League; but yet, with the inconsistency of the age, sometimes attacked other members of it. His furious energy was always disturbing the world, and Felix had no doubt he was now at war with some one or other, and that the war ship he had seen was on its way to assist him or his enemies. One of the possibilities which had impelled him to this voyage was that of taking service with some king or commander, and so perhaps gradually rising himself to command.

Such adventures were very common; knights often setting forth upon such expeditions when dissatisfied with their own rulers, and they were usually much welcomed as an addition to the strength of the camp they sought. But there was this difference, that such knights carried with them some substantial recommendation, either numerous retainers well armed and accustomed to battle, considerable treasure, or at least a reputation for prowess in the field. Felix had nothing to offer, and for nothing nothing is given.

The world does not recognise intrinsic worth, or potential genius. Genius must accomplish some solid result before it is applauded and received. The unknown architect may say: 'I have a design in my mind for an impregnable castle.' But the world cannot see or appreciate the mere design. If by any personal sacrifice of time, dignity, or self-respect the architect, after long years, can persuade some one to permit him to build the castle, to put his design into solid stone which squadrons may knock their heads against in vain, then he is acknowledged. There is then a tangible result.

Felix was in the position of the architect. He believed he had ideas; but he had nothing substantial, no result, to point to. He had therefore but little hope of success, and his natural hauteur and pride revolted against making application for enrolment which must be accompanied with much personal humiliation, since at best he could but begin in the common ranks. The very idea of asking was repugnant to him. The thought of Aurora, however, drew him on.

The pride was false, he said to himself, and arose from too high an estimate of his abilities; or it was the consequence of living so long entirely secluded from the world. He acknowledged to himself that he had not been beaten down to his level. Full of devotion to Aurora, he resolved to humble himself, to seek the humblest service in King Isembard's camp, to bow his spirit to the orders of men above him in rank but below in birth and ability, to submit to the numberless indignities of a common soldier's life.

He proceeded to launch the canoe, and had already placed the chest on board when it occurred to him that the difficulties he had encountered the previous evening, when his canoe was so nearly lost, arose from his ignorance of the channels. It would be advisable to ascend the hill, and carefully survey the coast as far as possible before setting forth. He did so. The war ship was still visible from the summit, but while he looked she was hidden by the intervening islands. The white foam and angry appearance of the distant open water direct to the eastward, showed how wise he had been not to attempt its exploration. Under the land the wind was steady; yonder, where the gale struck the surface with all its force, the waves were large and powerful.

From this spot he could see nearly the whole length of the strait, and, gazing up it in the direction he had come, he saw some boats crossing in the distance. As they moved so slowly, and appeared so broad, he conjectured that they were flat-bottomed punts, and, straining his eyes, he fancied he detected horses on board. He watched four cross, and presently the first punt returned, as if for another freight. He now noticed that there was a land route by which travellers or waggons came down from the northward, and crossed the strait by a ferry. It appeared that the ferry was not at the narrowest part of the strait, but nearer its western mouth, where the shores were flat, and covered with reeds and flags. He wondered that he had not seen anything of the landing-places, or of the ferry boats, or some sign of this traffic when he passed, but concluded that the track was hidden among the dense growth of reed and flag, and that the punts, not being in use that day, had been drawn up, and perhaps covered with green boughs to shelter them from the heat of the summer sun.

The fact of this route existing, however, gave additional importance to the establishment of a fort on the shore of the strait, as he had so long contemplated. By now, the first punt had obtained another load, and was re-crossing the channel. It was evident that a caravan of travellers or merchants had arrived, such persons usually travelling in large bodies for safety, so that the routes were often deserted for weeks together, and then suddenly covered with people. Routes, indeed, they were, and not roads; mere tracks worn through the forest and over the hills, often impassable from floods.

Still further satisfied that his original idea of a castle here was founded on a correct estimate of the value of the spot, Felix resolved to keep the conception to himself, and not again to hazard it to others, who might despise him, but adopt his design. With one long last glance at the narrow streak of water which formed the central part, as it were, of his many plans, he descended the hill, and pushed off in the canoe.

His course this time gave him much less trouble than the day before, when he had frequently to change his tack. The steady, strong breeze came off the land, to which he was too close for any waves to arise, and hour after hour passed without any necessity to shift the sail, further than to ease or tighten the sheets as the course of the land varied. By degrees the wind came more and more across his course, at right angles to it, and then began to fall aft as he described an arc, and the land projected northwards.

He saw several small villages on the shore, and passed one narrow bay, which seemed, indeed, to penetrate into the land deeper than he could actually see. Suddenly, after four or five hours sailing, he saw the tower of a church over the wooded hills. This he knew must indicate the position of Aisi. The question now came, whether he should sail into the harbour, when he would, of course, at once be seen, and have to undergo the examination of the officers; or should he land, and go on foot to the city? A minute's reflection assured him the latter was the better plan, for his canoe was of so unusual a construction, that it would be more than carefully examined, and not unlikely his little treasures would be discovered and appropriated. Without hesitation, therefore, and congratulating himself that there were no vessels in sight, he ran the canoe on shore among the flags and reeds which bordered it.

He drew her up as far as his strength permitted, and not only took down the sail, but unshipped the mast; then cutting a quantity of dead reeds, he scattered them over her, so that, unless a boat passed very close to the land, she would not be seen. While he had a meal he considered how he had better proceed. The only arms with which he excelled were the bow and arrow; clearly, therefore, if he wished an engagement, he should take these with him, and exhibit his skill. But well he knew the utter absence of law and justice except for the powerful. His bow, which he so greatly valued, and which was so well seasoned, and could be relied upon, might be taken from him.

His arrows, so carefully prepared from chosen wood, and pointed with steel, might be seized. Both bow and arrows were far superior to those used by the hunters and soldiery, and he dreaded losing them. There was his crossbow, but it was weak, and intended for killing only small game, as birds, and at short range. He could make no display with that. Sword he had none for defence; there remained only his boar-spear, and with this he resolved to be content, trusting to obtain the loan of a bow when the time came to display his skill, and that fortune would enable him to triumph with an inferior weapon.

After resting awhile and stretching his limbs, cramped in the canoe, he set out (carrying his boar-spear only) along the shore, for the thick growth of firs would not let him penetrate in the direction he had seen the tower. He had to force his way through the reeds and flags and brushwood, which flourished between the firs and the water's edge. It was hard work walking, or rather pushing through these obstacles, and he rejoiced when he emerged upon the slope of a down where there was an open sward, and but a few scattered groups of fir. The fact of it being open, and the shortness of the sward, showed at once that it was used for grazing purposes for cattle and sheep. Here he could walk freely, and soon reached the top. Thence the city was visible almost underneath him.

It stood at the base of a low narrow promontory, which ran a long way into the Lake. The narrow bank, near where it joined the mainland, was penetrated by a channel or creek, about a hundred yards wide, or less, which channel appeared to enter the land and was lost sight of among the trees. Beyond this channel a river ran into the lake, and in the Y, between the creek and the river, the city had been built.

It was surrounded with a brick wall, and there were two large round brick towers on the land side, which indicated the position of the castle and palace. The space enclosed by the walls was not more than half a mile square, and the houses did not occupy nearly all of it. There were open places, gardens, and even small paddocks among them. None of the houses were more than two storeys high, but what at once struck a stranger was the fact that they were all roofed with red tiles, most of the houses of that day being thatched or covered with shingles of wood. As Felix afterwards learnt, this had been effected during the reign of the present king, whose object was to protect his city from being set on fire by burning arrows. The encircling wall had become a dull red hue from long exposure to the weather, but the roofs were a brighter red. There was no ensign flying on either of the towers, from which he concluded that the king at that moment was absent.

CHAPTER XVI

THE CITY

SLOWLY descending towards the city, Felix looked in vain for any means of crossing the channel or creek, which extended upon this side of it, and in which he counted twenty-two merchant vessels at anchor, or moored to the bank, besides a number of smaller craft and boats. The ship of war, which had arrived before him, was beached close up by a gate of the city, which opened on the creek or port, and her crew were busily engaged discharging her stores. As he walked beside the creek trying to call the attention of some boatman to take him across, he was impressed by the silence, for though the city wall was not much more than a stone's throw distant, there was none of the usual hum which arises from the movements of people. On looking closer he noticed, too, that there were few persons on the merchant vessels, and not one gang at work loading or unloading. Except the warder stalking to and fro on the wall, and the crew of the war ship, there was no one visible. As the warder paced to and fro the blade of his partisan* gleamed in the sunshine. He must have seen Felix, but with military indifference did not pay the slightest heed to the latter's efforts to attract his attention.

He now passed the war ship, and shouted to the men at work, who were, he could see, carrying sheaves of arrows and bundles of javelins from the vessel and placing them on carts; but they did not trouble to reply. His common dress and ordinary appearance did not inspire them with any hope of payment from him if they obliged him with a boat. The utter indifference with which his approach was seen showed him the contempt in which he was held.

Looking round to see if there were no bridge or ferry, he caught sight of the grey church tower which he had observed from afar while sailing. It was quite a mile from the city, and isolated outside the walls. It stood on the slope of the hill, over whose summit the tower was visible. He wandered up towards it, as there were usually people

---

* A medieval polearm featuring a splayed or elaborately notched spearhead. Partisans are still used as a ceremonial weapon on occasion by the Queen's Yeoman of the Guard.

in or about the churches, which were always open day and night. If no one else, the porter in the lodge at the church door would be there, for he or his representative never left it, being always on the watch lest some thief should attempt to enter the treasury, or steal the sacred vessels.

But as he ascended the hill he met a shepherd, whose dogs prepared to fly at him, recognising a stranger. For a moment the man seemed inclined to let them wreak their will, if they could, for he also felt inclined to challenge a stranger, but, seeing Felix lower his spear, it probably occurred to him that some of his dogs would be killed. He therefore ordered them down, and stayed to listen. Felix learnt that there was no bridge across the creek, and only one over the river; but there was a ferry for anybody who was known. No strangers were allowed to cross the ferry; they must enter by the main road over the bridge.

'But how am I to get into the place, then?' said Felix. The shepherd shook his head, said he could not tell him, and walked away about his business.

Discouraged at these trifling vexations which seemed to cross his path at every step, Felix found his way to the ferry, but, as the shepherd had said, the boatman refused to carry him, being a stranger. No persuasion could move him; nor the offer of a small silver coin, worth about ten times his fare.

'I must then swim across,' said Felix, preparing to take off his clothes.

'Swim, if you like,' said the boatman, with a grim smile; 'but you will never land.'

'Why not?'

'Because the warder will let drive at you with an arrow.'

Felix looked, and saw that he was opposite the extreme angle of the city wall, a point usually guarded with care. There was a warder stalking to and fro; he carried a partisan, but, of course, might have his bow within reach, or could probably call to the soldiers of the guard.

'This *is* annoying,' said Felix, ready to give up his enterprise. 'How ever can I get into the city?'

The old boatman grinned, but said nothing, and returned to a net which he was mending. He made no answer to the further questions Felix put to him. Felix then shouted to the warder; the soldier looked once, but paid no more heed. Felix walked a little way and sat down on the grass. He was deeply discouraged. These repulses, trifles in themselves, assumed an importance, because his mind had long been strung up to a high pitch of tension. A stolid man would have thought nothing of them. After awhile he arose, again asking himself how should he become a leader, who had not the perseverance to enter a city in peaceful guise?

Not knowing what else to do, he followed the creek round the foot of the hill, and so onwards for a mile or more. This bank was steep, on account of the down; the other cultivated, the corn was already high. The cuckoo sang (she loves the near neighbourhood of man) and flew over the channel towards a little copse. Almost suddenly the creek wound round under a low chalk cliff, and in a moment Felix found himself confronted by another city. This had no wall; it was merely defended by a ditch and earthwork, without tower or bastion.

The houses were placed thickly together; there were, he thought, six or seven times as many as he had previously seen, and they were thatched or shingled, like those in his own country. It stood in the midst of the fields, and the corn came up to the fosse;* there were many people at work, but, as he noticed, most of them were old men bowed and feeble. A little way farther he saw a second boathouse; he hastened thither, and the ferrywoman, for the boat was poled across by a stout dame, made not the least difficulty about ferrying him over. So delighted was Felix at this unexpected fortune, that he gave her the small silver coin, at sight of which he instantly rose high in her estimation.

She explained to him, in answer to his inquiries, that this was also called Aisi; this was the city of the common folk. Those who were rich or powerful had houses in the walled city, the precinct of the Court. Many of the houses there, too, were the inns of great families who dwelt in the country in their castles, but when they came to the Court required a house. Their shields, or coats of arms, were painted over the doors. The walled city was guarded with such care, because so many attempts had been made to surprise it, and to assassinate the king, whose fiery disposition and constant wars had raised him up so many enemies. As much care was taken to prevent a single stranger entering as if he were the vanguard of a hostile army, and if he now went back (as he could do) to the bridge over the river, he would be stopped and questioned, and possibly confined in prison till the king returned.

'Where is the king?' asked Felix; 'I came to try and take service with him.'

'Then you will be welcome,' said the woman. 'He is in the field, and has just sat down before Iwis.'

'That was why the walled city seemed so empty, then,' said Felix.

---

* A defensive trench or moat, generally adjacent to a wall or fortification.

'Yes; all the people are with him; there will be a great battle this time.'

'How far is it to Iwis?' said Felix.

'Twenty-seven miles,' replied the dame; 'and if you take my advice, you had better walk twenty-seven miles there, than two miles back to the bridge over the river.'

Some one now called from the opposite bank, and she started with the boat to fetch another passenger.

'Thank you, very much,' said Felix, as he wished her good day; 'but why did not the man at the other ferry tell me I could cross here?'

The woman laughed outright. 'Do you suppose he was going to put a penny in my way when he could not get it himself?'

So mean and petty is the world! Felix entered the second city and walked some distance through it, when he recollected that he had not eaten for some time. He looked in vain for an inn, but upon speaking to a man who was leaning on his crutch at a doorway, he was at once asked to enter, and all that the house afforded was put before him. The man with the crutch sat down opposite, and remarked that most of the folk were gone to the camp, but he could not because his foot had been injured. He then went on to tell how it had happened, with the usual garrulity of the wounded. He was assisting to place the beam of a battering ram upon a truck (it took ten horses to draw it) when a lever snapped, and the beam fell. Had the beam itself touched him he would have been killed on the spot; as it was, only a part of the broken lever or pole hit him. Thrown with such force, the weight of the ram driving it, the fragment of the pole grazed his leg, and either broke one of the small bones that form the arch of the instep, or so bruised it that it was worse than broken. All the bone-setters and surgeons had gone to the camp, and he was left without attendance other than the women, who fomented the foot daily, but he had little hope of present recovery, knowing that such things were often months about.

He thought it lucky that it was no worse, for very few, he had noticed, ever recovered from serious wounds of spear or arrow. The wounded generally died; only the fortunate escaped. Thus he ran on, talking as much for his own amusement as that of his guest. He fretted because he could not join the camp and help work the artillery; he supposed the ram would be in position by now and shaking the wall with its blow. He wondered if Baron Ingulph would miss his face.

'Who's he?' asked Felix.

'He is captain of the artillery,' replied his host.

'Are you his retainer?'

'No; I am a servant.'

Felix started slightly, and did but just check himself from rising from the table. A 'servant' was a slave; it was the euphuism* used instead of the hateful word, which not even the most degraded can endure to hear. The class of the nobles to which he belonged deemed it a disgrace to sit down with a slave, to eat with him, even to accidentally touch him. With the retainers, or free men, they were on familiar terms, though despotic to the last degree; the slave was less than the dog. Then, stealing a glance at the man's face, Felix saw that he had no moustache; he had not noticed this before. No slaves were allowed to wear the moustache.

This man having been at home ill some days had neglected to shave, and there was some mark upon his upper lip. As he caught his guest's glance, the slave hung his head, and asked his guest in a low and humble voice not to mention this fault. With his face slightly flushed, Felix finished his meal; he was confused to the last degree. His long training and the tone of the society in which he had moved (though so despised a member of it) prejudiced him strongly against the man whose hospitality was so welcome. On the other hand, the ideas which had for so long worked in his mind in his solitary intercommunings in the forest were entirely opposed to servitude. In abstract principle he had long since condemned it, and desired to abolish it. But here was the fact.

He had eaten at a slave's table, and sat with him face to face. Theory and practice are often strangely at variance. He felt it an important moment; he felt that he was himself, as it were, on the balance; should he adhere to the ancient prejudice, the ancient exclusiveness of his class, or should he boldly follow the dictate of his mind? He chose the latter, and extended his hand to the servant as he rose to say goodbye. The act was significant; it recognised man as distinct from caste. The servant did not know the conflict that had taken place; but to be shaken hands with at all, even by a retainer as he supposed Felix to be, was indeed a surprise. He could not understand it; it was the first time his hand had been taken by any one of superior position since he had been born. He was dumb with amazement, and could scarcely point out the road when asked; nor did he take the small coin Felix offered, one of the few he possessed. Felix therefore left it on the table and again started.

Passing through the town, Felix followed the track which led in the

---

* Referring to a strongly mannered and artificial style of prose briefly popular in sixteenth-century England, euphuism more generally denotes artificial elegance of language. Jefferies seemingly uses the term here as a variant of euphemism.

direction indicated. In about half a mile it led him to a wider track, which he immediately recognised as the main way and road to the camp by the ruts and dust, for the sward had been trampled down for fifty yards wide, and even the corn was cut up by wheels and horses' hoofs. The army had passed, and he had but to follow its unmistakable trail.

CHAPTER XVII

THE CAMP

FELIX walked steadily on for nearly three hours, when the rough track, the dust, and heat began to tell upon him, and he sat down beside the way. The sun was now declining, and the long June day tending to its end. A horseman passed, coming from the camp, and as he wore only a sword, and had a leathern bag slung from his shoulder, he appeared to be a courier. The dust raised by the hoofs, as it rose and floated above the brushwood, rendered his course visible. Some time afterwards, while he still rested, being very weary with walking through the heat of the afternoon, he heard the sound of wheels, and two carts drawn by horses came along the track from the city.

The carts were laden with bundles of arrows, perhaps the same he had seen unloading that morning from the war ship, and were accompanied only by carters. As they approached he rose, feeling that it was time to continue his journey. His tired feet were now stiff, and he limped as he stepped out into the road. The men spoke, and he walked as well as he could beside them, using his boar-spear as a staff. There were two carters with each cart; and presently, noting how he lagged, and could scarce keep pace with them, one of them took a wooden bottle from the load on his cart, and offered him a draught of ale.

Thus somewhat refreshed, Felix began to talk, and learnt that the arrows were from the vessel in whose track he had sailed; that it had been sent loaded with stores for the king's use, by his friend the Prince of Quinton; that very great efforts had been made to get together a large army in this campaign: first, because the city besieged was so near home, and failure might be disastrous, and, secondly, because it was one of three which were all republics, and the other two would be certain to send it assistance. These cities stood in a plain, but a few miles apart, and in a straight line on the banks of the river. The king had just sat down before the first, vowing that he would knock them down, one after the other, like a row of ninepins. They asked him, in return, whose retainer he was, and he said that he was on his way to take service, and was under no banner yet.

'Then,' said the man who had given him a drink, 'if you are free like that, you had better join the king's levy, and be careful to avoid the barons' war. For if you join either of the barons' war, they will know you to be a stranger, and very likely, if they see that you are quick and active, they will not let you free again, and if you attempt to escape after the campaign, you will find yourself mightily mistaken. The baron's captain would only have to say you had always been his man; and, as for your word, it would be no more than a dog's bark. Besides which, if you rebelled, it would be only to shave off that moustache of yours, and declare you a slave, and as you have no friends in camp, a slave you would be.'

'That would be very unjust,' said Felix. 'Surely the king would not allow it?'

'How is he to know?' said another of the carters. 'My brother's boy was served just like that. He was born free, the same as all our family, but he was fond of roving, and when he reached Quinton, he was seen by Baron Robert, who was in want of men, and being a likely young fellow, they shaved his lip, and forced him to labour under the thong. When his spirit was cowed, and he seemed reconciled, they let him grow his moustache again, and there he is now, a retainer, and well treated. But still, it was against his will. Jack is right; you had better join the king's levy.'

The king's levy is composed of his own retainers from his estates, of townsmen, who are not retainers of the barons, of any knights and volunteers who like to offer their services; and a king always desires as large a levy as possible, because it enables him to overawe his barons. These, when their 'war', or forces, are collected together in camp, are often troublesome, and inclined to usurp authority. A volunteer is, therefore, always welcome in the king's levy.

Felix thanked them for the information they had given him, and said he should certainly follow their advice. He could now hardly keep up with the carts, having walked for so many hours, and undergone so much previous exertion. Finding this to be the case, he wished them good-night, and looked round for some cover. It was now dusk, and he knew he could go no farther. When they understood his intention, they consulted among themselves, and finally made him get up into one of the carts, and sit down on the bundles of arrows, which filled it like faggots. Thus he was jolted along, the rude wheels fitting but badly on the axle, and often sinking deep into a rut.

They were now in thick forest, and the track was much narrower, so that it had become worn into a hollow, as if it were the dry bed of a torrent. The horses and the carters were weary, yet they were obliged to plod on, as the arms had to be delivered before the morrow. They spoke little, except to urge the animals. Felix soon dropped into a reclining posture (uneasy as it was, it was a relief), and looking up, saw the white summer stars above. After a time he lost consciousness, and slept soundly, quite worn out, despite the jolting and creaking of the wheels.

The sound of a trumpet woke him with a start. His heavy and dreamless sleep for a moment had taken away his memory, and he did not know where he was. As he sat up two sacks fell from him; the carters had thrown them over him as a protection against the night dew. The summer morning was already as bright as noonday, and the camp about him was astir. In half a minute he came to himself, and getting out of the cart looked round. All his old interest had returned, the spirit of war entered into him, the trumpet sounded again, and the morning breeze extended the many-coloured banners.

The spot where he stood was in the rear of the main camp, and but a short distance from the unbroken forest. Upon either hand there was an intermingled mass of stores, carts, and waggons crowded together, sacks and huge heaps of forage, on and about which scores of slaves, drivers and others, were sleeping in every possible attitude, many of them evidently still under the influence of the ale they had drunk the night before. What struck him at once was the absence of any guard here in the rear. The enemy might steal out from the forest behind and help himself to what he chose, or murder the sleeping men, or, passing through the stores, fall on the camp itself. To Felix this neglect appeared inexplicable; it indicated a mental state which he could not comprehend, a state only to be described by negatives. There was no completeness, no system, no organisation; it was a kind of hap-hazard-ness, altogether opposite to his own clear and well-ordered ideas.

The ground sloped gently downwards from the edge of the forest, and the place where he was had probably been ploughed, but was now trodden flat and hard. Next in front of the stores he observed a long, low hut built of poles, and roofed with fir branches; the walls were formed of ferns, straw, bundles of hay, anything that had come to hand. On a standard beside it, a pale blue banner, with the device of a double hammer worked in gold upon it, fluttered in the wind. Twenty or thirty, perhaps more, spears leant against one end of this rude shed, their bright points projecting yards above the roof. To the right of the booth as many horses were picketed, and not far from them some soldiers were cooking at an open fire of logs. As Felix came slowly towards the booth, winding in and out among the carts and heaps of sacks, he saw that similar erections extended down the slope for a long distance.

There were hundreds of them, some large, some small, not placed in any order, but pitched where chance or fancy led, the first-comers taking the sites that pleased them, and the rest crowding round. Beside each hut stood the banner of the owner, and Felix knew from this that they were occupied by the barons, knights, and captains of the army. The retainers of each baron bivouacked as they might in the open air; some of them had hunter's hides, and others used bundles of straw to sleep on. Their fire was as close to their lord's hut as convenient, and thus there were always plenty within call.

The servants, or slaves, also slept in the open air, but in the rear of their owner's booth, and apart from the free retainers. Felix noticed, that although the huts were pitched anyhow and anywhere, those on the lowest ground seemed built along a line, and, looking closer, he found that a small stream ran there. He learnt afterwards that there was usually an emulation among the commanders to set up their standards as near the water as possible, on account of convenience, those in the rear having often to lead their horses a long distance to water. Beyond the stream the ground rose again as gradually as it had declined. It was open and cultivated up to the walls of the besieged city, which was not three-quarters of a mile distant. Felix could not for the moment distinguish the king's head-quarters. The confused manner in which the booths were built prevented him from seeing far, though from the higher ground it was easy to look over their low roofs.

He now wandered into the centre of the camp, and saw with astonishment groups of retainers everywhere eating, drinking, talking, and even playing cards or dice, but not a single officer of any rank. At last, stopping by the embers of a fire, he asked timidly if he might have breakfast. The soldiers laughed and pointed to a cart behind them, telling him to help himself. The cart was turned with the tail towards the fire, and laden with bread and sides of bacon, slices of which the retainers had been toasting at the embers.

He did as he was bid, and the next minute a soldier, not quite steady on his legs even at that hour, offered him the can, 'for,' said he, 'you had best drink whilst you may, youngster. There is always plenty of drink and good living at the beginning of a war, and very often not a drop or a bite to be got in the middle of it.' Listening to their talk as he ate his breakfast, Felix found the reason there were no officers about was because most of them had drunk too freely the night before. The king himself, they said, was put to bed as tight as a drum, and it took no small quantity to fill so huge a vessel, for he was a remarkably big man.

After the fatigue of the recent march, they had, in fact, refreshed themselves, and washed down the dust of the track. They thought that this siege was likely to be a very tough business, and congratulated themselves that it was not thirty miles to Aisi, so that so long as they stayed there they might, perhaps, get supplies of provisions with tolerable regularity. 'But if you're over the water, my lad,' said the old fellow with the can, picking his teeth with a twig, 'and have got to get your victuals by ship; by George, you may have to eat grass, or gnaw boughs like a horse.'

None of these men wore any arms, except the inevitable knife; their arms were piled against the adjacent booth, bows and quivers, spears, swords, bills and darts, thrown together just as they had cast them aside, and more or less rusty from the dew. Felix thought that had the enemy come suddenly down in force they might have made a clean sweep of the camp, for there were no defences, neither breastwork, nor fosse, nor any set guard. But he forgot that the enemy were quite as ill-organised as the besiegers, probably they were in still greater confusion, for King Isembard was considered one of the greatest, if not the very greatest military commander of his age.

The only sign of discipline he saw was the careful grooming of some horses, which he rightly guessed to be those ridden by the knights, and the equally careful polishing of pieces of armour before the doors of the huts. He wished now to inquire his way to the king's levy, but as the question rose to his lips he checked himself, remembering the caution the friendly carters had given him. He therefore determined to walk about the camp till he found some evidence that he was in the immediate neighbourhood of the king.

He rose, stood about a little while to allay any possible suspicion (quite needless precautions, for the soldiers were far too agreeably engaged to take the least notice of him), and then sauntered off with as careless an air as he could assume. Looking about him, first at a forge where the blacksmith was shoeing a horse, then at a grindstone, where a knight's sword was being sharpened, he was nearly knocked down by a horse, urged at some speed through the crowds. By a rope from the collar, three dead bodies were drawn along the ground, dusty and disfigured by bumping against stone and clod. They were those of slaves, hanged the preceding day, perhaps for pilfering, perhaps for a mere whim, since every baron had power of the gallows.

They were dragged through the camp, and out a few hundred yards beyond, and there left to the crows. This horrible sight, to which the rest were so accustomed and so indifferent that they did not even turn to look at it, deeply shocked him; the drawn and distorted features, the tongues protruding and literally licking the dust, haunted him for long after. Though his father, as a baron, possessed the same power, it had never been exercised during his tenure of the estate, so that Felix had not been hardened to the sight of executions, common enough elsewhere. Upon the Old House estate a species of negative humanity reigned; if the slaves were not emancipated, they were not hanged or cruelly beaten for trifles.

Hastening from the spot, Felix came across the artillery, which consisted of battering rams and immense crossbows; the bows were made from entire trees, or, more properly, poles. He inspected these clumsy contrivances with interest, and entered into conversation with some men who were fitting up the framework on which a battering ram was to swing. Being extremely conceited with themselves and the knowledge they had acquired from experience only (as the repeated blows of the block drive home the pile), they scarcely answered him. But, presently, as he lent a hand to assist, and bore with their churlishness without reply, they softened, and, as usual, asked him to drink, for here, and throughout the camp, the ale was plentiful, too plentiful for much progress.

Felix took the opportunity and suggested a new form of trigger for the unwieldy crossbows. He saw that as at present discharged it must require some strength, perhaps the united effort of several men, to pull away the bolt or catch. Such an effort must disconcert the aim; these crossbows were worked upon a carriage, and it was difficult to keep the carriage steady even when stakes were inserted by the low wheels. It occurred to him at once that the catch could be depressed by a lever, so that one man could discharge the bow by a mere pressure of the hand, and without interfering with the aim. The men soon understood him, and acknowledged that it would be a great improvement. One, who was the leader of the gang, thought it so valuable an idea that he went off at once to communicate with the lieutenant, who would in his turn carry the matter to Baron Ingulph, Master of the Artillery.

The others congratulated him, and asked to share in the reward that would be given to him for this invention. To whose 'war' did he belong? Felix answered, after a little hesitation, to the king's levy. At this they whispered among themselves, and Felix, again remembering the carters' caution, said that he must attend the muster (this was a pure guess), but that he would return directly afterwards. Never for a moment suspecting that he would avoid the reward they looked upon as certain, they made no opposition, and he hurried away. Pushing through the groups, and not in the least knowing where he was going, Felix stumbled at last upon the king's quarters.

CHAPTER XVIII

THE KING'S LEVY

THE king's booth stood apart from the rest; it was not much larger, but properly thatched with straw, and the wide doorway hung with purple curtains. Two standards stood beside it; one much higher than the other. The tallest bore the ensign of the kingdom; the lesser, the king's own private banner as a knight. A breastwork encircled the booth, enclosing a space about seventy yards in diameter, with a fosse, and stakes so planted as to repel assailants. There was but one gateway, opposite the general camp, and this was guarded by soldiers fully armed. A knight on horseback in armour, except his helmet, rode slowly up and down before the gate; he was the officer of the guard. His retainers, some thirty or forty men, were drawn up close by.

A distance of fifty yards intervened between this entrenchment and the camp, and was kept clear. Within the entrenchment Felix could see a number of gentlemen, and several horses caparisoned, but from the absence of noise and the fact that every one appeared to walk daintily and on tiptoe, he concluded that the king was still sleeping. The stream ran beside the entrenchment, and between it and the city; the king's quarters were at that corner of the camp highest up the brook, so that the water might not be fouled before it reached him.

The king's levy, however, did not seem to be hereabouts, for the booths nearest the head-quarters were evidently occupied by great barons, as Felix easily knew from their banners. There was here some little appearance of formality; the soldiery were not so noisy, and there were several officers moving among them. He afterwards discovered that the greater barons claimed the right to camp nearest the king, and that the king's levy was just behind their booths. But unable to discover the place, and afraid of losing his liberty if he delayed longer, Felix, after hesitating some time, determined to apply direct to the guard at the gate of the circular entrenchment.

As he crossed the open ground towards it, he noticed that the king's quarters were the closest to the enemy. Across the little stream were some corn-fields, and beyond these the walls of the city, scarcely half a mile distant. There was no outpost, the stream was but a brook, and could be crossed with ease. He marvelled at the lack of precaution; but he had yet to learn that the enemy, and all the armies of the age, were equally ignorant and equally careless.

With as humble a demeanour as he could assume, Felix doffed his cap and began to speak to the guard at the gateway of the entrenchment. The nearest man-at-arms immediately raised his spear and struck at him with the butt. The unexpected blow fell on his left shoulder, and with such force as to render it powerless. Before he could utter a remonstrance, a second had seized his boar-spear, snapped the handle across his knee, and hurled the fragments from him. Others then took him by the shoulders and thrust him back across the open space to the camp, where they kicked him and left him, bruised, and almost stupefied with indignation. His offence was approaching the king's ground with arms in his hands.

Later in the afternoon he found himself sitting on the bank of the stream far below the camp. He had wandered thither without knowing where he was going or what he was doing. His spirit for the time had been crushed, not so much by the physical brutality as by the repulse to his aspirations. Full of high hopes, and conscious of great ideas, he had been beaten like a felon hound.

From this spot beside the brook the distant camp appeared very beautiful. The fluttering banners, the green roofs of the booths (of ferns and reeds and boughs), the movement and life, for bodies of troops were now marching to and fro, and knights in gay attire riding on horseback, made a pleasant scene on the sloping ground with the forest at the back. Over the stream the sunshine lit up the walls of the threatened city, where, too, many flags were waving. Felix came somewhat to himself as he gazed, and presently acknowledged that he had only had himself to blame. He had evidently transgressed a rule, and his ignorance of the rule was no excuse, since those who had any right to be in the camp at all were supposed to understand it.

He got up, and returning slowly towards the camp, passed on his way the drinking-place, where a groom was watering some horses. The man called to him to help hold a spirited charger, and Felix mechanically did as he was asked. The fellow's mates had left him to do their work, and there were too many horses for him to manage. Felix led the charger for him back to the camp, and in return was asked to drink. He preferred food, and a plentiful supply was put before him. The groom, gossiping as he attended to his duties, said that he always welcomed the beginning of a war, for they were often half starved, and had to gnaw the bones, like the dogs, in peace. But when war was declared, vast quantities of provisions were got together, and everybody gorged at their will. The very dogs battened; he pointed to half a dozen who were tearing a raw shoulder of mutton to pieces. Before the campaign was over, those very dogs might starve. To what 'war' did Felix belong? He replied to the king's levy.

The groom said that this was the king's levy where they were; but under whose command was he? This puzzled Felix, who did not know what to say, and ended by telling the truth, and begging the fellow to advise him, as he feared to lose his liberty. The man said he had better stay where he was, and serve with him under Master Lacy, who was mean enough in the city, but liked to appear liberal when thus consorting with knights and gentlemen.

Master Lacy was a merchant of Aisi, an owner of vessels. Like most of his fellows, when war came so close home, he was almost obliged to join the king's levy. Had he not done so it would have been recorded against him as lack of loyalty. His privileges would have been taken from him, possibly the wealth he had accumulated seized, and himself reduced to slavery. Lacy, therefore, put on armour, and accompanied the king to the camp. Thus Felix, after all his aspirations, found himself serving as the knave of a mere citizen.

He had to take the horses down to water, to scour arms, to fetch wood from the forest for the fire. He was at the beck and call of all the other men, who never scrupled to use his services, and, observing that he never refused, put upon him all the more. On the other hand, when there was nothing doing, they were very kind and even thoughtful. They shared the best with him, brought him wine occasionally (wine was scarce, though ale plentiful) as a delicacy, and one, who had dexterously taken a purse, presented him with half-a-dozen copper coins as his share of the plunder. Felix, grown wiser by experience, did not dare refuse the stolen money, it would have been considered as the greatest insult; he watched his opportunity and threw it away.

The men, of course, quickly discovered his superior education, but that did not in the least surprise them, it being extremely common for unfortunate people to descend by degrees to menial offices, if once they left the estate and homestead to which they naturally belonged. There as cadets, however humble, they were certain of outward respect: once outside the influence of the head of the house, and they were worse off than the lowest retainer. His fellows would have resented any show of pride, and would speedily have made his life intolerable. As he showed none, they almost petted him, but at the same time expected him to do more than his share of the work.

Felix listened with amazement to the revelations (revelations to him) of the inner life of the camp and court. The king's weaknesses, his inordinate gluttony and continual intoxication, his fits of temper, his follies and foibles, seemed as familiar to these grooms as if they had dwelt with him. As for the courtiers and barons, there was not one whose vices and secret crimes were not perfectly well known to them. Vice and crime must have their instruments; instruments are invariably indiscreet, and thus secrets escape. The palace intrigues, the intrigues with other states, the influence of certain women, there was nothing which they did not know.

Seen thus from below, the whole society appeared rotten and corrupted, coarse to the last degree, and animated only by the lowest motives. This very gossip seemed in itself criminal to Felix, but he did not at the moment reflect that it was but the tale of servants. Had such language been used by gentlemen, then it would have been treason. As himself of noble birth, Felix had hitherto seen things only from the point of view of his own class. Now he associated with grooms, he began to see society from *their* point of view, and recognised how feebly it was held together by brute force, intrigue, cord and axe, and woman's flattery. But a push seemed needed to overthrow it. Yet it was quite secure, nevertheless, as there was none to give that push, and if any such plot had been formed, those very slaves who suffered the most would have been the very men to give information, and to torture the plotters.

Felix had never dreamed that common and illiterate men, such as these grooms and retainers, could have any conception of reasons of State, or the crafty designs of courts. He now found that, though they could neither write nor read, they had learned the art of reading man (the worst and lowest side of character) to such perfection that they at once detected the motive. They read the face; the very gait and gesture gave them a clue. They read man, in fact, as an animal. They understood men just as they understood the horses and hounds under their charge. Every mood and vicious indication in those animals was known to them, and so, too, with their masters.

Felix thought that he was himself a hunter, and understood woodcraft; he now found how mistaken he had been. He had acquired woodcraft as a gentleman; he now learned the knave's woodcraft. They taught him a hundred tricks of which he had had no idea. They stripped man of his dignity, and nature of her refinement. Everything had a blackguard side to them. He began to understand that high principles and abstract theories were only words with the mass of men.

One day he saw a knight coolly trip up a citizen (one of the king's levy) in the midst of the camp and in broad daylight, and quietly cut away his purse, at least a score of persons looking on. But they were only retainers and slaves; there was no one whose word would for a moment have been received against the knight's, who had observed this, and plundered the citizen with impunity. He flung the lesser coins to the crowd, keeping the gold and silver for himself, and walked off amid their plaudits.

Felix saw a slave nailed to a tree, his arms put round it so as to clasp it, and then nails driven through them. There he was left in his agony to perish. No one knew what his fault had been; his master had simply taken a dislike to him. A guard was set that no one should relieve the miserable being. Felix's horror and indignation could not have been expressed, but he was totally helpless.

His own condition of mind during this time was such as could not well be analysed. He did not himself understand whether his spirit had been broken, whether he was really degraded with the men with whom he lived, or why he remained with them, though there were moments when it dawned upon him that this education, rude as it was, was not without its value to him. He need not practise these evils, but it was well to know of their existence. Thus he remained, as it were, quiescent, and the days passed on. He really had not much to do, although the rest put their burdens upon him, for discipline was so lax, that the loosest attendance answered equally well with the most conscientious. The one thing all the men about him seemed to think of was the satisfying of their appetites; the one thing they rejoiced at was the fine dry weather, for, as his mates told him, the misery of camp life in rain was almost unendurable.

CHAPTER XIX

FIGHTING

TWICE Felix saw the king. Once there was a review of the horse outside the camp, and Felix, having to attend with his master's third charger (a mere show and affectation, for there was not the least chance of his needing it), was now and then very near the monarch. For that day at least he looked every whit what fame had reported him to be. A man of unusual size, his bulk rendered him conspicuous in the front of the throng. His massive head seemed to accord well with the possession of despotic power.

The brow was a little bare, for he was no longer young, but the back of his head was covered with thick ringlets of brown hair, so thick as to partly conceal the coronet of gold which he wore. A short purple cloak, scarcely reaching to the waist, was thrown back off his shoulders, so that his steel corselet glistened in the sun. It was the only armour he had on; a long sword hung at his side. He rode a powerful black horse, full eighteen hands high, by far the finest animal on the ground; he required it, for his weight must have been great. Felix passed near enough to note that his eyes were brown, and the expression of his face open, frank, and pleasing. The impression left upon the observer was that of a strong intellect, but a still stronger physique, which latter too often ran away with and controlled the former. No one could look upon him without admiration, and it was difficult to think that he could so demean himself as to wallow in the grossest indulgence.

As for the review, though it was a brilliant scene, Felix could not conceal from himself that these gallant knights were extremely irregular in their movements, and not one single evolution was performed correctly, because they were continually quarrelling about precedence, and one would not consent to follow the other. He soon understood, however, that discipline was not the object, nor regularity considered; personal courage and personal dexterity were everything. This review was the prelude to active operations, and Felix now hoped to have some practical lessons in warfare.

He was mistaken. Instead of a grand assault, or a regular approach, the fighting was merely a series of combats between small detachments and bodies of the enemy. Two or three knights with their retainers and slaves would start forth, cross the stream, and riding right past the besieged city endeavour to sack some small hamlet, or the homestead of a noble. From the city a sortie would ensue; sometimes the two bodies only threatened each other at a distance, the first retiring as the second advanced. Sometimes only a few arrows were discharged; occasionally they came to blows, but the casualties were rarely heavy.

One such party, while returning, was followed by a squadron of horsemen from the town towards the stream to within three hundred yards of the king's quarters. Incensed at this assurance, several knights mounted their horses and rode out to reinforce the returning detachment, which was loaded with booty. Finding themselves about to be supported, they threw down their spoils, faced about, and Felix saw for the first time a real and desperate *mêlée*. It was over in five minutes. The king's knights, far better horsed, and filled with desire to exhibit their valour to the camp, charged with such fury that they overthrew the enemy and rode over him.

Felix saw the troops meet; there was a crash and cracking as the lances broke, four or five rolled from the saddle on the trodden corn, and the next moment the entangled mass of men and horses unwound itself as the enemy hastened back to the walls. Felix was eager to join in such an affray, but he had no horse nor weapon. Upon another occasion early one bright morning four knights and their followers, about forty in all, deliberately set out from the camp, and advanced up the sloping ground towards the city. The camp was soon astir watching their proceedings; and the king, being made acquainted with what was going on, came out from his booth. Felix, who now entered the circular entrenchment without any difficulty, got up on the mound with scores of others, where, holding to the stakes, they had a good view.

The king stood on a bench and watched the troops advance, shading his eyes with his hand. As it was but half a mile to the walls they could see all that took place. When the knights had got within two hundred yards and arrows began to drop amongst them, they dismounted from their horses and left them in charge of the grooms, who walked them up and down, none remaining still a minute, so as to escape the aim of the enemy's archers. Then drawing their swords, the knights, who were in full armour, put themselves at the head of the band, and advanced at a steady pace to the wall. In their mail with their shields before them they cared not for such feeble archery, nor even for the darts that poured upon them when they came within reach. There was no fosse to the wall, so that, pushing forward, they were soon at the foot. So easily had they reached it that Felix almost thought the city already won. Now he saw blocks of stone, darts, and beams of wood cast at them from the parapet, which was not more than twelve feet above the ground.

Quite undismayed, the knights set up their ladders, of which they had but four, one each. The men-at-arms held these by main force against the wall, the besiegers trying to throw them away, and chopping at the rungs with their axes. But the ladders were well shod with iron to resist such blows, and in a moment Felix saw, with intense delight and admiration, the four knights slowly mount to the parapet and cut at the defenders with their swords. The gleam of steel was distinctly visible as the blades rose and fell. The enemy thrust at them with pikes, but seemed to shrink from closer combat, and a moment afterwards the gallant four stood on the top of the wall. Their figures, clad in mail and shield in hand, were distinctly seen against the sky. Up swarmed the men-at-arms behind them, and some seemed to descend on the other side. A shout rose from the camp and echoed over the woods. Felix shouted with the rest, wild with excitement.

The next minute, while yet the knights stood on the wall, and scarcely seemed to know what to do next, there appeared at least a dozen men in armour running along the wall towards them. Felix afterwards understood that the ease with which the four won the wall at first was owing to there being no men of knightly rank among the defenders at that early hour. Those who had collected to repulse the assault were citizens, retainers, slaves, any, in fact, who had been near. But now the news had reached the enemy's leaders, and some of them hastened to the wall. As these were seen approaching, the camp was hushed, and every eye strained on the combatants.

The noble four could not all meet their assailants, the wall was but wide enough for two to fight; but the other two had work enough the next minute, as eight or ten more men in mail advanced the other way. So they fought back to back, two facing one way, and two the other. The swords rose and fell. Felix saw a flash of light fly up into the air, it was the point of a sword broken off short. At the foot of the wall the men who had not had time to mount endeavoured to assist their masters by stabbing upwards with their spears.

All at once two of the knights were hurled from the wall; one seemed to be caught by his men, the other came heavily to the ground. While they were fighting their immediate antagonists, others within the wall had come with lances, and literally thrust them from the parapet. The other two still fought back to back for a moment; then, finding themselves overwhelmed, they sprang down among their friends.

The minute the two first fell, the grooms with the horses ran towards the wall, and despite the rain of arrows, darts, and stones from the parapet, Felix saw with relief three of the four knights placed on their chargers. One only could sit upright unassisted, two were supported in their saddles, and the fourth was carried by his retainers. Thus they retreated, and apparently without further hurt, for the enemy on the wall crowded so much together as to interfere with the aim of their darts, which, too, soon fell short. But there was a dark heap beneath the wall, where ten or twelve retainers and slaves, who wore no armour, had been slain or disabled. Upon these the loss invariably fell.

None attempted to follow the retreating party, who slowly returned towards the camp, and were soon apparently in safety. But suddenly a fresh party of the enemy appeared upon the wall, and the instant afterwards three retainers dropped, as if struck by lightning. They had been hit by sling stones, whirled with great force by practised slingers. These rounded pebbles come with such impetus as to stun a man at two hundred yards. The aim, it is true, is uncertain, but where there is a body of troops they are sure to strike some one. Hastening on, leaving the three fallen men where they lay, the rest in two minutes were out of range, and came safely into camp. Every one, as they crossed the stream, ran to meet them, the king included, and as he passed in the throng, Felix heard him remark that they had had a capital main of cocks* that morning.

Of the knights only one was much injured; he had fallen upon a stone, and two ribs were broken; the rest suffered from severe bruises, but had no wound. Six men-at-arms were missing, probably prisoners, for, as courageous as their masters, they had leapt down from the wall into the town. Eleven other retainers or slaves were slain, or had deserted, or were prisoners, and no trouble was taken about them. As for the three who were knocked over by the sling stones, there they lay till they recovered their senses, when they crawled into camp. This incident cooled Felix's ardour for the fray, for he reflected that, if injured thus, he too, as a mere groom, would be left. The devotion of the retainers to save and succour their masters was almost heroic. The mailed knights thought no more of their men, unless it was some particular favourite, than of a hound slashed by a boar's tusk in the chase.

When the first flush of his excitement had passed, Felix, thinking over the scene of the morning as he took his horses down to water at the stream, became filled at first with contempt, and then with indignation. That the first commander of the age should thus look on while

---

* The principal spectacle during bouts of cock-fighting, usually involving multiple birds bred by illustrious and often aristocratic patrons. In organised cock-fights, which were as much about betting as entertainment, bye-bouts (minor contests) often preceded the main of cocks.

the wall was won before his eyes, and yet never send a strong detachment, or move himself with his whole army to follow up the advantage, seemed past understanding. If he did not intend to follow it up, why permit such desperate ventures, which must be overwhelmed by mere numbers, and could result only in the loss of brave men? And if he did permit it, why did he not, when he saw they were overthrown, send a squadron to cover their retreat? To call such an exhibition of courage 'a main of cocks', to look on it as mere display for his amusement, was barbarous and cruel in the extreme. He worked himself up into a state of anger which rendered him less cautious than usual in expressing his opinions.

The king was not nearly so much at fault as Felix, arguing on abstract principles, imagined. He had had long experience of war, and he knew its extreme uncertainty. The issue of the greatest battle often hung on the conduct of a single leader, or even a single man-at-arms. He had seen walls won and lost before. To follow up such a venture with a strong detachment must result in one of two things, either the detachment in its turn must be supported by the entire army, or it must eventually retreat. If it retreated, the loss of prestige would be serious, and might encourage the enemy to attack the camp, for it was only his prestige which prevented them. If supported by the entire army, then the fate of the whole expedition depended upon that single day.

The enemy had the advantage of the wall, of the narrow streets and enclosures within, of the houses, each of which would become a fortress, and thus in the winding streets a repulse might easily happen. To risk such an event would be folly in the last degree, before the town had been dispirited and discouraged by the continuance of the siege, the failure of their provisions, or the fall of their chief leaders in the daily combats that took place.

The army had no discipline whatever, beyond that of the attachment of the retainer to his lord, and the dread of punishment on the part of the slave. There were no distinct ranks, no organised corps. The knights followed the greater barons, the retainers the knights; the greater barons followed the king. Such an army could not be risked in an assault of this kind. The venture was not ordered, nor was it discouraged; to discourage, indeed, all attempts would have been bad policy; it was upon the courage and bravery of his knights that the king depended, and upon that alone rested his hopes of victory.

The great baron whose standard they followed would have sent them assistance if he had deemed it necessary. The king, unless on the day of battle, would not trouble about such a detail. As for the remark, that they had had 'a good main of cocks that morning', he simply expressed the feeling of the whole camp. The spectacle Felix had seen was, in fact, merely an instance of the strength and of the weakness of the army and the monarchy itself.

Felix afterwards acknowledged these things to himself, but at the moment, full of admiration for the bravery of the four knights and their followers, he was full of indignation, and uttered his views too freely. His fellow-grooms cautioned him; but his spirit was up, and he gave way to his feelings without restraint. Now, to laugh at the king's weaknesses, his gluttony or follies, was one thing; to criticise his military conduct was another. The one was merely badinage, and the king himself might have laughed had he heard it; the other was treason, and, moreover, likely to touch the monarch on the delicate matter of military reputation.

Of this Felix quickly became aware. His mates, indeed, tried to shield him; but possibly the citizen, his master, had enemies in the camp, barons, perhaps, to whom he had lent money, and who watched for a chance of securing his downfall. At all events, early the next day Felix was rudely arrested by the provost in person, bound with cords, and placed in the provost's booth. At the same time, his master was ordered to remain within, and a guard was put over him.

CHAPTER XX

IN DANGER

HOPE died within Felix when he thus suddenly found himself so near the executioner. He had known so many butchered without cause, that he had, indeed, reason to despair. Towards the sunset he felt sure he should be dragged forth and hanged on the oak used for the purpose and which stood near where the track from Aisi joined the camp. Such would most probably have been his fate, had he been alone concerned in this affair, but by good fortune he was to escape so miserable an end. Still, he suffered as much as if the rope had finished him, for he had no means of knowing what would be the result.

His heart swelled with bitterness; he was filled with inexpressible indignation, his whole being rebelled against the blundering, as it were, of events which had thus thrown him into the jaws of death. In an hour or two, however, he sufficiently recovered from the shock to reflect that most probably they would give him some chance to speak for himself. There would not be any trial; who would waste time in trying so insignificant a wretch? But there might be some opportunity of speaking, and he resolved to use it to the utmost possible extent.

He would arraign the unskilful generalship of the king; he would not only point out his errors, but how the enemy could be defeated. He would prove that he had ideas and plans worthy of attention. He would, as it were, vindicate himself before he was executed, and he tried to collect his thoughts and to put them into form. Every moment the face of Aurora seemed to look upon him, lovingly and mournfully; but beside it he saw the dusty and distorted features of the corpse he had seen drawn by the horse through the camp. Thus, too, his tongue would protrude and lick the dust. He endured, in a word, those treble agonies which the highly wrought and imaginative inflict upon themselves.

The hours passed, and still no one came near him; he called, and the guard appeared at the door, but only to see what was the matter, and finding his prisoner safe, at once resumed his walk to and fro. The soldier did not, for his own sake, dare to enter into conversation with a prisoner under arrest for such an offence; he might be involved, or suspected. Had it been merely theft or any ordinary crime, he would have talked freely enough, and sympathised with his prisoner. As time went on, Felix grew thirsty, but his request for water was disregarded, and there he remained till four in the afternoon. They then marched him out; he begged to be allowed to speak, but the soldiery did not reply, simply hurrying him forward. He now feared that he should be executed without the chance being afforded him to say a word; but, to his surprise, he found in a few minutes that they were taking him in the direction of the king's quarters. New fears now seized him, for he had heard of men being turned loose, made to run for their lives, and hunted down with hounds for the amusement of the Court.

If the citizen's wealth had made him many enemies (men whom he had befriended, and who hoped, if they could but see him executed, to escape the payment of their debts), on the other hand, it had made him as many friends, that is, interested friends, who trusted by doing him service to obtain advances. These latter had lost no time, for greed is quite as eager as hate, and carried the matter at once to the king. What they desired was that the case should be decided by the monarch himself, and not by his chancellor, or a judge appointed for the purpose. The judge would be nearly certain to condemn the citizen, and to confiscate whatever he could lay hands on. The king might pardon, and would be content with a part only, where his ministers would grasp all.

These friends succeeded in their object; the king, who hated all judicial affairs because they involved the trouble of investigation, shrugged his shoulders at the request, and would not have granted it had it not come out that the citizen's servant had declared him to be an incapable commander. At this the king started. 'We are, indeed, fallen low,' said he, 'when a miserable trader's knave calls us incapable. We will see this impudent rascal.' He accordingly ordered that the prisoner should be brought before him after dinner.

Felix was led inside the entrenchment, unbound, and commanded to stand upright. There was a considerable assembly of the greater barons anxious to see the trial of the money-lender, who, though present, was kept apart from Felix lest the two should arrange their defence. The king was sleeping on a couch outside the booth in the shade; he was lying on his back breathing loudly with open mouth. How different his appearance to the time when he sat on his splendid charger and reviewed his knights! A heavy meal had been succeeded by as heavy a slumber. No one dared to disturb him; the assembly moved on tiptoe and conversed in whispers. The experienced divined that the prisoners were certain to be condemned, for the king would wake with indigestion, and vent his uneasy sensations upon them. Full an hour elapsed before the king awoke with a snort and called for a draught of water. How Felix envied that draught! He had neither eaten nor drunk since the night previous; it was a hot day, and his tongue was dry and parched.

The citizen was first accused; he denied any treasonable designs or expressions whatever; as for the other prisoner, till the time he was arrested he did not even know he had been in his service. He was some stroller whom his grooms had incautiously engaged, the lazy scoundrels, to assist them. He had never even spoken to him; if the knave told the truth he must acknowledge this.

'How now,' said the king, turning to Felix; 'what do you say?'

'It is true,' replied Felix, 'he has never spoken to me nor I to him. He knew nothing of what I said. I said it on my own account, and I say it again!'

'And pray, sir knave,' said the king, sitting up on his couch, for he was surprised to hear one so meanly dressed speak so correctly, and so boldly face him. 'What was it you did say?'

'If your majesty will order me a single drop of water,' said the prisoner, 'I will repeat it word for word, but I have had nothing the whole day, and I can hardly move my tongue.'

Without a word the king handed him the cup from which he had himself drunk. Never, surely, was water so delicious. Felix drained it to the bottom, handed it back (an officer took it), and with one brief thought of Aurora, he said: 'Your majesty, you are an incapable commander.'

'Go on,' said the king, sarcastically; 'why am I incapable?'

'You have attacked the wrong city; these three are all your enemies, and you have attacked the first. They stand in a row.'

'They stand in a row,' repeated the king; 'and we will knock them over like three nine-pins.'

'But you have begun with the end one,' said Felix, 'and that is the mistake. For after you have taken the first you must take the second, and still after that the third. But you might have saved much trouble and time if——'

'If what?'

'If you had assaulted the middle one first. For then, while the siege went on, you would have been able to prevent either of the other two towns from sending assistance, and when you had taken the first and put your garrison in it, neither of the others could have stirred, or reaped their corn, nor could they even communicate with each other, since you would be between them; and in fact you would have cut your enemies in twain.'

'By St. John!' swore the king; 'it is a good idea. I begin to think——but go on, you have more to say.'

'I think, too, your majesty, that by staying here as you have done this fortnight past without action, you have encouraged the other two cities to make more desperate resistance; and it seems to me that you are in a dangerous position, and may at any moment be overwhelmed with disaster, for there is nothing whatever to prevent either of the other two from sending troops to burn the open city of Aisi in your absence. And that danger must increase every day as they take courage by your idleness.'

'Idleness! There shall be idleness no longer. The man speaks the truth; we will consider further of this, we will move on Adelinton,' turning to his barons.

'If it please your majesty,' said Baron Ingulph, 'this man invented a new trigger for our carriage cross-bows, but he was lost in the crowd, and we have sought for him in vain; my serjeant here has this moment recognised him.'

'Why did you not come to us before, fellow?' said the king. 'Let him be released; let him be entertained at our expense; give him clothes and a sword. We will see you further.'

Overjoyed at this sudden turn of fortune, Felix forgot to let well alone. He had his audience with him for a moment; he could not resist as it were following up his victory. He thanked the king, and added that he could make a machine which would knock the walls yonder to pieces without it being necessary to approach nearer than half a bow-shot.

'What is this?' said the king. 'Ingulph, have you ever heard of such a machine?'

'There is no such thing,' said the Baron, beginning to feel that his professional reputation as the master of the artillery was assailed. 'There is nothing of the kind known.'

'It will shoot stones as big, as heavy as a man can lift,' said Felix eagerly, 'and knock towers to fragments.'

The king looked from one to another; he was incredulous. The Baron smiled scornfully. 'Ask him, your majesty, how these stones are to be thrown; no bow could do it.'

'How are the stones to be thrown?' said the king sharply. 'Beware how you play with us.'

'By the force of twisted ropes, your majesty.'

They all laughed. The Baron said: 'You see, your majesty, there is nothing of the kind. This is some jester.'

'The twisted rope should be a halter,' said another courtier, one of those who hoped for the rich man's downfall.

'It can be done, your majesty,' cried Felix, alarmed. 'I assure you, a stone of two hundred weight might be thrown a quarter of a mile.'

The assembly did not repress its contempt.

'The man is a fool,' said the king, who now thought that Felix was a jester who had put a trick upon him. 'But your joke is out of joint; I will teach such fellows to try tricks on us! Beat him out of camp.'

The provost's men seized him, and in a moment he was dragged off his feet, and bodily carried outside the entrenchment. Thence they pushed him along, beating him with the butts of their spears to make him run the faster; the groups they passed laughed and jeered; the dogs barked and snapped at his ankles. They hurried him outside the camp, and thrusting him savagely with their spear butts sent him headlong. There they left him, with the caution which he did not hear, being insensible, that if he ventured inside the lines he would be at once hanged. Like a dead dog they left him on the ground.

Some hours later, in the dusk of the evening, Felix stole from the spot, skirting the forest like a wild animal afraid to venture from its cover, till he reached the track which led to Aisi. His one idea was to reach his canoe. He would have gone through the woods, but that was not possible. Without axe or wood-knife to hew a way, the tangled brushwood he knew to be impassable, having observed how thick it was when coming. Aching and trembling in every limb, not so much with physical suffering as that kind of inward fever which follows unmerited injury, the revolt of the mind against it, he followed the track as fast as his weary frame would let him. He had tasted nothing that day but the draught from the king's cup, and a second draught when he recovered consciousness, from the stream that flowed past the camp. Yet he walked steadily on without pause; his head hung forward, and his arms were listless, but his feet mechanically plodded on. He walked, indeed, by his will, and not with his sinews. Thus, like a ghost, for there was no life in him, he traversed the shadowy forest.

The dawn came, and still he kept onwards. As the sun rose higher, having now travelled fully twenty miles, he saw houses on the right of the trail. They were evidently those of retainers or workmen employed on the manor, for a castle stood at some distance.

An hour later he approached the second or open city of Aisi, where the ferry was across the channel. In his present condition he could not pass through the town. No one there knew of his disgrace, but it was the same to him as if they had. Avoiding the town itself, he crossed the cultivated fields, and upon arriving at the channel at once stepped in, and swam across to the opposite shore. It was not more than sixty yards, but, weary as he was, it was an exhausting effort. He sat down, but immediately got up and struggled on.

The church tower on the slope of the hill was a landmark by which he easily discovered the direction of the spot where he had hidden the canoe. But he felt unable to push through the belt of brushwood, reeds, and flags beside the shore, and therefore struck through the firs, following a cattle track, which doubtless led to another grazing ground. This ran parallel with the shore, and when he judged himself about level with the canoe he left it, and entered the wood itself. For a little way he could walk, but the thick fir branches soon blocked his progress, and he could progress only on hands and knees, creeping beneath them. There was a hollow space under the lower branches free from brushwood.

Thus he painfully approached the Lake, and descending the hill, after an hour's weary work emerged among the rushes and reeds. He was within two hundred yards of the canoe, for he recognised the island opposite it. In ten minutes he found it undisturbed and exactly as he had left it, except that the breeze had strewn the dry reeds with which it was covered with willow leaves, yellow and dead (they fall while all the rest are green), which had been whirled from the branches. Throwing himself upon the reeds beside the canoe, he dropped asleep as if he had been dead.

He awoke as the sun was sinking and sat up, hungry in the extreme, but much refreshed. There were still some stores in the canoe, of which he ate ravenously. But he felt better now; he felt at home beside his boat. He could hardly believe in the reality of the hideous dream through which he had passed. But when he tried to stand, his feet, cut and blistered, only too painfully assured him of its reality. He took out his hunter's hide and cloak and spread himself a comfortable bed. Though he had slept so long he was still weary. He reclined in a semi-unconscious state, his frame slowly recovering from the strain it had endured, till by degrees he fell asleep again. Sleep, nothing but sleep, restores the over-taxed mind and body.

CHAPTER XXI

A VOYAGE

THE sun was up when Felix awoke, and as he raised himself the beauty of the Lake before him filled him with pleasure. By the shore it was so calm that the trees were perfectly reflected, and the few willow leaves that had fallen floated without drifting one way or the other. Farther out the islands were lit up with the sunlight, and the swallows skimmed the water, following the outline of their shores. In the Lake beyond them, glimpses of which he could see through the channel or passage between, there was a ripple where the faint south-western breeze touched the surface. His mind went out to the beauty of it. He did not question or analyse his feelings; he launched his vessel, and left that hard and tyrannical land for the loveliness of the water.

Paddling out to the islands he passed through between them, and reached the open Lake. There he hoisted the sail, the gentle breeze filled it, the sharp cutwater* began to divide the ripples, a bubbling sound arose, and steering due north, straight out to the open and boundless expanse, he was carried swiftly away.

The mallards, who saw the canoe coming, at first scarcely moved, never thinking that a boat would venture outside the islands, within whose line they were accustomed to see vessels, but when the canoe continued to bear down upon them, they flew up and descended far away to one side. When he had sailed past the spot where these birds had floated, the Lake was his own. By the shores of the islands the crows came down for mussels. Moorhens swam in and out among the rushes, water-rats nibbled at the flags, pikes basked at the edge of the weeds, summer-snipes ran along the sand, and doubtless an otter here and there was in concealment. Without the line of the shoals and islets, now that the mallards had flown, there was a solitude of water. It was far too deep for the longest weeds, nothing seemed to exist here. The very water-snails seek the shore, or are drifted by the currents into shallow corners. Neither great nor little care for the broad expanse.

The canoe moved more rapidly as the wind came now with its full force over the distant woods and hills, and though it was but a

* The forward edge of a ship's or boat's prow.

light southerly breeze, the broad sail impelled the taper vessel swiftly. Reclining in the stern, Felix lost all consciousness of aught but that he was pleasantly borne along. His eyes were not closed, and he was aware of the canoe, the Lake, the sunshine, and the sky, and yet he was asleep. Physically awake, he mentally slumbered. It was rest. After the misery, exertion, and excitement of the last fortnight it was rest, intense rest for body and mind. The pressure of the water against the handle of the rudder-paddle, the slight vibration of the wood, as the bubbles rushed by beneath, alone perhaps kept him from really falling asleep. This was something which could not be left to itself; it must be firmly grasped, and that effort restrained his drowsiness.

Three hours passed. The shore was twelve or fifteen miles behind, and looked like a blue cloud, for the summer haze hid the hills, more than would have been the case in clearer weather.

Another hour, and at last Felix, awakening from his slumberous condition, looked round and saw nothing but the waves. The shore he had left had entirely disappeared, gone down; if there were land more lofty on either hand, the haze concealed it. He looked again; he could scarcely comprehend it. He knew the Lake was very wide, but it had never occurred to him that he might possibly sail out of sight of land. This, then, was why the mariners would not quit the islands; they feared the open water. He stood up and swept the horizon carefully, shading his eyes with his hand; there was nothing but a mist at the horizon. He was alone with the sun, the sky, and the Lake. He could not surely have sailed into the ocean without knowing it? He sat down, dipped his hand overboard and tasted the drops that adhered; the water was pure and sweet, warm from the summer sunshine.

There was not so much as a swift in the upper sky; nothing but slender filaments of white cloud. No swallows glided over the surface of the water. If there were fishes he could not see them through the waves, which were here much larger; sufficiently large, though the wind was light, to make his canoe rise and fall with their regular rolling. To see fishes a calm surface is necessary, and, like other creatures, they haunt the shallows and the shore. Never had he felt alone like this in the depths of the farthest forest he had penetrated. Had he contemplated beforehand the possibility of passing out of sight of land, when he found that the time had arrived he would probably have been alarmed and anxious for his safety. But thus stumbling drowsily into the solitude of the vast Lake, he was so astounded with his own discovery, so absorbed in thinking of the immense expanse, that the idea of danger did not occur to him.

Another hour passed, and he now began to gaze about him more eagerly for some sign of land, for he had very little provision with him, and he did not wish to spend the night upon the Lake. Presently, however, the mist on the horizon ahead appeared to thicken, and then became blue, and in a shorter time than he expected land came in sight. This arose from the fact of its being low, so that he had approached nearer than he knew before recognising it. At the time when he was really out of sight of the coast, he was much farther from the hilly land left behind than from the low country in front, and not in the mathematical centre, as he had supposed, of the Lake. As it rose and came more into sight, he already began to wonder what reception he should meet with from the inhabitants, and whether he should find them as hard of heart as the people he had just escaped from. Should he, indeed, venture among them at all? Or should he remain in the woods till he had observed more of their ways and manners? These questions were being debated in his mind, when he perceived that the wind was falling.

As the sun went past the meridian the breeze fell, till, in the hottest part of the afternoon, and when he judged that he was not more than eight miles from shore, it sank to the merest zephyr, and the waves by degrees diminished. So faint became the breeze in half-an-hour's time, and so intermittent, that he found it patience wasted even to hold the rudder-paddle. The sail hung and was no longer bellied out; as the idle waves rolled under, it flapped against the mast. The heat was now so intolerable, the light reflected from the water increasing the sensation, that he was obliged to make himself some shelter by partly lowering the sail, and hauling the yard athwart the vessel, so that the canvas acted as an awning. Gradually the waves declined in volume, and the gentle breathing of the wind ebbed away, till at last the surface was almost still, and he could feel no perceptible air stirring.

Weary of sitting in the narrow boat, he stood up, but he could not stretch himself sufficiently for the change to be of much use. The long summer day, previously so pleasant, now appeared scarcely endurable. Upon the silent water the time lingered, for there was nothing to mark its advance, not so much as a shadow beyond that of his own boat. The waves having now no crest, went under the canoe without chafing against it, or rebounding, so that they were noiseless. No fishes rose to the surface. There was nothing living near, except a blue butterfly, which settled on the mast, having ventured thus far from land. The vastness of the sky, over-arching the broad water, the sun, and the motionless filaments of cloud, gave no repose for his gaze, for they were seemingly still. To the weary glance motion is repose; the waving boughs, the foam-tipped waves, afford positive rest to look at. Such intense stillness as this of the summer sky was oppressive; it was like living in space itself, in the ether above. He welcomed at last the gradual downward direction of the sun, for, as the heat decreased, he could work with the paddle.

Presently he furled the sail, took his paddle, and set his face for the land. He laboured steadily, but made no apparent progress. The canoe was heavy, and the outrigger or beam which was of material use in sailing, was a drawback to paddling. He worked till his arms grew weary, and still the blue land seemed as far off as ever.

But by the time the sun began to approach the horizon, his efforts had produced some effect, the shore was visible, and the woods beyond. They were still five miles distant, and he was tired; there was little chance of his reaching it before night. He put his paddle down for refreshment and rest, and while he was thus engaged, a change took place. A faint puff of air came; a second, and a third; a tiny ripple ran along the surface. Now he recollected he had heard that the mariners depended a great deal on the morning and the evening, the land and the Lake, breeze as they worked along the shore. This was the first breath of the land breeze. It freshened after awhile, and he re-set his sail.

An hour or so afterwards he came near the shore; he heard the thrushes singing, and the cuckoo calling, long before he landed. He did not stay to search about for a creek, but ran the canoe on the strand, which was free of reeds or flags, a sign that the waves often beat furiously there, rolling as they must for so many miles. He hauled the canoe up as high as he could, but presently when he looked about him he found that he was on a small and narrow island, with a channel in the rear. Tired as he was, yet anxious for the safety of his canoe, he pushed off again, and paddled round and again beached her with the island between her and the open Lake. Else he feared if a south wind should blow she might be broken to pieces on the strand before his eyes. It was prudent to take the precaution, but, as it happened, the next day the Lake was still.

He could see no traces of human occupation upon the island, which was of small extent and nearly bare, and therefore, in the morning, paddled across the channel to the mainland, as he thought. But upon exploring the opposite shore, it proved not to be the mainland, but merely another island. Paddling round it, he tried again, but with the same result; he found nothing but island after island, all narrow, and bearing nothing except bushes. Observing a channel which seemed to go straight in among these islets, he resolved to follow it, and did so (resting at noon-time) the whole morning. As he paddled slowly in, he found the water shallower, and weeds, bulrushes, and reeds became thick, except quite in the centre.

After the heat of midday had gone over, he resumed his voyage, and still found the same; islets and banks, more or less covered with hawthorn bushes, willow, elder, and alder, succeeded to islets, fringed round their edges with reeds and reed canary-grass. When he grew weary of paddling, he landed and stayed the night; the next day he went on again, and still for hour after hour rowed in and out among these banks and islets, till he began to think he should never find his way out.

The farther he penetrated the more numerous became the waterfowl. Ducks swam among the flags, or rose with a rush and splashing. Coots and moorhens dived and hid in the reeds. The lesser grebe sank at the sound of the paddle like a stone. A strong northern diver raised a wave as he hurried away under the water, his course marked by the undulation above him. Sedge-birds chirped in the willows; black-headed buntings sat on the trees, and watched him without fear. Bearded titmice were there, clinging to the stalks of the sedges, and long-necked herons rose from the reedy places where they love to wade. Blue dragonflies darted to and fro, or sat on water-plants as if they were flowers. Snakes swam across the channels, vibrating their heads from side to side. Swallows swept over his head. Pike 'stuck' from the verge of the thick weeds as he came near. Perch rose for insects as they fell helpless into the water.

He noticed that the water, though so thick with reeds, was as clear as that in the open Lake; there was no scum such as accumulates in stagnant places. From this he concluded that there must be a current, however slight, perhaps from rivers flowing into this part of the Lake. He felt the strongest desire to explore farther till he reached the mainland, but he reflected that mere exploration was not his object; it would never obtain Aurora for him. There were no signs whatever of human habitation, and from reeds and bulrushes, however interesting, nothing could be gained. Reluctantly, therefore, on the third morning, having passed the night on one of the islets, he turned his canoe, and paddled southwards towards the Lake.

He did not for a moment attempt to retrace the channel by which he had entered; it would have been an impossibility; he took advantage of any clear space to push through. It took him as long to get out as it had to get in; it was the afternoon of the fourth day when he at last regained the coast. He rested the remainder of the afternoon, wishing to start fresh in the morning, having determined to follow the line of the shore eastwards, and so gradually to circumnavigate the Lake. If he succeeded in nothing else, that at least would be something to relate to Aurora.

The morning rose fair and bright, with a southwesterly air rather than a breeze. He sailed before it; it was so light that his progress could not have exceeded more than three miles an hour. Hour after hour passed away, and still he followed the line of the shore, now going a short way out to skirt an island, and now nearer in to pass between sandbanks. By noon he was so weary of sitting in the canoe that he ran her ashore, and rested awhile.

It was the very height of the heat of the day when he set forth again, and the wind lighter than in the morning. It had, however, changed a little, and blew now from the west, almost too exactly abaft to suit his craft. He could not make a map while sailing, or observe his position accurately, but it appeared to him that the shore trended towards the south-east, so that he was gradually turning an arc. He supposed from this that he must be approaching the eastern end of the Lake. The water seemed shallower, to judge from the quantity of weeds. Now and then he caught glimpses between the numerous islands of the open Lake, and there, too, the weeds covered the surface in many places.

In an hour or two the breeze increased considerably, and travelling so much quicker, he found it required all his dexterity to steer past the islands and clear the banks upon which he was drifting. Once or twice he grazed the willows that overhung the water, and heard the keel of the canoe drag on the bottom. As much as possible he bore away from the mainland, steering south-east, thinking to find deeper water, and to be free of the islets. He succeeded in the first, but the islets were now so numerous that he could not tell where the open Lake was. The farther the afternoon advanced, the more the breeze freshened, till occasionally, as it blew between the islands, it struck his mast almost with the force of a gale. Felix welcomed the wind, which would enable him to make great progress before evening. If such favouring breezes would continue, he could circumnavigate the waters in a comparatively short time, and might return to Aurora, so far, at least, successful. Hope filled his heart, and he sang to the wind.

The waves could not rise among these islands, which intercepted them before they could roll far enough to gather force, so that he had all the advantage of the gale without its risks. Except a light haze all round the horizon, the sky was perfectly clear, and it was pleasant now the strong current of air cooled the sun's heat. As he came round the islands he constantly met and disturbed parties of waterfowl, mallards, and coots. Sometimes they merely hid in the weeds, sometimes they rose, and when they did so passed to his rear.

CHAPTER XXII

DISCOVERIES

THIS little circumstance of the mallards always flying over him and away behind, when flushed, presently made Felix speculate on the cause, and he kept a closer watch. He now saw (what had, indeed, been going on for some time) that there was a ceaseless stream of waterfowl, mallards, ducks, coots, moorhens, and lesser grebes coming towards him, swimming to the westward. As they met him they parted and let him through, or rose and went over. Next he noticed that the small birds on the islands were also travelling in the same direction, that is against the wind. They did not seem in any haste, but flitted from islet to islet, bush to tree, feeding and gossiping as they went; still the movement was distinct.

Finches, linnets, blackbirds, thrushes, wrens, and whitethroats, and many others, all passed him, and he could see the same thing going on to his right and left. Felix became much interested in this migration, all the more singular as it was the nesting-time, and hundreds of these birds must have left their nests with eggs or young behind them. Nothing that he could think of offered an adequate explanation. He imagined he saw shoals of fishes going the same way, but the surface of the water being ruffled, and the canoe sailing rapidly, he could not be certain. About an hour after he first observed the migration the stream of birds ceased suddenly.

There were no waterfowls in the water, and no finches in the bushes. They had evidently all passed. Those in the van of the migratory army were no doubt scattered and thinly distributed, so that he had been meeting the flocks a long while before he suspected it. The nearer he approached their centre the thicker they became, and on getting through that he found a solitude. The weeds were thicker than ever, so that he had constantly to edge away from where he supposed the mainland to lie. But there were no waterfowls and no birds on the islets. Suddenly as he rounded a large island he saw what for the moment he imagined to be a line of white surf, but the next instant he recognised a solid mass, as it were, of swallows and martins flying just over the surface of the water straight towards him. He had no time to notice how far they extended before they had gone by him with a rushing sound.

Turning to look back, he saw them continue directly west in the teeth of the wind.

Like the water and the islands, the sky was now cleared of birds, and not a swallow remained. Felix asked himself if he were running into some unknown danger, but he could not conceive any. The only thing that occurred to him was the possibility of the wind rising to a hurricane; that gave him no alarm, because the numerous islands would afford shelter. So complete was the shelter in some places, that as he passed along his sail drew above, while the surface of the water, almost surrounded with bushes and willows, was smooth. No matter to how many quarters of the compass the wind might veer, he should still be able to get under the lee of one or other of the banks.

The sky remained without clouds; there was nothing but a slight haze, which he sometimes fancied looked thicker in front or to the eastward. There was nothing whatever to cause the least uneasiness; on the contrary, his curiosity was aroused, and he was desirous of discovering what it was that had startled the birds. After a while the water became rather more open, with sandbanks instead of islands, so that he could see around him for a considerable distance. By a large bank, behind which the ripple was stilled, he saw a low wave advancing towards him, and moving against the wind. It was followed by two others at short intervals, and though he could not see them, he had no doubt shoals of fishes were passing and had raised the undulations.

The sedges on the sandbanks appeared brown and withered, as if it had been autumn instead of early summer. The flags were brown at the tip, and the aquatic grasses had dwindled. They looked as if they could not grow, and had reached but half their natural height. From the low willows the leaves were dropping, faded and yellow, and the thorn-bushes were shrivelled and covered with the white cocoons of caterpillars. The farther he sailed the more desolate the banks seemed, and trees ceased altogether. Even the willows were fewer and stunted, and the highest thorn-bush was not above his chest. His vessel was now more exposed to the wind, so that he drove past the banks and scattered islands rapidly, and he noticed that there was not so much as a crow on them. Upturned mussel-shells, glittering in the sunshine, showed where crows had been at work, but there was not one now visible.

Felix thought the water had lost its clearness and had become thick, which he put down to the action of the wavelets disturbing the sand in the shallows. Ahead the haze, or mist, was now much thicker, and was apparently not over a mile distant. It hid the islands and concealed everything. He expected to enter it immediately, but it receded

as he approached. Along the strand of an island he passed there was
a dark line like a stain, and in still water under the lee the surface was
covered with a floating scum. Felix, on seeing this, at once concluded
that he had unknowingly entered a gulf, and had left the main Lake,
for the only place he had ever seen scum before was at the extremity of a creek near home, where the water was partly stagnant on a
marshy level. The water of the Lake was proverbial for its purity and
clearness.

He kept, therefore, a sharp look-out, expecting every moment to
sight the end of the gulf or creek in which he supposed himself sailing,
so that he might be ready to lower his sail. By degrees the wind had
risen till it now blew with fury, but the numerous sandflats so broke
up the waves that he found no inconvenience from them. One solitary
gull passed over at a great height, flying steadily westwards against the
wind. The canoe now began to overtake fragments of scum drifting
before the wind, and rising up and down on the ripples. Once he saw
a broad piece rise to the surface together with a quantity of bubbles.
None of the sandbanks now rose more than a foot or so above the surface, and were entirely bare, mere sand and gravel.

The mist ahead was sensibly nearer, and yet it eluded him; it was
of a faint yellow, and though so thin, obscured everything where it
hovered. From out of the mist there presently appeared a vast stretch
of weeds. They floated on the surface and undulated to the wavelets, a
pale yellowish green expanse. Felix was hesitating whether to lower his
sail or attempt to drive over them, when, as he advanced and the mist
retreated, he saw open water beyond. The weeds extended on either
hand as far as he could see, but they were only a narrow band, and
he hesitated no longer. He felt the canoe graze the bottom once as he
sailed over the weeds. The water was free of sandbanks beyond them,
but he could see large islands looming in several directions.

Glancing behind him he perceived that the faint yellow mist had
closed in and now encircled him. It came within two or three hundred
yards, and was not affected by the wind, rough as it was. Quite suddenly he noticed that the water on which the canoe floated was black.
The wavelets which rolled alongside were black, and the slight spray
that occasionally flew on board was black, and stained the side of
the vessel. This greatly astonished and almost shocked him; it was so
opposite and contrary to all his ideas about the Lake, the very mirror
of purity. He leant over, and dipped up a little in the palm of his hand;
it did not appear black in such a small quantity, it seemed a rusty
brown, but he became aware of an offensive odour. The odour clung
to his hand, and he could not remove it, to his great disgust. It was like

nothing he had ever smelt before, and not in the least like the vapour of marshes.

By now being some distance from any island, the wavelets increased in size, and spray flew on board, wetting everything with this black liquid. Instead of level marshes and the end of the gulf, it appeared as if the water were deep, and also as if it widened. Exposed to the full press of the gale, Felix began to fear that he should not be able to return very easily against it. He did not know what to do. The horrid blackness of the water disposed him to turn about and tack out; on the other hand, having set out on a voyage of discovery, and having now found something different to the other parts of the Lake, he did not like to retreat. He sailed on, thinking to presently pass these loathsome waters.

He was now hungry, and indeed thirsty, but was unable to drink because he had no water-barrel. No vessel sailing on the Lake ever carried a water-barrel, since such pure water was always under their bows. He was cramped, too, with long sitting in the canoe, and the sun was perceptibly sloping in the west. He determined to land and rest, and with this purpose steered to the right under the lee of a large island, so large, indeed, that he was not certain it was not part of the mainland or one side of the gulf. The water was deep close up to the shore, but, to his annoyance, the strand appeared black, as if soaked with the dark water. He skirted along somewhat farther, and found a ledge of low rocks stretching out into the Lake, so that he was obliged to run ashore before coming to these.

On landing, the black strand, to his relief, was fairly firm, for he had dreaded sinking to the knees in it; but its appearance was so unpleasant that he could not bring himself to sit down. He walked on towards the ledge of rocks, thinking to find a pleasanter place there. They were stratified, and he stepped on them to climb up, when his foot went deep into the apparently hard rock. He kicked it, and his shoe penetrated it as if it had been soft sand. It was impossible to climb up the reef. The ground rose inland, and curious to see around him as far as possible, he ascended the slope.

From the summit, however, he could not see farther than on the shore, for the pale yellow mist rose up round him, and hid the canoe on the strand. The extreme desolation of the dark and barren ground repelled him; there was not a tree, bush, or living creature, not so much as a buzzing fly. He turned to go down, and then for the first time noticed that the disk of the sun was surrounded with a faint blue rim, apparently caused by the yellow vapour. So much were the rays shorn of their glare, that he could look at the sun without any distress, but its heat seemed to have increased, though it was now late in the afternoon.

Descending towards the canoe, he fancied the wind had veered considerably. He sat down in the boat, and took some food; it was without relish, as he had nothing to drink, and the great heat had tired him. Wearily, and without thinking, he pushed off the canoe; she slowly floated out, when, as he was about to hoist up the sail, a tremendous gust of wind struck him down on the thwarts,* and nearly carried him overboard. He caught the mast as he fell, or over he must have gone into the black waves. Before he could recover himself, she drifted against the ledge of rocks, which broke down and sank before the blow, so that she passed over uninjured.

Felix got out a paddle, and directed the canoe as well as he could; the fury of the wind was irresistible, and he could only drive before it. In a few minutes, as he was swept along the shore, he was carried between it and another immense reef. Here, the waves being broken and less powerful, he contrived to get the heavy canoe ashore again, and, jumping out, dragged her up as far as he could on the land. When he had done this, he found to his surprise that the gale had ceased. The tremendous burst of wind had been succeeded by a perfect calm, and the waves had already lost their violent impetus.

This was a relief, for he had feared that the canoe would be utterly broken to pieces; but soon he began to doubt if it were an unmixed benefit, as without a wind he could not move from this dismal place that evening. He was too weary to paddle far. He sat on the canoe to rest himself, and, whether from fatigue or other causes, fell asleep. His head heavily drooping on his chest partly woke him several times, but his lassitude overcame the discomfort, and he slept on. When he got up he felt dazed and unrefreshed, as if sleeping had been hard work. He was extremely thirsty, and oppressed with the increasing heat. The sun had sunk, or rather was so low that the high ground hid it from sight.

* A structural cross-piece in a boat or canoe used as a seat for the rower(s).

CHAPTER XXIII

STRANGE THINGS

THE thought struck Felix that perhaps he might find a spring somewhere in the island, and he started at once up over the hill. At the top he paused. The sun had not sunk, but had disappeared as a disk. In its place was a billow of blood, for so it looked, a vast up-heaved billow of glowing blood surging on the horizon. Over it flickered a tint of palest blue, like that seen in fire. The black waters reflected the glow, and the yellow vapour around was suffused with it. Though momentarily startled, Felix did not much heed these appearances; he was still dazed and heavy from his sleep.

He went on, looking for a spring, sometimes walking on firm ground, sometimes sinking to the ankle in a friable soil like black sand. The ground looked, indeed, as if it had been burnt, but there were no charred stumps of timber such as he had seen on the sites of forest fires. The extreme dreariness seemed to oppress his spirits, and he went on and on in a heavy waking dream. Descending into a plain, he lost sight of the flaming sunset and the black waters. In the level plain the desolation was yet more marked; there was not a grass blade or plant; the surface was hard, black, and burned, resembling iron, and indeed in places it resounded to his feet, though he supposed that was the echo from hollow passages beneath.

Several times he shook himself, straightened himself up, and endeavoured to throw off the sense of drowsy weight which increased upon him. He could not do so; he walked with bent back, and crept, as it were, over the iron land which radiated heat. A shimmer like that of water appeared in front; he quickened his pace, but could not get to it, and he realised presently that it was a mirage which receded as he advanced. There was no pleasant summer twilight; the sunset was succeeded by an indefinite gloom, and while this shadow hung overhead the yellow vapour around was faintly radiant. Felix suddenly stopped, having stepped, as he thought, on a skeleton.

Another glance, however, showed that it was merely the impression of one, the actual bones had long since disappeared. The ribs, the skull, and limbs were drawn on the black ground in white lines as if it had been done with a broad piece of chalk. Close by he found three or four more, intertangled and superimposed as if the unhappy beings had fallen partly across each other, and in that position had mouldered away leaving nothing but their outline. From among a variety of objects that were scattered about Felix picked up something that shone; it was a diamond bracelet of one large stone, and a small square of blue china-tile with a curious heraldic animal drawn on it. Evidently these had belonged to one or other of the party who had perished.

Though startled at the first sight, it was curious that Felix felt so little horror; the idea did not occur to him that he was in danger as these had been. Inhaling the gaseous emanations from the soil and contained in the yellow vapour, he had become narcotised, and moved as if under the influence of opium, while wide awake, and capable of rational conduct. His senses were deadened, and did not carry the usual vivid impression to the mind; he saw things as if they were afar off. Accidentally looking back, he found that his footmarks, as far as he could see, shone with a phosphoric light like that of 'touchwood' in the dark. Near at hand they did not shine; the appearance did not come till some few minutes had elapsed. His track was visible behind till the vapour hid it. As the evening drew on the vapour became more luminous, and somewhat resembled an aurora.

Still anxious for water he proceeded as straight ahead as he could, and shortly became conscious of an indefinite cloud which kept pace with him on either side. When he turned to look at either of the clouds, the one looked at disappeared. It was not condensed enough to be visible to direct vision, yet he was aware of it from the corner of his eye. Shapeless and threatening, the gloomy thickness of the air floated beside him like the vague monster of a dream. Sometimes he fancied that he saw an arm or a limb among the folds of the cloud, or an approach to a face; the instant he looked it vanished. Marching at each hand these vapours bore him horrible company.

His brain became unsteady, and flickering things moved about him; yet, though alarmed, he was not afraid; his senses were not acute enough for fear. The heat increased, his hands were intolerably hot as if he had been in a fever, he panted, but did not perspire. A dry heat like an oven burned his blood in his veins. His head felt enlarged, and his eyes seemed alight; he could see these two globes of phosphoric light under his brows. They seemed to stand out so that he could see them. He thought his path straight, it was really curved; nor did he know that he staggered as he walked.

Presently a white object appeared ahead; and on coming to it, he found it was a wall, white as snow, with some kind of crystal. He touched it, when the wall fell immediately with a crushing sound as if pulverised, and disappeared in a vast cavern at his feet. Beyond this chasm he came to more walls like those of houses, such as would be left if the roofs fell in. He carefully avoided touching them, for they seemed as brittle as glass, and merely a white powder having no consistency at all. As he advanced these remnants of buildings increased in number, so that he had to wind in and out and round them. In some places the crystallised wall had fallen of itself, and he could see down into the cavern; for the house had either been built partly underground, or, which was more probable, the ground had risen. Whether the walls had been of bricks or stone or other material he could not tell; they were now like salt.

Soon wearying of winding round these walls, Felix returned and retraced his steps till he was outside the place, and then went on towards the left. Not long after, as he still walked in a dream and without feeling his feet, he descended a slight slope and found the ground change in colour from black to a dull red. In his dazed state he had taken several steps out into this red before he noticed that it was liquid, unctuous and slimy, like a thick oil. It deepened rapidly and was already over his shoes; he returned to the black shore and stood looking out over the water, if such it could be called.

The luminous yellow vapour had now risen a height of ten or fifteen feet, and formed a roof both over the land and over the red water, under which it was possible to see for a great distance. The surface of the red oil or viscid liquid was perfectly smooth, and, indeed, it did not seem as if any wind could rouse a wave on it, much less that a swell should be left after the gale had gone down. Disappointed in his search for water to drink, Felix mechanically turned to go back.

He followed his luminous footmarks, which he could see a long way before him. His trail curved so much that he made many short cuts across the winding line he had left. His weariness was now so intense that all feeling had departed. His feet, his limbs, his arms, and hands were numbed. The subtle poison of the emanations from the earth had begun to deaden his nerves. It seemed a full hour or more to him till he reached the spot where the skeletons were drawn in white upon the ground.

He passed a few yards to one side of them, and stumbled over a heap of something which he did not observe, as it was black like the level ground. It emitted a metallic sound, and looking he saw that he had kicked his foot against a great heap of money. The coins were black as ink; he picked up a handful and went on. Hitherto Felix had accepted all that he saw as something so strange as to be unaccountable. During his advance into this region in the canoe he had in fact become slowly stupefied by the poisonous vapour he had inhaled. His mind was partly in abeyance; it acted, but only after some time had elapsed. He now at last began to realise his position; the finding of the heap of blackened money touched a chord of memory. These skeletons were the miserable relics of men who had ventured, in search of ancient treasures, into the deadly marshes over the site of the mightiest city of former days. The deserted and utterly extinct city of London was under his feet.

He had penetrated into the midst of that dreadful place, of which he had heard many a tradition: how the earth was poison, the water poison, the air poison, the very light of heaven, falling through such an atmosphere, poison. There were said to be places where the earth was on fire and belched forth sulphurous fumes, supposed to be from the combustion of the enormous stores of strange and unknown chemicals collected by the wonderful people of those times. Upon the surface of the water there was a greenish-yellow oil, to touch which was death to any creature; it was the very essence of corruption. Sometimes it floated before the wind, and fragments became attached to reeds or flags far from the place itself. If a moorhen or duck chanced to rub the reed, and but one drop stuck to its feathers, it forthwith died. Of the red waters he had not heard, nor of the black, into which he had unwittingly sailed.

Ghastly beings haunted the site of so many crimes, shapeless monsters, hovering by night, and weaving a fearful dance. Frequently they caught fire, as it seemed, and burned as they flew or floated in the air. Remembering these stories, which in part, at least, seemed now to be true, Felix glanced aside, where the cloud still kept pace with him, and involuntarily put his hands to his ears lest the darkness of the air should whisper some horror of old times. The earth on which he walked, the black earth, leaving phosphoric footmarks behind him, was composed of the mouldered bodies of millions of men who had passed away in the centuries during which the city existed. He shuddered as he moved; he hastened, yet could not go fast, his numbed limbs would not permit him.

He dreaded lest he should fall and sleep and wake no more, like the searchers after treasure; treasure which they had found only to lose for ever. He looked around, supposing that he might see the gleaming head and shoulders of the half-buried giant, of which he recollected he had been told. The giant was punished for some crime by being buried to the chest in the earth; fire incessantly consumed his head and played about it, yet it was not destroyed. The learned thought, if such a thing really existed, that it must be the upper part of an ancient brazen statue, kept bright by the action of acid in the atmosphere, and shining with reflected light. Felix did not see it, and shortly afterwards surmounted the hill, and looked down upon his canoe. It was on fire.

CHAPTER XXIV

FIERY VAPOURS

FELIX tried to run, but his feet would not rise from the ground; his limbs were numb as in a nightmare; he could not get there. His body would not obey his will. In reality he did move, but more slowly than when he walked. By degrees approaching the canoe his alarm subsided, for although it burned it was not injured; the canvas of the sail was not even scorched. When he got to it the flames had disappeared, like Jack-o'-the-lantern, the phosphoric fire receded from him. With all his strength he strove to launch her, yet paused, for over the surface of the black water, now smooth and waveless, played immense curling flames, stretching out like endless serpents, weaving, winding, rolling over each other. Suddenly they contracted into a ball, which shone with a steady light, and was as large as the full moon. The ball swept along, rose a little, and from it flew out long streamers till it was unwound in fiery threads.

But remembering that the flames had not even scorched the canvas, he pushed the canoe afloat, determined at any risk to leave this dreadful place. To his joy he felt a faint air rising, it cooled his forehead, but was not enough to fill the sail. He paddled with all the strength he had left. The air seemed to come from exactly the opposite direction to what it had previously blown, some point of east he supposed. Labour as hard as he would, the canoe moved slowly, being so heavy. It seemed as if the black water was thick and clung to her, retarding motion. Still, he did move, and in time (it seemed, indeed, a time) he left the island, which disappeared in the luminous vapours. Uncertain as to the direction, he got his compass, but it would not act; the needle had no life, it swung and came to rest, pointing any way as it chanced. It was demagnetised. Felix resolved to trust to the wind, which he was certain blew from the opposite quarter, and would therefore carry him out. The stars he could not see for the vapour, which formed a roof above him.

The wind was rising, but in uncertain gusts; however, he hoisted the sail, and floated slowly before it. Nothing but excitement could have kept him awake. Reclining in the canoe, he watched the serpent-like flames playing over the surface, and forced himself by sheer power of will not to sleep. The two dark clouds which had accompanied him to the shore now faded away, and the cooling wind enabled him to bear up better against his parching thirst. His hope was to reach the clear and beautiful Lake; his dread that in the uncertain light he might strike a concealed sandbank and become firmly fixed.

Twice he passed islands, distinguishable as masses of visible darkness. While the twisted flames played up to the shore, and the luminous vapour overhung the ground, the island itself appeared as a black mass. The wind became by degrees steadier, and the canoe shot swiftly over the water. His hopes rose; he sat up and kept a keener look-out ahead. All at once the canoe shook as if she had struck a rock. She vibrated from one end to the other, and stopped for a moment in her course. Felix sprang up alarmed. At the same instant a bellowing noise reached him, succeeded by a frightful belching and roaring, as if a volcano had burst forth under the surface of the water; he looked back but could see nothing. The canoe had not touched ground; she sailed as rapidly as before.

Again the shock, and again the hideous roaring, as if some force beneath the water were forcing itself up, vast bubbles rising and bursting. Fortunately it was at a great distance. Hardly was it silent before it was reiterated for the third time. Next Felix felt the canoe heave up, and he was aware that a large roller had passed under him. A second and a third followed. They were without crests, and were not raised by the wind; they obviously started from the scene of the disturbance. Soon afterwards the canoe moved quicker, and he detected a strong current setting in the direction he was sailing.

The noise did not recur, nor did any more rollers pass under. Felix felt better and less dazed, but his weariness and sleepiness increased every moment. He fancied that the serpent flames were less brilliant or farther apart, and that the luminous vapour was thinner. How long he sat at the rudder he could not tell; he noticed that it seemed to grow darker, the serpent flames faded away, and the luminous vapour was succeeded by something like the natural gloom of night. At last he saw a star overhead, and hailed it with joy. He thought of Aurora; the next instant he fell back in the canoe firm asleep.

His arm, however, still retained the rudder-paddle in position, so that the canoe sped on with equal swiftness. She would have struck more than one of the sandbanks and islets had it not been for the strong current that was running. Instead of carrying her against the banks this warded her off, for it drew her between the islets in the channels where it ran fastest, and the undertow, where it struck the shore, bore her back from the land. Driving before the wind, the canoe swept onward steadily to the west. In an hour it had passed the line of the black water, and entered the sweet Lake. Another hour and all trace of the marshes had utterly disappeared, the last faint glow of the vapour had vanished. The dawn of the coming summer's day appeared, and the sky became a lovely azure. The canoe sailed on, but Felix remained immovable in slumber.

Long since the strong current had ceased, it scarcely extended into the sweet waters, and the wind only impelled the canoe. As the sun rose the breeze gradually fell away, and in an hour or so there was only a light air. The canoe had left most of the islets and was approaching the open Lake when, as she passed almost the last, the yard caught the overhanging branch of a willow, the canoe swung round and grounded gently under the shadow of the tree. For some time the little wavelets beat against the side of the boat, gradually they ceased, and the clear and beautiful water became still. Felix slept till nearly noon, when he awoke and sat up. At the sudden movement a pike struck, and two moorhens scuttled out of the water into the grass on the shore. A thrush was singing sweetly, whitethroats were busy in the bushes, and swallows swept by overhead.

Felix drew a long deep breath of intense relief; it was like awaking in Paradise. He snatched up a cup, dipped, and satisfied his craving thirst, then washed his hands over the side, and threw the water over his face. But when he came to stand up and move, he found that his limbs were almost powerless. Like a child he tottered, his joints had no strength, his legs tingled as if they had been benumbed. He was so weak he crawled on all fours along to the mast, furled the sail kneeling, and dragged himself rather than stepped ashore with the painter. The instant he had fastened the rope to a branch, he threw himself at full length on the grass, and grasped a handful of it. Merely to touch the grass after such an experience was intense delight.

The song of the thrush, the chatter of the whitethroats, the sight of a hedge-sparrow, gave him inexpressible pleasure. Lying on the sward he watched the curves traced by the swallows in the sky. From the sedges came the curious cry of the moorhen; a bright kingfisher went by. He rested as he had never rested before. His whole body, his whole being was resigned to rest. It was fully two hours before he rose and crept on all fours into the canoe for food. There was only sufficient left for one meal, but that gave him no concern now he was out of the marshes; he could fish and use his crossbow.

He now observed what had escaped him during the night, the canoe was black from end to end. Stem, stern, gunwale,* thwart, outrigger,

* The upper edge or lip of a ship or boat.

mast and sail were black. The stain did not come off on being touched, it seemed burnt in. As he leaned over the side to dip water, and saw his reflection, he started; his face was black, his clothes were black, his hair black. In his eagerness to drink, the first time, he had noticed nothing. His hands were less dark; contact with the paddle and ropes had partly rubbed it off, he supposed. He washed, but the water did not materially diminish the discoloration.

After eating, he returned to the grass and rested again; and it was not till the sun was sinking that he felt any return of vigour. Still weak, but able now to walk, leaning on a stick, he began to make a camp for the coming night. But a few scraps, the remnant of his former meal, were left; on these he supped after a fashion, and long before the white owl began his rounds Felix was fast asleep on his hunter's hide from the canoe. He found next morning that the island was small, only a few acres; it was well-wooded, dry, and sandy in places. He had little inclination or strength to resume his expedition; he erected a booth of branches, and resolved to stay a few days till his strength returned.

By shooting wildfowl, and fishing, he fared very well, and soon recovered. In two days the discoloration of the skin had faded to an olive tint, which, too, grew fainter. The canoe lost its blackness, and became a rusty colour. By rubbing the coins he had carried away he found they were gold; part of the inscription remained, but he could not read it. The blue china-tile was less injured than the metal; after washing it, it was bright. But the diamond pleased him most; it would be a splendid present for Aurora. Never had he seen anything like it in the palaces; he believed it was twice the size of the largest possessed by any king or prince.

It was as big as his finger nail, and shone and gleamed in the sunlight, sparkling and reflecting the beams. Its value must be very great. But well he knew how dangerous it would be to exhibit it; on some pretext or other he would be thrown into prison, and the gem seized. It must be hidden with the greatest care till he could produce it in Thyma Castle, when the Baron would protect it. Felix regretted now that he had not searched further; perhaps he might have found other treasures for Aurora; the next instant he repudiated his greed, and was only thankful that he had escaped with his life. He wondered and marvelled that he had done so, it was so well known that almost all who had ventured in had perished.

Reflecting on the circumstances which had accompanied his entrance to the marshes, the migration of the birds seemed almost the most singular. They were evidently flying from some apprehended danger, and that most probably would be in the air. The gale at that time, however, was blowing in a direction which would appear to ensure safety to them; into, and not out of, the poisonous marshes. Did they, then, foresee that it would change? Did they expect it to veer like a cyclone and presently blow east with the same vigour as it then blew west? That would carry the vapour from the inky waters out over the sweet Lake, and might even cause the foul water itself to temporarily encroach on the sweet. The more he thought of it, the more he felt convinced that this was the explanation; and, as a fact, the wind, after dropping, did arise again and blow from the east, though, as it happened, not with nearly the same strength. It fell, too, before long, fortunately for him. Clearly the birds had anticipated a cyclone, and that the wind turning would carry the gases out upon them to their destruction. They had therefore hurried away, and the fishes had done the same.

The velocity of the gale which had carried him into the black waters had proved his safety, by driving before it the thicker and most poisonous portion of the vapour, compressing it towards the east, so that he had entered the dreaded precincts under favourable conditions. When it dropped, while he was on the black island, he soon began to feel the effect of the gases rising imperceptibly from the soil, and had he not had the good fortune to escape so soon no doubt he would have fallen a victim. He could not congratulate himself sufficiently upon his good fortune. The other circumstances appeared to be due to the decay of the ancient city, to the decomposition of accumulated matter, to phosphorescence and gaseous exhalations. The black rocks that crumbled at a touch were doubtless the remains of ancient buildings saturated with the dark water and vapours. Inland similar remains were white, and resembled salt.

But the great explosions which occurred as he was leaving, and which sent heavy rollers after him, were not easily understood, till he remembered that in Sylvester's 'Book of Natural Things' it was related that 'the ancient city had been undermined with vast conduits, sewers, and tunnels, and that these communicated with the sea'. It had been much disputed whether the sea did or did not still send its tides up to the site of the old quays. Felix now thought that the explosions were due to compressed air, or more probably to gases met with by the ascending tide.

CHAPTER XXV

THE SHEPHERDS

FOR four days Felix remained on the island recovering his strength. By degrees the memory of the scenes he had witnessed grew less vivid, and his nerves regained their tone. The fifth morning he sailed again, making due south with a gentle breeze from the west, which suited the canoe very well. He considered that he was now at the eastern extremity of the Lake, and that by sailing south he should presently reach the place where the shore turned to the east again. The sharp prow of the canoe cut swiftly through the waves, a light spray flew occasionally in his face, and the wind blew pleasantly. In the cloudless sky swallows and swifts were wheeling, and on the water half-a-dozen mallards moved aside to let him pass.

About two hours after he started he encountered a mist which came softly over the surface of the water with the wind, and in an instant shut out all view. Even the sun was scarcely visible. It was very warm, and left no moisture. In five minutes he passed through and emerged again in the bright sunlight. These dry warm mists are frequently seen on the Lake in summer, and are believed to portend a continuance of fine weather.

Felix kept a good distance from the mainland, which was hilly and wooded, and with few islands. Presently he observed in the extreme distance, on his right hand, a line of mountainous hills, which he supposed to be the southern shore of the Lake, and that he was sailing into a gulf or bay. He debated with himself whether he should alter his course and work across to the mountains, or continue to trace the shore. Unless he did trace the shore, he could scarcely say that he had circumnavigated the Lake, as he would leave this great bay unexplored. He continued, therefore, to sail directly south.

The wind freshened towards noon, and the canoe flew at a great pace. Twice he passed through similar mists. There were now no islands at all, but a line of low chalk cliffs marked the shore. Considering that it must be deep, and safe to do so, Felix bore in closer to look at the land. Woods ran along the hills right to the verge of the cliff, but he saw no signs of inhabitants, no smoke, boat, or house. The sound of the surf beating on the beach was audible, though the waves were not large. High over the cliff he noticed a kite soaring, with forked tail, at a great height.

Immediately afterwards he ran into another mist or vapour, thicker, if anything, and which quite obscured his view. It seemed like a great cloud on the surface of the water, and broader than those he had previously entered. Suddenly the canoe stopped with a tremendous jerk, which pitched him forward on his knees, the mast cracked, and there was a noise of splitting wood. As soon as he could get up, Felix saw, to his bitter sorrow, that the canoe had split longitudinally; the water came up through the split, and the boat was held together only by the beams of the outrigger. He had run aground on a large sharp flint imbedded in a chalk floor, which had split the poplar wood of the canoe like an axe. The voyage was over, for the least strain would cause the canoe to part in two, and if she were washed off the ground she would be water-logged. In half a minute the mist passed, leaving him in the bright day, shipwrecked.

Felix now saw that the waters were white with suspended chalk, and sounding with the paddle, found that the depth was but a few inches. He had driven at full speed on a reef. There was no danger, for the distance to the shore was hardly two hundred yards, and judging by the appearance of the water, it was shallow all the way. But his canoe, the product of so much labour, and in which he had voyaged so far, his canoe was destroyed. He could not repair her; he doubted whether it could have been done successfully even at home with Oliver to help him. He could sail no farther; there was nothing for it but to get ashore and travel on foot. If the wind rose higher, the waves would soon break clean over her, and she would go to pieces.

With a heavy heart, Felix took his paddle and stepped overboard. Feeling with the paddle, he plumbed the depth in front of him, and, as he expected, walked all the way to the shore, no deeper than his knees. This was fortunate, as it enabled him to convey his things to land without loss. He wrapped up the tools and MSS. in one of his hunter's hides. When the whole cargo was landed, he sat down sorrowfully at the foot of the cliff, and looked out at the broken mast and sail, still flapping uselessly in the breeze.

It was a long time before he recovered himself, and set to work mechanically to bury the crossbow, hunter's hides, tools, and MSS. under a heap of pebbles. As the cliff, though low, was perpendicular, he could not scale it, else he would have preferred to conceal them in the woods above. To pile pebbles over them was the best he could do for the present; he intended to return for them when he discovered a path up the cliff. He then started, taking only his bow and arrows.

But no such path was to be found; he walked on and on till weary, and still the cliff ran like a wall on his left hand. After an hour's rest, he started again; and, as the sun was declining, came suddenly to a gap in the cliff, where a grassy sward came down to the shore. It was now too late, and he was too weary, to think of returning for his things that evening. He made a scanty meal, and endeavoured to rest. But the excitement of losing the canoe, the long march since, the lack of good food, all tended to render him restless. Weary, he could not rest, nor move farther. The time passed slowly, the sun sank, the wind ceased; after an interminable time the stars appeared, and still he could not sleep. He had chosen a spot under an oak on the green slope. The night was warm, and even sultry, so that he did not miss his covering, but there was no rest in him. Towards the dawn, which comes very early at that season, he at last slept, with his back to the tree. He awoke with a start in broad daylight, to see a man standing in front of him armed with a long spear.

Felix sprang to his feet, instinctively feeling for his hunting-knife; but he saw in an instant that no injury was meant, for the man was leaning on the shaft of his weapon, and, of course, could, if so he had wished, have run him through while sleeping. They looked at each other for a moment. The stranger was clad in a tunic and wore a hat of plaited straw. He was very tall and strongly built; his single weapon, a spear of twice his own length. His beard came down on his chest. He spoke to Felix in a dialect the latter did not understand. Felix held out his hand as a token of amity, which the other took. He spoke again. Felix, on his part, tried to explain his shipwreck, when a word the stranger uttered recalled to Felix's memory the peculiar dialect used by the shepherd race on the hills in the neighbourhood of his home.

He spoke in this dialect, which the stranger in part at least understood, and the sound of which at once rendered him more friendly. By degrees they comprehended each other's meaning the easier, as the shepherd had come the same way and had seen the wreck of the canoe. Felix learned that the shepherd was a scout sent on ahead to see that the road was clear of enemies. His tribe were on the march with their flocks, and to avoid the steep woods and hills which there blocked their course, they had followed the level and open beach at the foot of the cliff, aware, of course, of the gap which Felix had found. While they were talking, Felix saw the cloud of dust raised by the sheep as the flocks wound round a jutting buttress of cliff.

His friend explained that they marched in the night and early morning to avoid the heat of the day. Their proposed halting-place was close at hand; he must go on and see that all was clear. Felix accompanied him, and found within the wood at the summit a grassy coombe, where a spring rose. The shepherd threw down his spear, and began to dam up the channel of the spring with stones, flints, and sods of earth, in order to form a pool at which the sheep might drink. Felix assisted him, and the water speedily began to rise.

The flocks were not allowed to rush tumultuously to the water, they came in about fifty at a time, each division with its shepherds and their dogs, so that confusion was avoided and all had their share. There were about twenty of these divisions, besides eighty cows and a few goats. They had no horses; their baggage came on the backs of asses.

After the whole of the flocks and herds had been watered several fires were lit by the women, who in stature and hardihood scarcely differed from the men. Not till this work was over did the others gather about Felix to hear his story. Finding that he was hungry they ran to the baggage for food, and pressed on him a little dark bread, plentiful cheese and butter, dried tongue, and horns of mead. He could not devour a fiftieth part of what these hospitable people brought him. Having nothing else to give them, he took from his pocket one of the gold coins he had brought from the site of the ancient city, and offered it.

They laughed, and made him understand that it was of no value to them; but they passed it from hand to hand, and he noticed that they began to look at him curiously. From its blackened appearance they conjectured whence he had obtained it; one, too, pointed to his shoes, which were still blackened, and appeared to have been scorched. The whole camp now pressed on him, their wonder and interest rising to a great height. With some trouble Felix described his journey over the site of the ancient city, interrupted with constant exclamations, questions, and excited conversation. He told them everything, except about the diamond.

Their manner towards him perceptibly altered. From the first they had been hospitable; they now became respectful, and even reverent. The elders and their chief, not to be distinguished by dress or ornament from the rest, treated him with ceremony and marked deference. The children were brought to see and even to touch him. So great was their amazement that any one should have escaped from these pestilential vapours, that they attributed it to divine interposition, and looked upon him with some of the awe of superstition. He was asked to stay with them altogether, and to take command of the tribe.

The latter Felix declined; to stay with them for awhile, at least, he was, of course, willing enough. He mentioned his hidden possessions, and got up to return for them, but they would not permit him. Two men started at once. He gave them the bearings of the spot, and they had not the least doubt but that they should find it, especially as, the wind being still, the canoe would not yet have broken up, and would guide them. The tribe remained in the green coombe the whole day, resting from their long journey. They wearied Felix with questions, still he answered them as copiously as he could; he felt too grateful for their kindness not to satisfy them. His bow was handled, his arrows carried about so that the quiver for the time was empty, and the arrows scattered in twenty hands. He astonished them by exhibiting his skill with the weapon, striking a tree with an arrow at nearly three hundred yards.

Though familiar, of course, with the bow, they had never seen shooting like that, nor, indeed, any archery except at short quarters. They had no other arms themselves but spears and knives. Seeing one of the women cutting the boughs from a fallen tree, dead and dry, and, therefore, preferable for fuel, Felix naturally went to help her, and, taking the axe, soon made a bundle, which he carried for her. It was his duty as a noble to see that no woman, not a slave, laboured; he had been bred in that idea, and would have felt disgraced had he permitted it. The women looked on with astonishment, for in these rude tribes the labour of the women was considered valuable and appraised like that of a horse.

Without any conscious design, Felix thus in one day conciliated and won the regard of the two most powerful parties in the camp, the chief and the women. By his refusing the command the chief was flattered, and his possible hostility prevented. The act of cutting the wood and carrying the bundle gave him the hearts of the women. They did not, indeed, think their labour in any degree oppressive; still, to be relieved of it was pleasing.

The two men who had gone for Felix's buried treasure did not return till breakfast next morning. They stepped into the camp, each with his spear reddened and dripping with fresh blood. Felix no sooner saw the blood than he fainted. He quickly recovered, but he could not endure the sight of the spears, which were removed and hidden from his view. He had seen blood enough spilt at the siege of Iwis, but this came upon him in all its horror unrelieved by the excitement of war.

The two shepherds had been dogged by gipsies, and had been obliged to make a round to escape. They took their revenge by climbing into trees, and as their pursuers passed under thrust them through with their long spears. The shepherds, like all their related tribes, had been at feud with the gipsies for many generations. The gipsies followed them to and from their pastures, cut off stragglers, destroyed or stole their sheep and cattle, and now and then overwhelmed a whole tribe. Of late the contest had become more sanguinary and almost ceaseless.

Mounted on swift, though small, horses, the gipsies had the advantage of the shepherds. On the other hand, the shepherds, being men of great stature and strength, could not be carried away by a rush if they had time to form a circle, as was their custom of battle. They lost many men by the javelins thrown by the gipsies, who rode up to the edge of the circle, cast their darts and retreated. If the shepherds left their circle they were easily ridden over; while they maintained formation they lost individuals, but saved the mass. Battles were of rare occurrence; the gipsies watched for opportunities and executed raids, the shepherds retaliated, and thus the endless war continued. The shepherds invariably posted sentinels, and sent forward scouts to ascertain if the way were clear. Accustomed to the horrid scenes of war from childhood, they could not understand Felix's sensitiveness.

They laughed, and then petted him like a spoilt child. This galled him exceedingly; he felt humiliated, and eager to reassert his manhood. He was willing to stay with them before for awhile, nothing would have induced him to leave them now till he had vindicated himself in their sight. The incident happened soon after sunrise, which is very early at the end of June. The camp had only waited for the return of these men, and on their appearance began to move. The march that morning was not a long one, as the sky was clear and the heat soon wearied the flocks. Felix accompanied the scout in advance, armed with his bow, eager to encounter the gipsies.

CHAPTER XXVI

BOW AND ARROW

THREE mornings the shepherds marched in the same manner, when they came in view of a range of hills so high that to Felix they appeared mountains. The home of the tribe was in these hills, and once there they were comparatively safe from attack. In early spring when the herbage on the downs was scarce, the flocks moved to the meadow-like lands far in the valleys; in summer they returned to the hills; in autumn they went to the vales again. Soon after noon on the third day the scouts reported that a large body of gipsies were moving in a direction which would cut off their course to the hills on the morrow.

The chief held a council, and it was determined that a forced march should be made at once by another route, more to the left, and it was thought that in this way they might reach the base of the slopes by evening. The distance was not great, and could easily have been traversed by the men; the flocks and herds, however, could not be hurried much. A messenger was despatched to the hills for assistance, and the march began. It was a tedious movement. Felix was wearied, and walked in a drowsy state. Towards six o'clock, as he guessed, the trees began to thin, and the column reached the first slopes of the hills. Here about thirty shepherds joined them, a contingent from the nearest camp. It was considered that the danger was now past, and that the gipsies would not attack them on the hill; but it was a mistake.

A large body almost immediately appeared, coming along the slope on the right, not less than two hundred; and from their open movements and numbers it was evident that they intended battle. The flocks and herds were driven hastily into a coombe, or narrow valley, and there left to their fate. All the armed men formed in a circle; the women occupied the centre. Felix took his stand outside the circle by a gnarled and decayed oak. There was just there a slight rise in the ground, which he knew would give him some advantage in discharging his arrows, and would also allow him a clear view. His friends earnestly entreated him to enter the circle, and even sought to bring him within it by force, till he explained to them that he could not shoot if so surrounded, and promised if the gipsies charged to rush inside.

Felix unslung his quiver, and placed it on the ground before him;

a second quiver he put beside it; four or five arrows he stuck upright in the sward, so that he could catch hold of them quickly; two arrows he held in his left hand, another he fitted to the string. Thus prepared, he watched the gipsies advance. They came walking their short wiry horses to within half-a-mile, when they began to trot down the slope; they could not surround the shepherds because of the steep-sided coombe and some brushwood, and could advance only on two fronts. Felix rapidly became so excited that his sight was affected, and his head whirled. His heart beat with such speed that his breath seemed going. His limbs tottered, and he dreaded lest he should faint.

His intensely nervous organisation, strung up to its highest pitch, shook him in its grasp, and his will was powerless to control it. He felt that he should disgrace himself once more before these rugged but brave shepherds, who betrayed not the slightest symptom of agitation. For one hour of Oliver's calm courage and utter absence of nervousness he would have given years of his life. His friends in the circle observed his agitation, and renewed their entreaties to him to come inside it. This only was needed to complete his discomfiture. He lost his head altogether; he saw nothing but a confused mass of yellow and red rushing towards him, for each of the gipsies wore a yellow or red scarf, some about the body, some over the shoulder, others round the head. They were now within three hundred yards.

A murmur from the shepherd spearmen. Felix had discharged an arrow. It stuck in the ground about twenty paces from him. He shot again; it flew wild and quivering, and dropped harmlessly. Another murmur; they expressed to each other their contempt for the bow. This immediately restored Felix; he forgot the enemy as an enemy, he forgot himself; he thought only of his skill as an archer, now in question. Pride upheld him. The third arrow he fitted properly to the string, he planted his left foot slightly in advance, and looked steadfastly at the horsemen before he drew his bow.

At a distance of one hundred and fifty yards they had paused, and were widening out so as to advance in loose open rank and allow each man to throw his javelin. They shouted; the spearmen in the circle replied, and levelled their spears. Felix fixed his eye on one of the gipsies who was ordering and marshalling the rest, a chief. He drew the arrow swiftly but quietly, the string hummed, the pliant yew obeyed, and the long arrow shot forward in a steady swift flight like a line of gossamer drawn through the air. It missed the chief, but pierced the horse he rode just in front of the rider's thigh. The maddened horse reared and fell backwards on his rider.

The spearmen shouted. Before the sound could leave their lips another arrow had sped; a gipsy threw up his arms with a shriek; the arrow had gone through his body. A third, a fourth, a fifth; six gipsies rolled on the sward. Shout upon shout rent the air from the spearmen. Utterly unused to this mode of fighting, the gipsies fell back. Still the fatal arrows pursued them, and ere they were out of range three others fell. Now the rage of battle burned in Felix; his eyes gleamed, his lips were open, his nostrils wide like a horse running a race. He shouted to the spearmen to follow him, and snatching up his quiver ran forward. Gathered together in a group, the gipsy band consulted.

Felix ran at full speed; swift of foot, he left the heavy spearmen behind. Alone he approached the horsemen; all the Aquila courage was up within him. He kept the higher ground as he ran, and stopped suddenly on a little knoll or tumulus. His arrow flew, a gipsy fell. Again, and a third. Their anger gave them fresh courage; to be repulsed by one only! Twenty of them started to charge and run him down. The keen arrows flew faster than their horses' feet. Now the horse and now the man met those sharp points. Six fell; the rest returned. The shepherds came running; Felix ordered them to charge the gipsies. His success gave him authority; they obeyed; and as they charged, he shot nine more arrows; nine more deadly wounds. Suddenly the gipsy band turned and fled into the brushwood on the lower slopes.

Breathless, Felix sat down on the knoll, and the spearmen swarmed around him. Hardly had they begun to speak to him than there was a shout, and they saw a body of shepherds descending the hill. There were three hundred of them; warned by the messenger, the whole country had risen to repel the gipsies. Too late to join in the fight, they had seen the last of it. They examined the field. There were ten dead and six wounded, who were taken prisoners; the rest escaped, though hurt. In many cases the arrow had gone clean through the body. Then, for the first time, they understood the immense power of the yew bow in strong and skilful hands.

Felix was overwhelmed; they almost crushed him with their attentions; the women fell at his feet and kissed them. But the archer could scarcely reply; his intense nervous excitement had left him weak and almost faint; his one idea was to rest. As he walked back to the camp between the chiefs of the shepherd spearmen, his eyes closed, his limbs tottered, and they had to support him. At the camp he threw himself on the sward, under the gnarled oak, and was instantly fast asleep. Immediately the camp was stilled, not to disturb him.

His adventures in the marshes of the buried city, his canoe, his archery, were talked of the livelong night. Next morning the camp set out for their home in the mountains, and he was escorted by nearly four hundred spearmen. They had saved for him the ornaments of the gipsies who had fallen, golden earrings and nose-rings. He gave them to the women, except one, a finger ring, set with turquoise, and evidently of ancient make, which he kept for Aurora. Two marches brought them to the home of the tribe, where the rest of the spearmen left them. The place was called Wolfstead.

Felix saw at once how easily this spot might be fortified. There was a deep and narrow valley like a groove or green trench opening to the south. At the upper end of the valley rose a hill, not very high, but steep, narrow at the ridge, and steep again on the other side. Over it was a broad, wooded, and beautiful vale; beyond that again the higher mountains. Towards the foot of the narrow ridge here, there was a succession of chalk cliffs, so that to climb up on that side in the face of opposition would be extremely difficult. In the gorge of the enclosed narrow valley a spring rose. The shepherds had formed eight pools, one after the other, water being of great importance to them; and farther down, where the valley opened, there were forty or fifty acres of irrigated meadow. The spring then ran into a considerable brook, across which was the forest.

Felix's idea was to run a palisade along the margin of the brook, and up both sides of the valley to the ridge. There he would build a fort. The edges of the chalk cliffs he would connect with a palisade or a wall, and so form a complete enclosure. He mentioned his scheme to the shepherds; they did not greatly care for it, as they had always been secure without it, the rugged nature of the country not permitting horsemen to penetrate. But they were so completely under his influence that to please him they set about the work. He had to show them how to make a palisade; they had never seen one, and he made the first part of it himself. At building a wall with loose stones, without mortar, the shepherds were skilful; the wall along the verge of the cliffs was soon up, and so was the fort on the top of the ridge. The fort consisted merely of a circular wall, breast high, with embrasures or crenellations.*

When this was finished, Felix had a sense of mastership, for in this fort he felt as if he could rule the whole country. From day to day shepherds came from the more distant parts to see the famous archer, and to admire the enclosure. Though the idea of it had never occurred to them, now they saw it they fully understood its advantages, and two other chiefs began to erect similar forts and palisades.

---

* An embrasure is generally an opening, such as an arrow slit, in a defensive wall. A crenellation usually refers to a series of regular notches at the top of a defensive parapet. Jefferies appears to merge the two terms here.

CHAPTER XXVII

SURPRISED

FELIX was now anxious to continue his journey, yet he did not like to leave the shepherds, with whom his life was so pleasant. As usual, when deliberating, he wandered about the hills, and thus into the forest. The shepherds at first insisted on at least two of their number accompanying him; they were fearful lest the gipsies should seize him, or a Bushman assassinate him. This company was irksome to Felix. In time he convinced them that he was a much better hunter than any of the tribe, and they permitted him to roam alone. During one of these excursions into the forest he discovered a beautiful lake. He looked down on the water from the summit of one of the green mountains.

It was, he thought, half a mile across, and the opposite shore was open woodland, grassy and meadow-like, and dotted with fine old oaks. By degrees these closed together, and the forest succeeded; beyond it again, at a distance of two miles, were green hills. A little clearing only was wanted to make the place fit for a castle and enclosure. Through the grass land opposite he traced the course of a large brook down to the lake; another entered it on the right, and the lake gradually narrowed to a river on his left. Could he erect a tower there, and bring Aurora to it, how happy he would be! A more beautiful spot he had never seen, nor one more suited for every purpose of life.

He followed the course of the stream which left the lake, every now and then disturbing wild goats from the cliffs, and twice he saw deer under the oaks across it. On rounding a spur of down he saw that the river debouched into a much wider lake, which he conjectured must be the Sweet Waters. He went on till he reached the mouth of the river, and had then no doubt that he was standing once more on the shore of the Sweet Water sea. On this, the southern side, the banks were low; on the other, a steep chalky cliff almost overhung the river, and jutted out into the lake, curving somewhat towards him. A fort on that cliff would command the entrance to the river; the cliff was a natural breakwater, so that there was a haven at its base. The river appeared broad and deep enough for navigation, so that vessels could pass from the great Lake to the inland water; about six or seven miles, he supposed.

Felix was much taken with this spot; the beauty of the inland lake, the evident richness of the soil, the river communicating with the great Lake, the cliff commanding its entrance; never, in all his wanderings, had he seen a district so well suited for a settlement and the founding of a city. If he had but a thousand men! How soon he would bring Aurora there, and build a tower, and erect a palisade! So occupied was he with the thought that he returned the whole distance to the spot where he had made the discovery. There he remained a long time, designing it all in his mind.

The tower he would build yonder, threequarters of a mile, perhaps a mile, inland from the opposite shore, on a green knoll, at the base of which the brook flowed. It would be even more pleasant there than on the shore of the lake. The forest he would clear back a little, and put up a stout palisade, enclosing at least three miles of grassy land. By the shore of the lake he would build his town, so that his vessels might be able to go forth into the great Sweet Water sea. So strongly did imagination hold him that he did not observe how near it was to sunset, nor did he remark the threatening aspect of the sky. Thunder awoke him from his dream; he looked, and saw a storm rapidly coming from the north-east.

He descended the hill, and sheltered himself as well as possible among some thick fir trees. After the lightning, the rain poured so heavily that it penetrated the branches, and he unstrung his bow and placed the string in his pocket, that it might not become wet. Instantly there was a whoop on either side, and two gipsies darted from the undergrowth towards him. While the terrible bow was bent they had followed him, tracking his footsteps; the moment he unstrung the bow, they rushed out. Felix crushed through between the firs, by main force getting through, but only opening a passage for them to follow. They could easily have thrust their darts through him, but their object was to take him alive, and gratify the revenge of the tribes with torture.

Felix doubled from the firs, and made towards the far-distant camp; but he was faced by three more gipsies. He turned again and made for the steep hill he had descended. With all his strength he raced up it; his lightness of foot carried him in advance, and he reached the summit a hundred yards ahead; but he knew he must be overtaken presently, unless he could hit upon some stratagem. In the instant that he paused to breathe on the summit a thought struck him. Like the wind he raced along the ridge, making for the great Sweet Water, the same path he had followed in the morning. Once on the ridge the five pursuers shouted; they knew they should have him now there were no more hills to breast. It was not so easy as they imagined.

Felix was in splendid training; he kept his lead, and even drew a little on them. Still he knew in time he must succumb, just as the stag, though swifter of foot, ultimately succumbs to the hounds. They would track him till they had him. If only he could gain enough to have time to string and bend his bow! But with all his efforts he could not get away more than the hundred yards, and that was not far enough. It could be traversed in ten seconds, they would have him before he could string it and fit an arrow. If only he had been fresh as in the morning! But he had had a long walk during the day and not much food. He knew that his burst of speed must soon slacken, but he had a stratagem yet.

Keeping along the ridge till he reached the place where the lake narrowed to the river, suddenly he rushed down the hill towards the water. The edge was encumbered with brushwood and fallen trees; he scrambled over and through anyhow; he tore a path through the bushes and plunged in. But his jacket caught in a branch; he had his knife out and cut off the shred of cloth. Then with the bow and knife in one hand he struck out for the opposite shore. His hope was that the gipsies, being horsemen, and passing all their lives on their horses, might not know how to swim. His conjecture was right; they stopped on the brink, and yelled their loudest. When he had passed the middle of the slow stream their rage rose to a shriek, startling a heron far down the water.

Felix reached the opposite shore in safety, but the bow-string was now wet and useless. He struck off at once straight across the grass lands, past the oaks he had admired, past the green knoll where in imagination he had built his castle and brought Aurora, through the brook, which he found was larger than it appeared at a distance, and required two or three strokes to cross. A few more paces and the forest sheltered him. Under the trees he rested, and considered what course to pursue. The gipsies would expect him to endeavour to regain his friends, and would watch to cut off his return. Felix determined to make, instead, for another camp farther east, and to get even there by a detour.

Bitterly he reproached himself for his folly in leaving the camp, knowing that gipsies were about, with no other weapon than the bow. The knife at his belt was practically no weapon at all, useful only in the last extremity. Had he had a short sword, or javelin, he would have faced the two gipsies who first sprang towards him. Worse than this was the folly of wandering without the least precaution into a territory at that time full of gipsies, who had every reason to desire his capture. If he had used the ordinary precautions of woodcraft, he would have noticed their traces, and he would not have exposed himself in full view on the ridges of the hills, where a man was visible for miles. If he perished through his carelessness, how bitter it would be! To lose Aurora by the merest folly would, indeed, be humiliating.

He braced himself to the journey before him, and set off at a good swinging hunter's pace, as it is called, that is, a pace rather more than a walk and less than a run, with the limbs somewhat bent, and long springy steps. The forest was in the worst possible condition for movement; the rain had damped the fern and undergrowth, and every branch showered raindrops upon him. It was now past sunset and the dusk was increasing; this he welcomed as hiding him. He travelled on till nearly dawn, and then, turning to the right, swept round, and regained the line of the mountainous hills after sunrise. There he rested, and reached a camp about nine in the morning, having walked altogether since the preceding morning fully fifty miles. This camp was about fifteen miles from that of his friends; the shepherds knew him, and one of them started with the news of his safety. In the afternoon ten of his friends came over to see him, and to reproach him.

His weariness was so great that for three days he scarcely moved from the hut, during which time the weather was wet and stormy, as is often the case in summer after a thunderstorm. On the fourth morning it was fine, and Felix, now quite restored to his usual strength, went out with the shepherds. He found some of them engaged in throwing up a heap of stones, flint, and chalk lumps near an oak tree in a plain at the foot of the hill. They told him that during the thunderstorm two cows and ten sheep had been killed there by lightning, which had scarcely injured the oak.

It was their custom to pile up a heap of stones wherever such an event occurred, to warn others from staying themselves, or allowing their sheep or cattle to stay, near the spot in thunder, as it was observed that where lightning struck once it was sure to strike again, sooner or later. 'Then,' said Felix, 'you may be sure there is water there!' He knew from his study of the knowledge of the ancients that lightning frequently leaped from trees or buildings to concealed water, but he had no intention of indicating water in that particular spot. He meant the remark in a general sense.

But the shepherds, ever desirous of water, and looking on Felix as a being of a different order to themselves, took his casual observation in its literal sense. They brought their tools and dug, and, as it chanced, found a copious spring. The water gushed forth and formed a streamlet. Upon this the whole tribe gathered, and they saluted Felix as one almost divine. It was in vain that he endeavoured to repel this homage, and to explain the reason of his remark, and that it was only in a general way that he intended it. Facts were too strong for him. They had heard his words, which they considered an inspiration, and there was the water. It was no use; there was the spring, the very thing they most wanted. Perforce Felix was invested with attributes beyond nature.

The report spread; his own old friends came in a crowd to see the new spring, others journeyed from afar. In a week, Felix having meanwhile returned to Wolfstead, his fame had for the second time spread all over the district. Some came a hundred miles to see him. Nothing he could say was listened to; these simple, straightforward people understood nothing but facts, and the defeat of the gipsies and the discovery of the spring seemed to them little less than supernatural. Besides which, in innumerable little ways Felix's superior knowledge had told upon them. His very manners spoke of high training. His persuasive voice won them. His constructive skill and power of planning, as shown in the palisades and enclosure, showed a grasp of circumstances new to them. This was a man such as they had never before seen.

They began to bring him disputes to settle; he shrank from this position of judge, but it was useless to struggle; they would wait as long as he liked, but his decision they would have, and no other. Next came the sick begging to be cured. Here Felix was firm; he would not attempt to be a physician, and they went away. But, unfortunately, it happened that he let out his knowledge of plants, and back they came. Felix did not know what course to pursue; if by chance he did any one good, crowds would beset him; if injury resulted, perhaps he would be assassinated. This fear was quite unfounded; he really had not the smallest idea how high he stood in their estimation.

After much consideration, Felix hit upon a method which would save him from many inconveniences. He announced his intention of forming a herb-garden in which to grow the best kind of herbs, and at the same time said he would not administer any medicine himself, but would tell their own native physicians and nurses all he knew, so that they could use his knowledge. The herbgarden was at once begun in the valley; it could not contain much till next year, and meantime if any diseased persons came Felix saw them, expressed his opinion to the old shepherd who was the doctor of the tribe, and the latter carried out his instructions. Felix did succeed in relieving some small ailments, and thereby added to his reputation.

CHAPTER XXVIII

FOR AURORA

FELIX now began to find out for himself the ancient truth, that difficulties always confront man. Success only changes them, and increases their number. Difficulties faced him in every direction; at home it had seemed impossible for him to do anything. Now that success seemed to smile on him and he had become a power, instead of everything being smooth and easy, new difficulties sprang up for solution at every point. He wished to continue his journey, but he feared that he would not be permitted to depart. He would have to start away in the night, in which case he could hardly return to them again, and yet he wished to return to these, the first friends he had had, and amongst whom he hoped to found a city.

Another week slipped away, and Felix was meditating his escape, when one afternoon a deputation of ten spearmen arrived from a distant tribe, who had nominated him their king, and sent their principal men to convey the intelligence. Fame is always greatest at a distance, and this tribe in the mountains of the east had actually chosen him as king, and declared that they would obey him whether he took up his residence with them or not. Felix was naturally greatly pleased; how delighted Aurora would be! but he was in perplexity what to do, for he could not tell whether the Wolfstead people would be favourably inclined or would resent his selection.

He had not long to consider. There was an assembly of the tribe, and they, too, chose him by common consent as their king. Secretly they were annoyed that another tribe had been more forward than themselves, and were anxious that Felix should not leave them. Felix declined the honour; in spite of his refusal, he was treated as if he were the most despotic monarch. Four days afterwards two other tribes joined the movement, and sent their acceptance of him as their monarch. Others followed, and so quickly now that a day never passed without another tribe sending a deputation.

Felix thought deeply on the matter. He was, of course, flattered, and ready to accept the dignity, but he was alive to considerations of policy. He resolved that he would not use the title, nor exercise the functions of a king as usually understood. He explained his plan to the chiefs; it was that he should be called simply 'Leader', the Leader of the War; that he should only assume royal authority in time of war; that the present chiefs should retain their authority, and each govern as before, in accordance with ancient custom. He proposed to be king only during war-time. He would, if they liked, write out their laws for them in a book, and so give their customs cohesion and shape. To this plan the tribes readily agreed; it retained all the former customs, it left the chiefs their simple patriarchal authority, and it gave all of them the advantage of combination in war. As the Leader, Felix was henceforth known.

In the course of a fortnight, upwards of six thousand men had joined the Confederacy, and Felix wrote down the names of twenty tribes on a sheet of parchment which he took from his chest. A hut had long since been built for him; but he received all the deputations, and held the assemblies which were necessary, in the circular fort. He was so pressed to visit the tribes that he could not refuse to go to the nearest, and thus his journey was again postponed. During this progress from tribal camp to tribal camp, Felix gained the adhesion of twelve more, making a total of thirty-two names of camps, representing about eight thousand spearmen. With pride Felix reflected that he commanded a far larger army than the Prince of Ponze. But he was not happy.

Months had now elapsed since he had parted from Aurora. There were no means of communicating with her. A letter could be conveyed only by a special messenger; he could not get a messenger, and even if one had been forthcoming, he could not instruct him how to reach Thyma Castle. He did not know himself; the country was entirely unexplored. Except that the direction was west, he had no knowledge whatever. He had often inquired of the shepherds, but they were perfectly ignorant. Anker's Gate was the most westerly of all their settlements, which chiefly extended eastwards. Beyond Anker's Gate was the trackless forest, of which none but the Bushmen knew anything. They did not understand what he meant by a map; all they could tell him was that the range of mountainous hills continued westerly and southerly for an unascertained distance, and that the country was uninhabited except by wandering gipsy tribes.

South was the sea, the salt water; but they never went down to it, or near it, because there was no sustenance for their flocks and herds. Till now, Felix did not know that he was near the sea; he resolved at once to visit it. As nearly as he could discover, the great fresh water Lake did not reach any farther south; Wolfstead was not far from its southern margin. He concluded, therefore, that the shore of the Lake must run continually westward, and that if he followed it he should ultimately reach the very creek from which he had started in the canoe. How far it was he could not reckon.

There were none of the shepherds who could be sent with a letter; they were not hunters, and were unused to woodcraft; there was not one capable of the journey. Unless he went himself he could not communicate with Aurora. Two routes were open to him, one straight through the forest on foot, the other by water, which latter entailed the construction of another canoe. Journey by water, too, he had found was subject to unforeseen risks. Till he could train some of the younger men to row a galley, he decided not to attempt the voyage. There was but the forest route left, and that he resolved to attempt; but when? And how, without offending his friends?

Meantime, while he revolved the subject in his mind, he visited the river and the shore of the great Lake, this time accompanied by ten spears. The second visit only increased his admiration of the place and his desire to take possession of it. He ascended a tall larch, from whose boughs he had a view out over the Lake; the shore seemed to go almost directly west. There were no islands, and no land in sight; the water was open and clear. Next day he started for the sea; he wished to see it for its own sake, and, secondly, because if he could trace the trend of the shore, he would perhaps be able to put together a mental map of the country, and so assure himself of the right route to pursue when he started for Thyma Castle.

His guides took him directly south, and in three marches (three days) brought him to the strand. This journey was not in a straight line; they considered it was about five-and-thirty or forty miles to the sea, but the country was covered with almost impenetrable forests, which compelled a circuitous path. They had also to avoid a great ridge of hills, and to slip through a pass or river valley, because these hills were frequently traversed by the gipsies who were said, indeed, to travel along them for hundreds of miles. Through the river valley, therefore, which wound between the hills, they approached the sea, so much on a level with it that Felix did not catch a distant glimpse.

In the afternoon of the third day they heard a low murmur, and soon afterwards came out from the forest itself upon a wide bed of shingle, thinly bordered with scattered bushes on the inland side. Climbing over this, Felix saw the green line of the sea rise and extend itself on either hand; in the glory of the scene he forgot his anxieties and his hopes, they fell from him together, leaving the mind alone with itself and love. For the memory of Aurora rendered the beauty before him still more beautiful; love, like the sunshine, threw a glamour over the waves. His old and highest thoughts returned to him in all their strength. He must follow them, he could not help himself. Standing where the foam came nearly to his feet, the resolution to pursue his aspirations took possession of him as strong as the sea. When he turned from it, he said to himself, 'This is the first step homewards to her; this is the first step of my renewed labour.' To fulfil his love and his ambition was one and the same thing. He must see her, and then again endeavour with all his abilities to make himself a position which she could share.

Towards the evening, leaving his escort, he partly ascended the nearest slope of the hills to ascertain more perfectly than was possible at a lower level the direction in which the shore trended. It was nearly east and west, and as the shore of the inland Lake ran west, it appeared that between them there was a broad belt of forest. Through this he must pass, and he thought if he continued due west he should cross an imaginary line drawn south from his own home through Thyma Castle; then by turning to the north he should presently reach that settlement. But when he should cross this line, how many days' travelling it would need to reach it, was a matter of conjecture, and he must be guided by circumstances, the appearance of the country, and his hunter's instinct.

On the way back to Wolfstead Felix was occupied in considering how he could leave his friends, and yet be able to return to them and resume his position. His general idea was to build a fortified house or castle at the spot which had so pleased him, and to bring Aurora to it. He could then devote himself to increasing and consolidating his rule over these people, and perhaps in time organise a kingdom. But without Aurora the time it would require would be unendurable; by some means he must bring her. The whole day long as he walked he thought and thought, trying to discover some means by which he could accomplish these things, yet the more he considered the more difficult they appeared to him. There seemed no plan that promised success; all he could do would be to risk the attempt.

But two days after returning from the sea it chanced towards the afternoon he fell asleep, and on awaking found his mind full of ideas which he felt sure would succeed if anything would. The question had solved itself during sleep; the mind, like a wearied limb, strained by too much effort, had recovered its elasticity and freshness, and he saw clearly what he ought to do.

He convened an assembly of the chief men of the nearest tribes, and addressed them in the circular fort. He asked them if they could place sufficient confidence in him to assist him in carrying out certain plans, although he should not be able to altogether disclose the object he had in view.

They replied as one man that they had perfect confidence in him, and would implicitly obey.

He then said that the first thing he wished was the clearing of the land by the river in order that he might erect a fortified dwelling suitable to his position as their Leader in war. Next he desired their permission to leave them for two months, at the end of which he would return. He could not at that time explain his reasons, but until this journey had been made he could not finally settle among them.

To this announcement they listened in profound silence. It was evident that they disliked his leaving them, yet did not wish to seem distrustful by expressing the feeling.

Thirdly, he continued, he wanted them to clear a path through the forest, commencing at Anker's Gate and proceeding exactly west. The track to be thirty yards wide in order that the undergrowth might not encroach upon it, and to be carried on straight to the westward until his return. The distance to which this path was cleared he should take as the measure of their loyalty to him.

They immediately promised to fulfil this desire, but added that there was no necessity to wait till he left them, it should be commenced the very next morning. To his reiterated request for leave of absence they preserved an ominous silence, and as he had no more to say, the assembly then broke up.

It was afternoon, and Felix, as he watched the departing chiefs, reflected that these men would certainly set a watch upon him to prevent his escape. Without another moment's delay he entered his hut, and took from their hidingplace the diamond bracelet, the turquoise ring, and other presents for Aurora. He also secured some provisions, and put two spare bowstrings in his pocket. His bow of course he carried.

Telling the people about that he was going to the next settlement, Bedeston, and was anxious to overtake the chief from that place who had attended the assembly, he started. So soon as he knew he could not be seen from the settlement he quitted the trail, and made a wide circuit till he faced westwards. Anker's Gate was a small outlying post, the most westerly from Wolfstead; he went near it to get a true direction, but not sufficiently near to be observed. This was on the fourth of September. The sun was declining as he finally left the country of his friends, and entered the immense forest which lay between him and Aurora. Not only was there no track, but no one had ever traversed it, unless indeed it were Bushmen, who to all intents might be confused with the wild animals which it contained.

Yet his heart rose as he walked rapidly among the oaks; already he saw her, he felt the welcoming touch of her hand; the danger of Bushman or gipsy was as nothing. The forest at the commencement consisted chiefly of oaks, trees which do not grow close together, and so permitted of quick walking. Felix pushed on, absorbed in thought. The sun sank; still onward; and as the dusk fell he was still moving rapidly westwards.

THE END

Appendix 1

Richard Jefferies, 'The Great Snow' (fragment, 1876)

Much difficulty was experienced in locomotion. Trains were delayed but there was no interruption of the service, for the wind being still, there was no drift. All day and night of the seventeenth, eighteenth, nineteenth, and the twentieth the snow came steadily down, and on the twenty-first, despite all efforts to clear it, was twenty-seven inches deep. Traffic in the streets was now suspended, and the steamers ceased to ply, partly from want of passengers, and partly because of the dangerous obscurity. Most of the lines were blocked, and on the twenty-second when the snow had even depth of thirty-three inches, not a train reached London. Business was at an end. Till now the snow had been treated as a good joke by the populace who pelted each other in high spirits at their holiday, but when the trains ceased to arrive a species of desponding stupor seemed to fall upon them. The twenty-third was a windy day, the breeze increasing from the east, till in the evening it blew almost a hurricane. The grains of frozen snow lifted up and driven by the wind rushed up the streets like pellets from a gun. The narrow portals of Temple Bar were impassable, so vehement was the blast, and those who attempted to get through describe the hard snow as cutting the skin of their faces in a painful manner. This gale drifted the snow in huge mounds. On the morning of the twenty-fourth the western side of Trafalgar Square was eighteen feet deep in snow, the entrance to the Haymarket was blocked up, and Regent Street near the Quadrant was buried under more than twenty feet. The Thames Embankment was quite clear – the wind having an uninterrupted sweep up it – but the Houses of Parliament formed a dam across the stream of snow and against the eastern side there rose a mound at least twenty-seven feet high. The fleet of merchantmen at the mouth of the Thames were driven onshore, and the whole northern and eastern coasts were strewn with wreckage. Many of these incidents were not ascertained till long afterwards, for the telegraph posts were blown down, the wires snapped, and all communication at an end. The bitter wind lasted five days, and is described as causing an insupportable cold which neither walls, nor curtains, nor roaring fires could overcome. It penetrated through everything. Smith says in his journal: 'We cowered round the fire, but could get no heat. We dragged our beds downstairs, and arranged them in a semi-circle round the fireplace on the carpet. Behind these we placed chairs hung with a screen of thick carpets and matting. Crouching in our beds we drew over us a heavy counterpane, and thus formed a tent indoors. Despite all this my bones felt chilled to the marrow. Etty bore it well, but my poor wife shivered incessantly, and complained that her skin was dried up and shrivelled. Emma suffered most having a weak chest, and it was clear to me that her delicate constitution would not long withstand this strain. If this was the case in our well-appointed, and even luxurious house, how dreadful must have been the sufferings of the poor. Our cellars were full of coal and we had plenty of wine. Fortunately some friends in the country had sent us two tons of excellent potatoes as a present: and to these potatoes our ultimate preservation was due.'

On the twenty-ninth the gale moderated, but meantime snow had fallen unceasingly, and it had now reached a uniform depth of ten feet. With slight variations it continued at this depth but the drifts of course were of enormous height. The National Gallery was wholly hidden under a mound of snow. The dome of St. Paul's was alone visible, rising up like the roof of a huge Esquimoux hut. The great gilt cross on the top had been torn off by the violence of the wind. An intense frost set in, but the sky remained covered with a leaden pall of cloud, and the sun was invisible. All round the coasts there was an impenetrable wall of fog, and eight or ten icebergs are recorded to have come ashore. A berg of immense size, after beating and grinding for days against Portland break-water, at last worked its way into the harbour, and grounded. Another got up the Solent, and two white bears swam to land from it. A third iceberg of smaller size drifted along the south coast, and after sweeping away the Brighton piers, was carried out to sea again by the tide, and lost in the fog. Not a vessel could make her port: and none dared to put out to sea, so that communication with the Continent was totally interrupted. The depth of ten feet extended over the country. Railways, canals, roads, paths, fields, all were buried to that depth, and in places the drifts rose to one-hundred-and-fifty feet. Sheep and cattle were overwhelmed and perished by thousands. Those in stalls were in a few instances kept alive for a little while by the farmers, and herdsmen cutting holes down to them. The Thames was frozen, and on the second of March the ice was seven feet thick off the Tower. Below Gravesend the tides carried huge blocks up and down, dashing them against each other, and against the edge of the fixed ice with a most horrible noise. During the first days of this visitation a stupor fell upon the millions of London. The upper and middle classes shut themselves up in their houses. The poorer ranks flooded the taverns in crowds, and drank in silence huddled round the fires. But in a short time the pressure of hunger made itself felt. The meat markets were buried out of sight. The trains with carcasses from the north and provinces generally had long ceased to arrive, and the stock at the butcher's was speedily exhausted. Still another day or two and meat went up to fancy prices. Thirty pounds was given for a leg of mutton. Smith notes the payment of eighteen pounds for a bullock's heart – the last piece of butcher's meat they had, for those who still possessed a few joints refused to part with them at any price, fearful of starvation. The supply of bread was exhausted still more quickly. Bakers ceased to deliver on the fourth day, on the seventh the stocks were gone, on the eleventh a pound of flour was sold for three guineas. London had for so long been accustomed to depend upon a constant influx of provisions that ten days' interruption of traffic emptied the warehouses. Potatoes and vegetables of all kinds could not be bought at any price. The poor supported life mainly upon beer: but after a while the beer began to fail. Then the demon of plunder entered the minds of the populace hitherto patient. The East rose and threw itself en masse upon the West. The fashionable quarters were invaded by an army of ravening wretches who had climbed over the mounds of frozen snow, and in a moment the houses were swept clean of everything eatable. Smith foresaw this and provided against this. He writes: 'The potatoes were our only resource. To preserve them was all my thought: and at last I hit upon a plan. The snow came up to our first floor windows. I opened one of these, and dug a large cave in the snow. We carried the potatoes and hid them in this hole, and then covered up the entrance. Subsequently we enlarged the cave, and on more than one occasion took refuge in it, when the miserable people became bloodthirsty. The first gang that came were quite civil and quiet, yet their fearful aspect seemed to threaten every violence. Their faces I shall never forget. The temple seemed drawn in, and the cheekbones protruded: the teeth showed like a dogs about to bite, the lips being drawn back, and the gums blue with cold and lack of blood.'

About this time the bonded warehouses of spirits and wine were broken into. In these vaults scenes were enacted not to be surpassed in the annals of madness. Insane already with starvation frantic crowds swallowed the ardent liquors, and fell to dancing and singing. Men and women died in heaps, till the vaults were choked with corpses from which arose a horrible stench. The snow itself had buried and destroyed hundreds, hundreds more had fallen from starvation and exposure, but the cold preserved the bodies from decomposition. Those only decayed which were saturated with liquor in the warm vaults. Children especially died in unrecorded numbers. As the days went by the crowd grew violent – men naturally good or well disposed were turned into fiends by hunger. Roaming in bands they scrambled over the frozen snow, the drifts enabling them to enter the houses by the front or second floor windows, and even by the sky-lights. Armed with rifles and revolvers they demanded food, and if it was not produced fired indiscriminately upon all. The possession of a single potato was sufficient incitement for murder. They learnt to discern from the faces of people whether they had lately had food or not. In one instance a mother who had preserved a little for her children was tortured to reveal her store. Failing all other means the ruffians partially denuded her of clothing and held her down upon the fire. The heroic woman was faithful unto death. Suicides were of hourly occurrence. Whole families perished of starvation lying on the floor before the fire. Dogs, cats, parrots, even canaries were eaten, but afforded a brief respite only. The sparrows dropped dead upon the snow unable to find any sustenance, and were eagerly seized, and devoured. It is possible that had there been any organization much misery might have been avoided, and the stores made to last for a while. But there was no central authority, and the much vaunted local bodies broke down as they always do under pressure of great calamities or disturbance. In the country entire villages were blotted out. Here and there a well-provisioned farmhouse withstood the snow for awhile, like a castle in a state of siege; the farmers and men digging out the carcasses of sheep and bullocks from huge drifts. But there issued from the metropolis gangs of wolves in human shape, and these few farmhouses fell an early prey. After devouring all they found the thieves themselves perished miserably. Many tried to escape from the coast in boats and vessels: but could not shape a course through the fog, and were either driven back by the storms or crushed between floating ice. In London no water could be got except by boiling snow, which required coal, and coal was rapidly exhausted. Then chairs and tables were burnt, and furniture stripped of their elegant and valuable contents to boil the pot. Furniture failing, the flooring of the houses was torn up. Utter darkness prevailed at night for the gas stokers had long deserted their posts, and indeed no coal could have been obtained. On the fifth of March the heavy fog which enveloped the coasts came inland, and the city was in almost total darkness for three days. The mental depression caused by the obscurity equalled the physical sufferings which were at the same time undergone. The mob set fire to houses and burnt streets down to the level of the snow, not so much for warmth as for light. Many went raving mad, and ran about naked until they dropped and died. Fanatics preached unheeded to the crowds. 'Where now' they cried, 'Where now is your mighty city that defied nature and despised the conquered elements – where now is your pride when so simple and contemptible an agent as a few flakes of snow can utterly destroy it? Where are your steam-engine, your telegraphs, and your printing-presses – all powerless and against what – only a little snow! Of what use is your bank reserve of £20,000,000 sterling against the soft noiseless snow?' Such men often cast themselves into the flames of the burning houses, and there roasted bodies were eaten by the miserable creatures around. Others exclaimed that they saw armies fighting in the clouds ...

Appendix 2

Richard Jefferies, ['Alone in London'] (Untitled fragment, undated MS, British Library, Add. MSS 58817).*

I am the only man in London who is not quite decided. Everyone else has fully made up his mind and knows exactly what he is going to do. They come along the pavement in the Strand, one after the other, thicker than a crowd, for that is all bunched up together, but these march in ceaseless succession hour by hour. They are all going somewhere. All have got something to do. Upon their faces there is a set determination to get there and do it: each pushes past the other. If one hesitates a moment to glance at a window another seizes the opportunity to slip ahead. Someone is always waiting to slip by somebody; someone is always overtaking someone. Very little pushing, no jostling, simply moving on, bent on the execution of the business in hand. Everyone stern, serious, rapt in the duty of hastening onwards.

It makes me feel little. I look in the faces and can get no consolation, for they are all so thoroughly convinced; without a doubt, on they go. They have 'learned at the school', they have acquired a fixed knowledge, they have judged this life and the world and are firm of opinion. They know they are right, and that there is nothing else, or more possible, and on they go.

As I walk the pressure of this silent but immense energy around begins to fill me with all manner of difficulties. I came up to Town to purchase a small article in Piccadilly, and it seemed when I started very reasonable to go direct to the warehouse or manufactory for it. But ought I to have come at all? How very little and despicable my paltry object beside this stream of determined people bent on matters of consequence. I ought to have work at home, or I ought to enter an office or go down on the Docks if I can do nothing else and help unload the vessels. Something real, tangible, work in short, to hasten to and fro. To spend the money on a railway ticket was waste: it ought to have been put in the savings bank. I could have walked so short a distance. Had I not better go home as it is, and set to do something?

* First published in *Richard Jefferies Society Journal*, 1 (1992), 2–3. The *RJSJ* editors added the title. Internal evidence somewhat suggests that this may have been written after Jefferies's 1877 relocation to Surbiton.

Change my whole life, my whole scheme of existence is wrong. I must do something else, for all these faces are a reproach to me. Here is a portmanteau shop. I will go in and buy an overland trunk and start for India, or better still for Central Africa, and open up new ground. Here is a china shop, could I not invent a new pottery? There would be something in that. Someone would write my life and explain what an extraordinary benefactor I had been, and how the example of my self-denial and perseverance was in itself a gain to the moral universe. Here is a toy shop: perhaps I could make toys; nothing greater surely than to draw laughter from children to make thousands happy. I am drifting west, I ought to face around and start for the city; the warehouse and office of the world and do something. A hundred thousand clerks at this moment are pushing out for dinner; they do not hesitate: they crowd the restaurants and eat heartily, satisfied that they have done a good part and are entitled to this meal. There is no doubt about it. 'But you?' says my mental mentor, 'You are a detestable being, you have done nothing. You do not even know where you are going. You finger your money in your pocket and you cannot make up your mind whether you ought to buy that little engraving you set your mind on or not. Why don't you go and eat with a hearty goodwill?' 'Because I am not hungry,' I feebly respond, answering myself. 'Then you ought to be. Everybody else is. Look in at that buffet. Listen to the chink of plates. See the waiters rushing. Hearken to the pops of corks. They all know they're hungry. They're all quite certain they're hungry and go and do it. As for you.' I shudder at my own sneer at myself, and look again for consolation in the faces that are streaming by.

None whatever. They have no doubt; they are in no difficulty. A set determination is marked on every one; the expression is identical as if they were replicas of the same plaster cast. They all know everything. Each one could tell me what I was made for, what I ought to be doing, resolve for me every question. I can see it in the swing of their coat tails. It is visible in the precision of their neckties. They have all got boots that fit them and they have all got fitted into this society. I cannot understand it. I begin to feel creepy and queer. Something odd about me. Perhaps my trouser ends are frayed, my coat does not sit properly, my hat is tilted a trifle, my pockets bulged out of shape with a newspaper (wish I could throw it away). No one else has got an umbrella but me. I do not like this singularity. I keep running up against people – there again, and now a man has stepped on my heels. What's that boy running for? How he darts in and out and round folk and slips ahead! What's his message; something very special. Come make up your mind.

Rolled along by the current like a log in a shallow stream, I am washed up at last ashore, and take refuge in the niche of a doorway where I can stand flattened against the door and let people go by without getting in their way. That is something at all costs to be out of the way; so delightful to know one is right in something.